The principles of economics

The principles of economics
Some lies my teachers told me

Lawrence A. Boland
Simon Fraser University

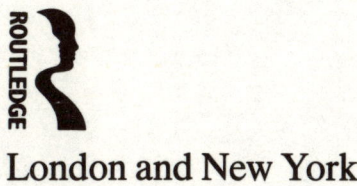

London and New York

First published 1992
by Routledge
11 New Fetter Lane, London EC4P 4EE

Simultaneously published in the USA and Canada
by Routledge
a division of Routledge, Chapman and Hall, Inc.
29 West 35th Street, New York, NY 10001

© 1992 Lawrence A. Boland

Printed and bound in Great Britain by
Mackays of Chatham PLC, Chatham, Kent

All rights reserved. No part of this book may be reprinted or
reproduced or utilized in any form or by any electronic,
mechanical, or other means, now known or hereafter
invented, including photocopying and recording, or in any
information storage or retrieval system, without permission in
writing from the publishers.

British Library Cataloguing in Publication Data
A catalogue record for this book is available from the British Library.

Library of Congress Cataloging in Publication Data
Boland, Lawrence A.
    The principles of economics : some lies my teachers told me /
  Lawrence A. Boland.
    p. cm.
    Includes bibliographical references and index.
    ISBN 0-415-06433-3
    1. Neoclassical school of economics. I. Title.
HB98.2.B65   1992   91-31008
330.15'7-dc20   CIP

to Irene

Contents

Preface · xi
Acknowledgements · xv

Prologue: Understanding neoclassical economics through criticism · 1
Necessary vs sufficient reasons · 2
Explaining vs explaining away · 2
Internal vs external criticism of neoclassical economics · 3
The dangers of criticizing critiques · 5
Understanding and criticism: were my teachers lying to me? · 6
Notes · 8

Part I The essential elements

1 The neoclassical maximization hypothesis · 11
   Types of criticism and the maximization hypothesis · 12
   The logical basis for criticism · 13
   The importance of distinguishing between tautologies and metaphysics · 16
   Notes · 19

2 Marshall's 'Principles' and the 'element of Time' · 21
   The two explanatory 'Principles' · 22
   The 'element of Time' · 23
   Marshall's strategy · 27
   Inadequacies of Marshall's method vs problems created by his followers · 32
   Some critical considerations · 36
   Notes · 37

viii Principles of economics

3	Marshall's 'Principle of Continuity'	39
	Marshall's Principle of Continuity and his biological perspective	40
	Marshall's Principle of Substitution as a research programme	42
	Marshall's rejection of mechanics and psychology	42
	Comprehensive maximization models	44
	Notes	47
4	Axiomatic analysis of equilibrium states	48
	Analyzing the logical structures in economics	50
	Wald's axiomatic Walrasian model: a case study	52
	Completeness and theoretical criticism	60
	A theory of completeness	61
	Notes	62
5	Axiomatic analysis of disequilibrium states	64
	Competition between the short and long runs	65
	The 'perfect-competitor' firm in the long run: a review	66
	Profit maximization with constant returns to scale	68
	Linear homogeneity without perfect competition	70
	Possible alternative models of the firm	71
	Profit maximization	74
	On building more 'realistic' models of the firm	75
	Using models of disequilibrium	75
	Uniformities in explanations of disequilibria	81
	A general theory of disequilibria	84
	Notes	85

Part II Some neglected elements

6	Knowledge in neoclassical economic theory	91
	Maximization as 'rationality'	93
	The methodological problem of knowledge	94
	The epistemological problem of knowledge	98
	The interdependence of methodology and epistemology	100
	Concluding remarks on the Lachmann–Shackle epistemology	101
	Notes	104

7	A naive theory of technology and change	105
	Non-autonomy of technology	107
	Capital as embodied technology	108
	Capital and change	109
	Towards a theory of social change	109
	Notes	111

8	Knowledge and institutions in economic theory	112
	The neoclassical view of institutions	114
	A critique of neoclassical theories of institutional change	117
	A simple theory of social institutions	119
	Time, knowledge and successful institutions	124
	Notes	125

Part III Some missing elements

9	The foundations of Keynes' methodology	131
	General vs special cases	132
	Generality from Keynes' viewpoint	134
	Neoclassical methodology and psychologistic individualism	134
	Keynes' macro-variables vs neoclassical individualism	136
	The Marshallian background of constrained-optimization methodology	136
	The Keynes–Hicks methodology of optimum 'liquidity'	139
	The consequences of 'liquidity in general'	141
	On effective criticism	144
	Notes	146

10	Individualism without psychology	147
	Individualism vs psychologism	147
	Individualism and the legacy of eighteenth century rationalism	148
	Unity vs diversity in methodological individualism	150
	Unnecessary psychologism	152
	Notes	152

11	Methodology and the individual decision-maker	153
	Epistemics in Hayek's economics	154
	The methodology of decision-makers	158
	Notes	161

x *Principles of economics*

Part IV Some technical questions

12 Lexicographic orderings 165
L-orderings 166
The discontinuity problem 167
Orderings and constrained maximization 169
Ad hoc vs arbitrary 171
Multiple criteria vs L-orderings in a choice process 171
The infinite regress vs counter-critical 'ad hocery' 174
Utility functions vs L-orderings 175
Notes 176

13 Revealed Preference vs Ordinal Demand 177
Consumer theory and individualism 179
The logic of explanation 180
Price–consumption curves 182
Choice analysis with preference theory assumptions 186
Choice theory from Revealed Preference Analysis 188
Methodological epilogue 193
Notes 194

14 Giffen goods vs market-determined prices 196
A rational reconstruction of neoclassical demand theory 198
Ad hocery vs testability 205
Giffen goods and the testability of demand theory 207
Concluding remarks 210
Notes 211

Epilogue: Learning economic theory through criticism 213

Bibliography 217
Name index 225
Subject index 227

Preface

Most students who approach neoclassical economics with a critical eye usually begin by thinking that neoclassical theory is quite vulnerable. They think it will be a push-over. Unless they are lucky enough to interact with a competent and clever believer in neoclassical economics, they are likely to advance rather hollow critiques which survive in their own minds simply because they have never been critically examined.

Having just said this, some readers will say, 'Oh, here we go again with another defense of neoclassical theory which, as every open-minded person realizes, is obviously false.' This book is not a defense of neoclassical theory. It is an examination of the ways one can try to criticize neoclassical theory. In particular, it examines inherently unsuccessful ways as well as potentially successful ways.

As with the question, 'Is there sound in the forest when there is nobody there to listen?', there is equally a question of how one registers criticisms. Who is listening? Who does one wish to convince? Is the intended audience other people who will agree in advance with your criticisms? Or people who have something to gain by considering them, namely believers in the propositions you wish to criticize? If you write for the wrong audience there may be nobody there to listen!

My view has always been that whenever I have a criticism I try to convince a believer that he or she is wrong since only in this way will I be maximizing the possibilities for my learning. Usually when the believer is competent I learn the most. Sometimes I learn that I was simply wrong. Other times I learn what issues are really important and thus I learn how to focus my critique to make it more telling. I rarely learn anything by sharing my critiques with someone who already rejects what I am criticizing. Unfortunately, it is easier to get a non-believer to share your critique than to get a believer to listen. Nevertheless, this is the important challenge.

I am firmly convinced that any effective critique must begin by a thorough and sympathetic understanding. It is important to ask: What is the problem that neoclassical economics intends to solve? What constitutes an acceptable solution? With these two questions in mind, I continue to try to understand neoclassical economics. Over the last twenty-five years I have been fortunate to have many colleagues at Simon Fraser University who are neoclassical believers. While I began as a student who considered neoclassical economics to be a push-over, thanks to my colleagues I have come to respect both its sophisticated structure and its simplistic fundamentals. My colleagues have listened to my complaints in seminars and they have taken the time to read my papers. When they thought I was wrong they told me so. And when they did not agree, and particularly when they said they did not know how to answer, they told me so. I do not think one should expect any more from one's colleagues.

This book presents what I think remain as possible avenues for criticism of neoclassical economics. The simplicity of neoclassical economics is that it has only two essential ideas: (1) an assumption of maximizing behaviour and (2) an assumption about the nature of the circumstances and constraints that might impede such behaviour. The obvious avenue for criticism is to attack the assumption of maximization behaviour. As we shall see, this turns out to be the most difficult avenue. Moreover, since both types of assumptions are essential, there are many other possibilities. For example, the problem is not whether one can try to maximize one's utility in isolation but whether a society consisting of similarly motivated people can achieve a state of coordination that will permit them all to achieve their goals. What are the knowledge requirements for such coordination? What are the logical requirements for the configuration of constraints facing these individuals?

Once one recognizes that the acceptance and use of the maximizing hypothesis creates many difficulties for the model-builder, the number of avenues multiplies accordingly. Perhaps the idea of a coordinated society of maximizing individuals is not totally implausible. The question that we all face as economic theorists is whether we can build models that demonstrate such plausibility. Of course this raises the methodological question of one's standard of plausibility but for the most part I will not be concerned with this question. I will be more concerned instead with some technical issues even though questions of an epistemological or methodological nature cannot be totally avoided. It is in the two areas of epistemology and methodology that neoclassical critiques get very murky once one recognizes that to explain the behaviour of an individual decision-maker one must deal with how that individual knows what he or she needs to know in order to make a decision that will contribute to a coordinated society.

While knowledge, information and uncertainty are often recognized today, rarely is there more than lip-service given to a critical discussion of their theoretical basis. How does information reduce a decision-maker's uncertainty? What concept of knowledge or learning is presumed by the neoclassical theorist? Typically, the presumed theory is based on a seventeenth-century epistemology that was refuted two hundred years ago. If knowledge, information or uncertainty matter then it is important for us to understand these concepts.

This book is written for those who like me wish to understand neoclassical economics. In particular, it is for those who wish to develop a critical understanding whether one wishes to improve neoclassical theory or just criticize it. I cannot preclude true believers who are looking for research projects that would lead to needed repairs. They are welcome, too.

L.A.B.
Burnaby, British Columbia
29 November 1990

Acknowledgements

I wish to thank several people who kindly took the time to read the manuscript of this book. Those deserving pariticular praise are Irene Gordon, Richard Simson and Xavier DeVanssay. Geoffrey Newman, Paul Harrald, Zane Spindler and John Chant were most helpful with a couple of difficult chapters. I also wish to thank Ray Offord for editing the final version. Since I have taken the opporunty to use parts of some of my published papers, I wish to thank the managing editors of *American Economic Review*, *Australian Economic Papers*, *Eastern Economic Journal* and *Philosophy of the Social Sciences* for giving me permission to use copyright material.

Prologue

Understanding neoclassical economics through criticism

Far too often when one launches a criticism of a particular proposition or school of thought many bystanders jump to the conclusion that the critic is taking sides, that is, the critic is stating an opposing position. Sometimes, it is merely asked, 'Which side are you on?' Criticism need not be limited to such a context.

Since the time of Socrates we have known that criticism is an effective means of learning. Criticism as a means of learning recognizes that we offer theories to explain events or phenomena. One explains an event by stating one or more reasons which when logically conjoined imply that the event in question would occur. While some of the reasons involve known facts, making assumptions is unavoidable. Simply stated, we assume simply because we do not know.

Economics students are quite familiar with the task of using assumptions to form explanations of economic phenomena. But, some may ask, will just any assumptions suffice? Apart from requiring that the phenomena in question are logically entailed by the assumptions ventured, it might seem that anything goes. Such is not the case. The 'Principles of Economics' are essential ingredients of *every* acceptable explanation in modern neoclassical economics. For example, it would be difficult to see how one could give a *neoclassical* explanation of social phenomena that did not begin with an assumption that the phenomena in question were the results of maximizing behaviour on the part of the relevant decision-makers. Recognizing that the Principles are essential for any acceptable explanation is itself an important consideration for any criticism.

Whether one's purpose in criticizing is to dispute a proposition (or dispute an entire school of thought) or just to try to learn more, understanding what it takes logically to form an effective criticism would seem to be an important starting point.

NECESSARY VS SUFFICIENT REASONS

At the very minimum, explanations are logical arguments. The logic of explanation is simple. The ingredients of an argument are either assumptions or conclusions. The conclusions of an explanation include statements which are sometimes called necessary conditions.[1] One states explicit assumptions which are all assumed to be true and then one provides the logical structure which shows that for all the assumptions to be true the conclusion (regarding the events or phenomena to be explained) must *necessarily* be true. Despite how some early mathematical economics textbooks state the issues, there usually is no *single* assumption or conclusion which is a sufficient condition.[2] Usually, the sufficient condition is the conjunction (i.e. the compound statement formed by all) of the assumptions. The error of the early textbooks is that if there are n assumptions and $n-1$ are true, then the nth assumption appears to 'make' the conjunction into the sufficient compound statement. Of course, any one of the n assumptions could thus be a sufficient condition when all the others are given as true.[3] In short, the conclusions are necessary and the *conjunction* of all the assumptions is sufficient.

What is not always recognized is that it is the presumed necessity of the *individual assumptions* forming the conjunction that is put at stake in any claim to have provided an explanation which could form the basis for *understanding* the events or phenomena in question (e.g. 'Ah, now I understand, it is because people always do X'). This may seem rather complicated, so let me explain. We offer explanations in order to understand phenomena. To accept an explanation as a basis for understanding, one would have to have all assumptions of the explanation be true (or at least not known to be false). Otherwise, the logic of the explanation has no force. The logic of the explanation is that whenever all the assumptions are true then the events or phenomena in question will occur. There is nothing that one can say when one or more of the assumptions is false since the logic of explanation requires true assumptions.

EXPLAINING VS EXPLAINING AWAY

A key aspect of the above discussion of explanation is that the events or phenomena in question are accepted as 'reality' (rather than mere 'appearances'). For example, the Law of Demand (i.e. the proposition that demand curves are *universally* downward sloping) was often taken as a fact of reality and thus we were compelled to offer explanations of it. Today, on the other hand, disequilibrium phenomena such as 'involuntary unemployment' may be *explained away* as mere appearances. Supposedly, in the latter case, if we could see all the costs (such as transaction costs) then we could see that what appears to be a disequilibrium is really an equilibrium.[4]

The distinction between explaining and explaining away involves one's presumptions. If one thinks the decision-maker is always maximizing then any appearance of 'irrationality' can be explained away by demonstrating that the true utility function is more complicated [e.g. Becker 1962]. Explaining away takes the truth of one's explanation for granted; thus whatever one may think reality is can be seen to be mere appearance (e.g. apparently irrational behaviour). Moreover, reality is seen to be the utility function that would have to exist to maintain the truth of one's explanation. If one wishes to explain (as opposed to engaging in explaining away) then one's assumption regarding the *a priori* form of the objective function must be stated in advance and thus put at stake (i.e. not made dependent on the observed behaviour). In this sense, one's explanation makes maximization a necessary assumption (although not necessarily true – its truth status is still open to question). The claim is that we understand the behaviour simply *because we assume* maximization. For most of our considerations here, it will not matter whether we are explaining or explaining away since in either case one must put either the truth status of one's assumptions or the logical validity of one's argument at stake and thus open to criticism.

INTERNAL VS EXTERNAL CRITICISM OF NEOCLASSICAL ECONOMICS

Given the observations so far, if one wishes to criticize an argument, there are basically two general approaches depending on whether or not one is willing to accept the aim of the argument even if only for the purposes of discussion. If one accepts the aim of the argument then one can offer *internal* criticism, that is, criticism that examines the internal logic of the argument without introducing any new or external considerations. In contrast, methodologists will often refer to their favourite philosophical authorities to quibble with the purpose of one's argument rather than try to find faults in the logic of the argument. This, of course, leads to arguments at cross-purposes and usually carries little weight with the proponents of the argument. For example, advocates of a methodology that stresses the utility of simplicity (e.g. Friedman's Instrumentalism) might wish to develop explanations based on perfect competition while those who wish to maximize generality are more likely to see virtue in developing imperfectly competitive models which see perfect competition as a special case. Criticizing perfect competition models for not being general enough or criticizing imperfect competition models for not being simple enough does not seem to be very useful. Nevertheless, the history of economics is populated by many such disputes based on such *external* critiques.

Internal critiques focus on two considerations. The most obvious consideration is the truth status of the assumptions since they must all be true for an explanation to be true. The other concerns the sufficiency of the argument. If one wished to criticize an explanation directly, one would have to either empirically refute one or more of the assumptions or cleverly show that the argument was logically insufficient. If one could refute one of the assumptions, one would thereby criticize the possibility of claiming to *understand* the events or phenomena in question with the given argument. Much of the criticism of neoclassical economics involves such a direct form of criticism. Unfortunately, many of the assumptions of neoclassical economics are not directly testable and others are, by the very construction of neoclassical methodology, put beyond question (this matter of putting assumptions beyond question will be discussed in Chapter 1).

Even when an assumption cannot be refuted, one can criticize its adequacy to serve as a basis for *understanding* by showing that it is not necessary for the sufficiency of the explanation. To refute the necessity of an assumption one would have to build an alternative explanation that does not use the assumption in question and thereby prove that it is not necessary. To refute the sufficiency of an argument one must prove that it is possible to have the conclusion be false even when all of the assumptions are true. This latter approach is most common in criticisms of equilibrium models where one would try to show that even if all the behavioural assumptions were true there still might not exist a possible equilibrium state.

It might be thought that the criticism most telling for the argument as a whole would be to criticize the truth of one's conclusion. But since explanations are offered to explain the *given* truth of the conclusion, such a brute force way of criticizing is usually precluded. However, an indirect criticism could involve showing that other conclusions entailed by the argument are false. This approach to criticism is not commonly followed in economics.

If the theorist offering the explanation has done his or her job, there will not be any problem with the sufficiency of the logic of the argument. Thus, theoretical criticism usually concerns whether the argument has hidden assumptions (or ones taken for granted) which are not plausible or are known to be false. Such a critique is usually presented in a form of axiomatic analysis where each assumption is explicitly stated. The most common concerns of a critical nature involve either the mechanics of equilibria or the knowledge requirements of the decision-makers of neoclassical models. I will pursue various essential aspects of maximization and equilibrium in Chapters 1 to 5 and I will examine the questioning of the adequacy of the essential elements of individual decision-making in Chapters 6 to 14.

THE DANGERS OF CRITICIZING CRITIQUES

There is another level of discussion that it is not often attempted. When a particular argument has generated many *accepted* critiques, obviously there arises the opportunity to critically examine the critiques. Given the sociology of the economics profession this approach is rather dangerous. If you treat each critique as an internal critique (by accepting the aims of the argument) you leave yourself open to a claim that you are defending the original argument from *any* critique. This claim is a major source of confusion even though it is not obviously true. I have a first-hand familiarity with this confusion. When I published my critique of the numerous critiques of Friedman's famous 1953 essay on methodology [Boland 1979a], far too many methodologists jumped to the conclusion that I was defending Friedman. My 1979 argument was simply that the *existing* critiques were all flawed. Moreover, while I defended Friedman's *essay* from specific existing critiques it does not follow that I was defending him from *any* conceivable critique. A similar situation occurred in response to my general criticism of existing arguments against the assumption of maximizing behaviour [Boland 1981]. Many readers jumped to the conclusion that I was defending the truth status of this assumption. Herbert Simon has often told me I was wrong. But again, facing the facts of how the maximization assumption is used in economics, and in particular why it is put beyond question, in no way implies an assertion about the assumption's truth status – even though the assumption might actually be false.

The difficulty with my two critical papers about accepted critiques is that too often the economics profession requires one to take sides in methodological disputes while at the same time not allowing open discussion of methodology. Specifically, those economists who side with Friedman's version of Chicago School economics were thrilled with my 1979 paper but those who oppose Friedman rejected it virtually sightunseen. Clearly few of the anti-Chicago School critics actually finished reading my paper. I reach this conclusion because at the end of my paper I explicitly stated how to form an effective criticism. Only one of the critics whom I criticized responded [see Rotwein 1980]. My paper apparently disrupted the complacency among those opposed to Friedman's methodology – it appears that they were left exposed on the methodology flank without a defense against Friedman's essay. This is particularly so since by my restating Friedman's methodology, and thereby showing that it is nothing more than commonplace Instrumentalism, it was probably clear to Friedman's opponents that their methodological views did not differ much from his.

While there is the potential for everyone to learn from critiques of critiques, if the audience are too eager to believe any critique of their favourite boogey-man they read, then all the clearly stated logical arguments in the world will not have much effect. Despite the confusion, and regardless of whether anyone else learned from my two papers on effective criticism, certainly I think I learned a lot. Unfortunately, I probably learned more about the sociology of the economics profession than anything else!

UNDERSTANDING AND CRITICISM: WERE MY TEACHERS LYING TO ME?

Even after having recognized the dangers, I wish to stress that I still think criticism is an effective means of learning and understanding. Moreover, understanding without criticism is hollow. As a student I think I learned much more in classes where teachers allowed me to challenge and criticize them on the spot. Sometimes I thought they were telling me 'lies' and most of the time I was wrong. Of course, I doubt very much that teachers intentionally lie to their students. Nevertheless, many textbooks do contain lies with regard to the essential nature of neoclassical economics and students and their teachers would learn more by challenging their textbooks.

Each of the following chapters is concerned with a specific 'lie', that is, with an erroneous notion that has been foisted on us by various textbook writers and teachers. The first such notion I discuss in Chapter 1 which is about the claim by many critics of neoclassical economics that the assumption of maximization is a tautology and thus *inherently* untestable. I will explain why this claim is false. The remaining chapters explore various theoretical avenues for criticism of neoclassical economics that have interested me over the last twenty-five years. With the exception of Chapters 5, 7 and 9, my discussion will focus primarily on consumer demand theory since neoclassical economists give more attention to demand theory than they do to the theory of supply.

In Chapters 2 and 3 I begin by determining the nature of the essential ingredients of neoclassical economics, namely, the Principles of Economics, starting with Alfred Marshall's view of these principles. While it may not be possible to simply deny that people maximize, we can question the necessary conditions for maximization along lines suggested by Marshall. Chapter 2 is concerned with the lie perpetrated by some critics that neoclassical economics is inherently 'timeless'. Chapter 3 is concerned with the lie perpetrated by friends of neoclassical economics who, by ignoring one of the fundamental requirements for any maximization-based explanation, suggest that the maximization assumption is universally applicable. As Marshall pointed out long ago, maximization presumes the Principle of Continuity, that is, a sufficiently free range of choice if maximization is to explain choice.

The logical requirements for equilibrium are examined in Chapters 4 and 5 with an eye on how equilibrium models can be construed as bases for understanding economic phenomena. Chapter 4 is concerned with the common misleading notion that model-builders need to assure only that the number of unknown variables equals the number of equations in the model. Chapter 5 is about the erroneous notion that models of imperfect competition can be constructed from perfect competition models by merely relaxing only the price-taker assumption.

Chapters 6 to 8 are concerned with two neglected elements of every neoclassical model. Specifically, they are about the knowledge and institutional conditions needed for decision-making and how these requirements can be used as a basis for criticizing neoclassical economics. Chapter 6 examines the claim that Austrian economics is superior to neoclassical theories because the former explicitly recognizes the necessity of dealing with the knowledge required for utility or profit maximization. It is argued that both versions of economics suffer from the inability to handle knowledge dynamics. Chapter 7 examines the questionable notion that the Principles of Economics can be applied to technology when explaining the historical developments of an economy. And Chapter 8 questions the applicability of Marshall's Principles to a similar question concerning the development of the institutions of an economy.

Chapters 9 to 11 consider some critiques which claim there are missing elements in neoclassical economics particularly with regard to the role of the individual in neoclassical theory. While some proponents of Post-Keynesian economics claim that Keynes offered a blueprint for a different approach to explaining economic behaviour, in Chapter 9 I argue that such a view may be misleading readers of his famous book. I think his *General Theory* is better understood as a critique of neoclassical economics, one that was written to convince believers in neoclassical economics rather than provide the desired revolutionary blueprint. Chapter 10 explains why neoclassical economics does not need an infusion of social psychology as some critics claim. And Chapter 11 pushes beyond Chapter 6 to challenge those neoclassical theorists who think the behaviour of individuals can be explained without dealing with how individuals know they are maximizing.

Chapters 12 to 14 deal with a few technical questions raised by those economists who attempt to construct logically complete formal models of consumer choice. Chapter 12 examines the common lie that lexicographic orderings are not worthy of consideration by a neoclassical model-builder even though many of us may think that they are certainly plausible. Chapter 13 examines the alleged equivalence of Paul Samuelson's revealed preference analysis and the ordinal demand theory of R.G.D. Allen and John Hicks. For many decades the critical issue of consumer theory has been whether we can explain why demand curves are downward sloping. Today many theorists think demand theory can be developed without reference to downward sloping demand curves. In Chapter 14 I show why downward sloping demand curves have to be explained in any neoclassical theory of prices.

Each of these chapters represents the understanding of neoclassical economics that I have acquired from various attempts on my part and others' to criticize the logical sufficiency of neoclassical explanations. The criticisms in question are almost always ones which argue that there are hidden presumptions that might not survive exposure to the light of day. One thing which will be evident is that I will often be discussing articles published in the 1930s. This is no accident, as I think that many of the problems considered in those 'years of high theory' were the most interesting and critical. However, my interest in these old papers is not historical. Many of the problems discussed during that period unfortunately remain unresolved today. If I had my way we would all go back to that period of 'high theory' and start over at the point where things were interrupted by the urgencies of a world war.

NOTES

1 For example, for a differentiable function to be maximized, the 'necessary conditions' are (1) that its first derivative must be zero and (2) that its second derivative be negative. These two necessary conditions merely follow from what we mean by maximization.
2 Years ago, it was typically said that for a differentiable function, given a zero first derivative, the function's second derivative being negative is the 'sufficient condition' for maximization [e.g. see Chiang 1974, p. 258].
3 The only time a single assumption is sufficient is when there is just one assumption. The statement 'all swans are white' is sufficient to conclude that the next swan you see will be white.
4 See further Robert Solow's [1979] examination of the usual ways disequilibria are explained away in macroeconomics.

Part I

The essential elements

1 The neoclassical maximization hypothesis

> At present the maximization postulate has an unusually strong hold on the mind set of economists... Suffice it to say that in my view the belief in favor of maximization does not depend on strong evidence that people are in fact maximizers... The main argument against the maximization postulate is an empirical one – namely, people frequently do not maximize. Of course, this standpoint argues that while postulates simplify reality, we are not free to choose counterfactual postulates. Hence, from this point of view a superior postulate would be one under which maximizing behavior is a special case, but non-maximization is accommodated for as a frequent mode of behavior.
>
> Harvey Leibenstein [1979, pp. 493–4]

> If by rational we mean demonstrably optimal, it follows that conduct in order to be rational must be relevantly fully informed.
>
> George Shackle [1972, p. 125]

> The assumption of maximization may also place a heavy (often unbearable) computational burden on the decision maker.
>
> Herbert Simon [1987, p. 267]

The assumption of maximization is a salient feature of every neoclassical explanation. Obviously, then, if one wanted to criticize neoclassical economics it would seem that the most direct way would be to criticize the assumption of universal maximization. Several approaches have been taken. Harvey Leibenstein [1979] offered an external criticism. He argued for a 'micro-micro theory' on the grounds that profit maximization is not necessarily the objective of the actual decision-makers in a firm and that a complete explanation would require an explanation of intrafirm behaviour. He also gave arguments for why maximization of anything may not be realistic or is at best a special case. Similarly, Herbert Simon has argued that individuals do not actually maximize anything – they 'satisfice' – and yet they still make decisions.[1] And of course, George Shackle has for many years argued that maximization is not even possible.

Some anti-neoclassical economists are very encouraged by these arguments, but I think these arguments are unsuccessful. For anyone opposed to neoclassical theory, a misdirected criticism, which by its failure only adds apparent credibility to neoclassical theory, will be worse than the absence of criticism. The purpose of this chapter is to explain why, although the neoclassical hypothesis is *not a tautology* and thus may be false, no criticism of that hypothesis will ever be successful. My arguments will be based first on the possible types of theoretical criticism and the logic of those criticisms, and second on the methodological status of the maximization hypothesis in neoclassical explanations.

TYPES OF CRITICISM AND THE MAXIMIZATION HYPOTHESIS

There are only two types of *direct* criticism of any behavioural hypothesis once its logical validity has been established. One can argue against the *possibility* of the hypothesized behaviour or one can argue against the *empirical* truth of the premise of the hypothesis. In the case of the neoclassical maximization hypothesis, virtually everyone accepts the logical validity of the hypothesis. For example, everyone can accept that *if* the consumer is a utility maximizer, then for the particular bundle of goods chosen: (a) the marginal utility is zero, and (b) the slope of the marginal utility curve at the point representing the chosen bundle is non-positive and usually negative.[2] That is to say, necessarily the marginal increment to the objective must be zero and falling (or not rising) whenever (i.e. without exception) the maximization premise is actually true. Of course, one could substitute the word 'profit' for the word 'utility' and the logic of the hypothesis still holds. With either form, (a) and (b) are the 'necessary conditions' for maximization. Note again that there are no 'sufficient conditions' for maximization. Rather, the maximization premise is the sufficient condition for (a) and (b).

Parenthetically, I should note that economists often refer to the *conjunction* of (a) and (b) as a sufficient condition for maximization. This is a common error.[3] Even if (a) and (b) are both true, only *local* maximization is assured. However, maximization in general (i.e. global) is what the premise explicitly asserts and that is not assured by (a) and (b) alone. I will return to this below when I discuss the methodological uses of the maximization hypothesis.

THE LOGICAL BASIS FOR CRITICISM

As stated above, there are two types of direct criticism of the maximization hypothesis: the possibilities criticism and the empirical criticism. In this section I will examine the logical bases of these critiques, namely of the possibilities argument which concerns only the necessary conditions and of the empirical argument which concerns only the statements which form the sufficient conditions. In each case I will also discuss the possible logical defense for these criticisms.

The possibilities critique: can the necessary conditions be fulfilled?

The possibilities critique builds on the difference between necessary and sufficient conditions. Specifically, what is criticized is the possibility of fulfilling all of the necessary conditions for maximization. Of course, this type of critique begs the question as to what are all the necessary conditions. Are there more conditions than the (a) and (b) listed above? Shackle, following Friedrich Hayek and John Maynard Keynes, argues that maximization also presumes that the knowledge necessary for the process of choosing the 'best' alternative has been acquired.[4] For Shackle, maximization is always a deliberate act. Shackle argues that for maximization to be a behavioural hypothesis (i.e. about the behaviour of decision-makers), the actor must have acquired all of the information necessary to determine or calculate which alternative maximizes utility (or profit, etc.) and he argues that such an acquisition is impossible, hence deliberate maximization is an impossible act.

Although this argument appears to be quite strong, it is rather elementary. A closer examination will show it to be overly optimistic because it is epistemologically presumptive. One needs to ask: Why is the possession of the necessary knowledge impossible? This question clearly involves one's epistemology – that is, one's theory of knowledge. The answer, I think, is quite simple. Shackle's argument (also Hayek's and Keynes') presumes that the truth of one's knowledge requires an inductive proof. And as everyone surely knows today, there is no way to prove one's knowledge inductively whenever the amount of information is finite or it is otherwise incomplete (e.g. information about the future).[5]

The strength of Shackle's argument is actually rather vulnerable. Inductive proofs (and hence inductive logic) are not necessary for true knowledge. One's knowledge (i.e. one's theory) can be true even though one does not know it to be true – that is, even if one does not have proof. But I think there is an even stronger objection to the 'true knowledge is necessary for maximization' argument. True knowledge is not necessary for maximization! Consumers, for example, only have to think that their theory of what is the shape of their utility function is true. Once a consumer picks the 'best' option there is no reason to deviate or engage in 'disequilibrium behaviour' unless he or she is prone to testing his or her own theories.[6]

In summary, Shackle's inductivist argument against the possibility of a true maximization hypothesis is a failure. Inductive proofs are not necessary for true knowledge and true knowledge (by any means) is not necessary for successful or determinate decision-making. Maximizing behaviour cannot be ruled out as a logical impossibility.

The empirical critiques: are the sufficient premises true?

Simon and Leibenstein argue against the maximization hypothesis in a more straightforward way. While accepting the logical validity of the hypothesis, they simply deny the truth of the premise of the hypothesis. They would allow that if the consumer is actually a maximizer, the hypothesis would be a true explanation of the consumer's behaviour but they say the premise is false; consumers are not necessarily maximizers hence their behaviour (e.g. their demand) would not necessarily be determinable on that basis. Leibenstein may allow that the consumer's behaviour can be determined, but it is an open question as to what is the determining factor – utility, prestige, social convention, etc.? Simon seems to reject as well the necessity of determinate explanation although he does discuss alternative decision rules to substitute for the maximization rule.[7]

A denial of the maximization hypothesis on empirical grounds raises the obvious question: How do the critics know the premise is false? Certain methodological considerations would seem to give an advantage to the critics over those who argue in its favour. Note that we can distinguish between those statements which are verifiable (i.e. when true, can be proven true) and those which are refutable (i.e. when false, can be proven false) on purely logical grounds. Furthermore, strictly universal statements – those of the form '*all* Xs have property Y' – are refutable (if false) but not verifiable (even if true). On the other hand, strictly existential statements – those of the form 'there are *some* Xs which have property Y' – are verifiable (if true) but not refutable (even if false). At first glance it would seem that the maximization hypothesis – 'all decision-makers are maximizers' – is straightforwardly a universal statement and hence is refutable but not verifiable. But the statistical and methodological problems of empirical refutation present many difficulties. Some of them are well known but, as I shall show a little later, the logical problems are insurmountable.

The methodological problems of empirical refutations of economic theories are widely accepted. In the case of utility maximization we realize that survey reports are suspect and direct observations of the decision-making process are difficult or impossible. In this sense behavioural maximization is not directly testable. The only objective part of the maximization hypothesis is the set of logical consequences such as the uniquely determinate choices. One might thus attempt an indirect test of maximization by examining the outcomes of maximization, namely the implied pattern of observable choices based on a presumption that there is a utility function and that utility is being maximized by the choices made.

If one wishes to avoid errors in logic, an indirect test of any behavioural hypothesis which is based on a direct examination of its logical consequences must be limited to attempting refutations of one or more of the necessary conditions for the truth of the hypothesis. For example, in the case of consumer theory, whenever utility maximization is the basis of observed choices, a necessary condition is that for any given pattern of choices the 'Slutsky Theorem' must hold.[8] It might appear then that the above methodological problems of observation could be easily overcome, since the Slutsky Theorem can in principle be made to involve only observable quantities and prices. And, if one could refute the Slutsky Theorem then one could indirectly refute the maximization hypothesis.[9] Unfortunately, even if from this perspective such an indirect refutation cannot be ruled out on logical grounds alone, the methodological problems concerning observations will remain.

The fundamental methodological problem of refuting any behavioural hypothesis indirectly is that of constructing a convincing refutation. Any indirect test of the utility maximization hypothesis will be futile if it is to be based on a test of any logically derived implication (such as the Slutsky Theorem). On the one hand, everyone – even critics of maximization – will accept the theorem's logical validity. On the other hand, given the numerous constraints involved in any concrete situation, the problems of observation will be far more complex than those outlined by the standard theory. Thus, it is not difficult to see that there are numerous obstacles in the way of constructing any convincing refutation of maximization, one which would be beyond question.

I now wish to offer some different considerations about the potential refutations of the neoclassical behavioural hypothesis. I will argue here that even if one could prove that a consumer is not maximizing utility or a producer is not maximizing profit, this would not constitute a refutation of the neoclassical hypothesis. The reason why is that the actual form of the neoclassical premise is not a strictly universal statement. Properly stated, the neoclassical premise is: 'For *all* decision-makers there is *something* they maximize.' This statement has the form which is called an incomplete 'all-and-some statement'. Incomplete all-and-some statements are neither verifiable nor refutable! As a universal statement claiming to be true for all decision-makers, it is unverifiable. But, although it is a universal statement and it should be logically possible to prove it is false when it is false (viz. by providing a counter-example) this form of universal statement cannot be so easily rejected. Any alleged counter-example is unverifiable even if true![10]

Let me be specific. Given the premise 'All consumers maximize *something*', the critic can claim to have found a consumer who is not maximizing anything. The person who assumed the premise is true can respond: 'You claim you have found a consumer who is not a maximizer but how do you *know* there is not *something* which he or she is maximizing?' In other words, the verification of the counter-example requires the refutation of a strictly existential statement; and as stated above, we all agree that one cannot refute strictly existential statements.

In summary, empirical arguments such as Simon's or Leibenstein's that deny the truth of the maximization hypothesis are no more testable than the hypothesis itself. Note well, the logical impossibility of proving or disproving the truth of any statement does not indicate anything about the truth of that statement. The neoclassical assumption of universal maximization could very well be false, but as a matter of logic we cannot expect ever to be able to prove that it is.

THE IMPORTANCE OF DISTINGUISHING BETWEEN TAUTOLOGIES AND METAPHYSICS

Some economists have charged that the maximization hypothesis should be rejected because, they argue, since the hypothesis is not testable it must then be a tautology, hence it is 'meaningless' or 'unscientific'. Although they may be correct about its testability, they are wrong about its being necessarily a tautology. Statements which are untestable are not necessarily tautologies because they may merely be metaphysical.

Distinguishing between tautologies and metaphysics

Tautologies are statements which are true by virtue of their logical form alone – that is, one cannot even conceive of how they could ever be false. For example, the statement 'I am here or I am not here' is true regardless of the meaning of the non-logical words 'I' or 'here'. There is no conceivable counter-example for this tautological statement. But the maximization hypothesis is not a tautology. It is conceivably false. Its truth or falsity is not a matter of logical form. The problem with the hypothesis is that it is treated as a metaphysical statement.

A statement which is a tautology is intrinsically a tautology. One cannot make it a non-tautology merely by being careful about how it is being used. A statement which is metaphysical is not intrinsically metaphysical. Its metaphysical status is a result of how it is used in a research programme. Metaphysical statements can be false but we may never know because they are the assumptions of a research programme which are deliberately put beyond question. Of course, a metaphysical assumption may be a tautology but that is not a necessity.

Typically, a metaphysical statement has the form of an existential statement (e.g. there is class conflict; there is a price system; there is an invisible hand; there will be a revolution; etc.). It would be an error to think that because a metaphysical existential statement is irrefutable it must also be a tautology. More important, a unanimous acceptance of the truth of any existential statement still does not mean it is a tautology.

Some theorists inadvertently create tautologies with their *ad hoc* attempts to overcome any possible informational incompleteness of their theories. For example, as an explanation, global maximization implies the adequacy of either the consumer's preferences or the consumer's theory of all conceivable bundles which in turn implies his or her acceptance of an unverifiable universal statement. Some theorists thus find global maximization uncomfortable as it expects too much of any decision-maker – but the usual reaction only makes matters worse. The maximization hypothesis is easily transformed into a tautology by limiting the premise to local maximization. Specifically, while the necessary conditions (a) and (b) are not sufficient for global maximization, they are sufficient for local maximization. If one then changes the premise to say, 'if the consumer is maximizing over the neighbourhood of the chosen bundle', one is only begging the question as to how the neighbourhood was chosen. If the neighbourhood is defined as that domain over which the rate of change of the slope of the marginal utility curve is monotonically increasing or decreasing, then at best the hypothesis is circular. But what is more important here, if one limits the premise to local maximization, one will severely limit the explanatory power or generality of the allegedly explained behaviour.[11] One would be better off maintaining one's metaphysics than creating tautologies to seal their defense.

Metaphysics vs methodology

Sixty years ago metaphysics was considered a dirty word but today most people realize that every explanation has its metaphysics. Every model or theory is merely another attempted test of the 'robustness' of a given metaphysics. Every research programme has a foundation of given behavioural or structural assumptions. Those assumptions are implicitly ranked according to their questionability. The last assumptions on such a rank-ordered list are the metaphysics of that research programme. They can even be used to define that research programme. In the case of neoclassical economics, the maximization hypothesis plays this methodological role. Maximization is considered fundamental to everything; even an assumed equilibrium need not actually be put beyond question as disequilibrium in a market is merely a consequence of the failure of all decision-makers to maximize. Thus, those economists who put maximization beyond question cannot 'see' any disequilibria.

The research programme of neoclassical economics is the challenge of finding a neoclassical explanation for any given phenomenon – that is, whether it is possible to show that the phenomenon can be seen as a logical consequence of maximizing behaviour – thus, maximization is beyond question for the purpose of accepting the challenge.[12] The only question of substance is whether a theorist is willing to say what it would take to convince him or her that the metaphysics used failed the test. For the reasons I have given above, no logical criticism of maximization can ever convince a neoclassical theorist that there is something intrinsically wrong with the maximization hypothesis.

Whether maximization should be part of anyone's metaphysics is a methodological problem. Since maximization is part of the metaphysics, neoclassical theorists too often employ *ad hoc* methodology to deflect possible criticism; thus any criticism or defense of the maximization hypothesis must deal with neoclassical methodology rather than the truth of the hypothesis. Specifically, when criticizing any given assumption of maximization it would seem that critics need only be careful to determine whether the truth of the assumption matters. It is true that for followers of Friedman's Instrumentalism the truth of the assumption does not matter, hence for strictly methodological reasons it is futile to criticize maximization. And the reasons are quite simple. Practical success does not require true knowledge and Instrumentalism presumes that the sole objective of research in economic theory is immediate solutions to practical problems. The truth of assumptions supposedly matters to those economists who reject Friedman's Instrumentalism, but for those economists interested in developing economic theory for its own sake I have argued here that it is still futile to criticize the maximization hypothesis. There is nothing *intrinsically* wrong with the maximization hypothesis. The only problem, if there is a problem, resides in the methodological attitude of most neoclassical economists.

The neoclassical maximization hypothesis 19

In summary, the general lesson to be learned here is that while it may seem useful to criticize what appear to be necessary elements of neoclassical economics, it may not be fruitful when the proponents of neoclassical economics are unwilling to accept such a line of criticism. External criticisms may be interesting for critical bystanders, but for someone interested only in attempting to see whether it is possible to develop a neoclassical model to explain some particular economic phenomenon, the questions of interest will usually only be the ones concerning particular techniques of model-building. They will usually be satisfied with minimalist concern for whether the model as a whole is testable and thus be satisfied to say that if you think you can do better with a non-neoclassical model (in particular, one which does not assume maximization), then you are quite welcome to try. When you are finished, the neoclassical economists will be willing to compare the results. Which model fits the data better? But until a viable competitor is created, the neoclassical economists will be uninterested in *a priori* discussions of the realism of assumptions which cannot be independently tested as is the case with the maximization assumption.

NOTES

1 Thus one might use Simon's argument to deny the necessity of the maximization assumption. But this denial is an indirect argument. It is also somewhat unreliable. It puts the onus on the critic to offer an equally sufficient argument that does not use maximization either explicitly or implicitly. Sometimes what might appear as a different argument can on later examination turn out to be equivalent to what it purports to replace. This is almost always the case when only one assumption is changed.
2 Note that any hypothesized utility function may already have the effects of constraints built in as is the case with the Lagrange multiplier technique.
3 This is not the error I discussed in the previous chapter, that is, the one where some people call (b) the sufficient condition.
4 Although Shackle's argument applies to the assumption of either local or global maximization, it is most telling in the case of global maximization.
5 Requiring an inductive proof of any claim to knowledge is called Inductivism. Inductivism is the view that all knowledge is logically derived generalizations that are based ultimately only on observations. The generalizations are not instantaneous but usually involve secondary assumptions which require more observations to verify these assumptions to ensure that the foundation of knowledge will be observations alone. This theory of knowledge presumes that any true claim for knowledge can be proven with singular statements of observation. Inductivism is the belief that one could actually prove that 'all swans are white' by means of observing white swans and without making any assumptions to help in the proof. It is a false theory of knowledge simply because there is no logic that can ever prove a strictly universal generality based solely on singular observations – *even when the generality is true* [see

further my 1982 book, Chapter 1].
6. Again this raises the question of the intended meaning of the maximization premise. If global maximization is the intended meaning, then the consumer must have a (theory of his or her) preference ordering over all conceivable alternative bundles. At a very minimum, the consumer must be able to distinguish between local maxima all of which satisfy both necessary conditions, (a) and (b).
7. Some people have interpreted Simon's view to be saying that the reason why decision-makers merely satisfice is that it would be 'too costly' to collect all the necessary information to determine the unique maximum. But this interpretation is inconsistent if it is a justification of assuming only 'satisficing' as it would imply *cost minimization* which of course is just the dual of utility maximization!
8. The Slutsky Theorem is about the income and substitution effects and involves an equation derived from a utility maximization model which shows that the slope of a demand curve can be *analyzed* into two basic terms. One represents the contribution of the substitution effect to the slope and the other the income effect's contribution. The equation is interpreted in such a manner that all the terms are in principle observable.
9. For example, if one could show that when the income effect is positive but the demand curve is positively sloped, then the Slutsky Theorem would be false or there is no utility maximization [see Lloyd 1965]. I will return to Lloyd's views of the testability of the Slutsky equation in Chapter 14.
10. The important point to stress here is that it is the incompleteness of the statement that causes problems. Whether one can make such statements verifiable or refutable depends on how one completes the statement. For example, if one completes the statement by appending assertions about the nature of the function being maximized (such as it being differentiable, transitive, reflexive, etc.) one can form a more complete statement that may be refutable [see Mongin 1986].
11. See note 6 above. If one interprets maximization to mean only local maximization, then the question is begged as to how a consumer has chosen between competing local maxima.
12. For these reasons the maximization hypothesis might be called the 'paradigm' according to Thomas Kuhn's view of science. But note that the existence of a paradigm or of a metaphysical statement in any research programme is not a psychological quirk of the researcher. Metaphysical statements are necessary because we cannot simultaneously explain everything. There must be some exogenous variables or some assumptions (e.g. universal statements) in every explanation whether it is scientific or not.

2 Marshall's 'Principles' and the 'element of Time'

> The Hatter was the first to break the silence. 'What day of the month is it?' he said, turning to Alice: he had taken his watch out of his pocket, and was looking at it uneasily, shaking it every now and then, holding it to his ear...
> 'Two days wrong!' sighed the Hatter. 'I told you butter wouldn't suit the works!' he added, looking angrily at the March Hare.
> 'It was the *best* butter,' the March Hare replied.
>
> Lewis Carroll

While it might not be possible to confront neoclassical theory by criticizing the maximization hypothesis, its main essential element, internal criticisms are still not ruled out. But internal criticisms of maximization are very difficult since too often utility as the objective of maximization is not directly observable. Are there any ancillary aspects of maximization that can be critically examined? Perhaps if there are, we can find them in the views that Marshall developed in his famous book *Principles of Economics* [1920/49]. Marshall, I *now* think, had a clear understanding of the limitations of what we know as neoclassical economics. Recognized limitations would seem to be a good starting point for a critical examination of neoclassical economics.

I say that I *now* have this view because as a product of the 1950s and 1960s I never learned to read originals – we were taught to be in a big hurry. Consequently I accepted the many second-hand reports which alleged that the contributions of Samuelson, Hicks, Robinson, Sraffa, Keynes, Chamberlin, Triffin and others represented major or revolutionary advances in economic science which displaced the contributions of Marshall. If the truth were told, economic theory is no better off – maybe it is even worse off.

With respect to Marshall's *Principles* the only apparent accomplishment of more modern writings is a monumental obfuscation of the problem that

Marshall's method of analysis was created to solve. A clear understanding of the methodological problem that concerned Marshall is absolutely essential for a clear understanding of the Marshallian version of neoclassical economics. Unfortunately, owing to our technically oriented training, we have lost the ability to appreciate Marshall's approach to the central problem of economic analysis which is based on the methodological role of the element of time. Having said this I do not want to lead anyone to think that I am simply saying that one can understand Marshall by mulling over each passage of everything he wrote. Reading the history of economic thought has its limitations, too. My main interest is improving my understanding of modern neoclassical economics, so I view historical works as a guide rather than a rule.[1] It is *my* understanding that is at issue, not Marshall's. Nevertheless, appreciating why Marshall saw problems with 'the element of Time' and its role in economic analysis can be a fruitful basis for a critical understanding of Marshall's version of neoclassical economics.

Unlike neo-Walrasian equilibrium models, which take time for granted, Marshall's economics allows time to play a central role.[2] Simply stated, the recognition of the element of time is Marshall's solution to the problem of explanation which all economists face. That problem can only be appreciated in relation to a specific explanatory principle or behavioural hypothesis. Such a relationship was introduced in the preface to Marshall's first edition where he refers to the Principle of Continuity. But he explains neither the role of continuity in the problem of explanation nor the problem itself. The problem, it turns out, results primarily from a second explanatory principle, the Principle of Substitution, which he introduces later (in Book V). I will argue here that Marshall saw an essential role for time in economic explanations for the simple reason that he wished to apply only these two principles to all economic problems.

THE TWO EXPLANATORY 'PRINCIPLES'

It seems surprising that there are only two explanatory principles stated by Marshall – the Principle of Substitution and the Principle of Continuity. These two explanatory principles are distinguished from 'laws' (or 'tendencies') which also play a role in his explanations. The principles are assumptions (we assume because we do not know) but Marshall considers 'laws' to be beyond doubt.

The Principle of Substitution is easily the more familiar of the two since it is merely what we now call the neoclassical maximization hypothesis. It says, *everyone is an optimizer* (i.e. a maximizer or minimizer) *given his or her situation* (including his or her endowment). But *by itself* it is not a sufficient explanation of phenomena. The Principle of Substitution presumes the truth of what Marshall calls the Principle of Continuity. Since Marshall wishes to apply the Principle of Substitution to everything, he needs to show that the Principle of Continuity applies to everything. In simple terms, the Principle of Continuity says everything is relatively a matter of degree. For Marshall there are no class differences, only matters of degree. He takes the same attitude towards the differences between 'city men' and 'ordinary people', between altruistic motives and selfish motives, between short runs and long runs, between cause and effect, between Rent and Interest, between man and his appliances, between productive and non-productive labour, between capital and non-capital, and even between needs and non-essentials. In all cases whether the degree in question is more or less is relative to how the distinction is being used *in an explanation*. For example, 'what is a short period for one problem, is a long period for another' [p. vii].[3]

Sometimes it seems that Marshall is probably the only neoclassical economist who fully appreciates the methodological problem of the applicability of the Principle of Substitution. To be sure of its applicability, he postpones its introduction until Book V, the fifth of six major parts of his book. The first four Books are devoted to convincing the reader that the assumption of maximization is applicable by demonstrating the universal applicability of the Principle of Continuity. There must be available a continuous range of options[4] over which there is free choice (i.e. substitutability is precluded whenever choice is completely limited), and the choice must not be an extreme (or special) case – otherwise the question would be begged as to what determines the constraining extreme limit.

THE 'ELEMENT OF TIME'

Marshall stresses (e.g. in his original preface) that the applicability of the Principle of Continuity (and consequently the applicability of the Principle of Substitution) depends heavily on 'the element of Time'. By ignoring the element of time, our teachers (and their textbooks) would have us believe that the Principle of Substitution is the only hypothetical aspect of the 'Principles'. If one could reduce everything to maximization then explanation would certainly be made at least formally easier. Samuelson saw that it was possible for even the notion of a stable equilibrium to be reduced to the Principle of Substitution [e.g. Samuelson 1947/65, p. 5], that is, to a matter of constrained maximization. Time, if considered at all, is deemed relevant only for the proofs of the stability of equilibria. Most of us have been trained not to see any difficulty with the element of time – for fear of being accused of incompetence.

Marshall's view is quite the contrary: the element of time is central. For instance, to presume that at any point in time a firm has chosen the best labour and capital mix presumes that time has elapsed since the relevant givens were established (viz. the technology, the prices, the market conditions, etc.), and that period of time was sufficient for the firm to vary those things over which it has control (viz. the labour hired and the capital purchased) prior to the decision or substitution. Even when its product's price has gone up the firm cannot respond immediately. Nor can it stop production and its employment of labour merely because the price has fallen [cf. p. 298]. Contrary to modern textbooks, in Marshall's economics very short-run market pressures are more 'the noise' than they are 'the signal' *when viewed from the perspective of the entrepreneur's decision process*.[5]

Time is an essential element in Marshall's method of explanation. Marshall tells us quite a lot about explanation in economics. He stresses the need to recognize the role of fixed 'conditions', but he also stresses that the 'fixity' is not independent of the defining 'time periods'.[6] Marshall's use of the term 'conditions' can lead to confusion, so it might be useful to examine his theory of explanation more specifically by distinguishing between dependent, independent and exogenous *variables*, and between fixed and exogenous *conditions*. These distinctions crucially involve the element of time.

The relationship between dependent and independent variables is supposed to be analogous to the relationship between causes and effects. Marshall, however, cautions us that all such distinctions are relative. For instance, in the very short period the market price is the dependent variable and, given the demand, the quantity supplied is the independent variable. But, in the usual short run, the market price is the independent variable and, given technology (i.e. the production function), the quantity supplied is the dependent variable.

In the preface to the *Principles* Marshall recognizes the usual type of interdependence as being an instance of the Principle of Continuity. He specifically credits Cournot with teaching us to face the difficulty of 'mutual determination'. Marshall calls this type of interdependence a mathematical conception of continuity although he refers to this conception only in regard to the relationship between causes and effects.[7] Today we might say that, in Marshall's short period, price and quantity are both endogenous variables and are *simultaneously determined* by the exogenously given technology and demand. Thus, the distinction between independent and dependent variables is only a matter of verbal convenience since both are endogenous.

Marshall regards 'conditions' as variables which are exogenously fixed during the period of time under consideration. He relies on their fixity in his explanation of behaviour where these fixed variables are the constraints in a maximization process. In this regard, Marshall's neoclassical programme is indistinguishable from the mathematical approach of his contemporary Leon Walras. However, in Walras' approach, as it is taught today, the constraints are given as stocks to be allocated between competing uses. And, of course, Walras is usually thought to consider all processes to be completed simultaneously as if the economy were a system of simultaneous equations. Nevertheless, although both approaches to explanation are 'scientific' in Marshall's sense, the mathematical conception of an economy is rejected [p. 297].

In Marshall's view the problem of explanation is that there are too many conceivable 'causes'. It is not that one has to rely on exogenous givens as being 'causes' in any hypothesized relationship, but rather that there are so many exogenous variables to consider. This problem was not the one faced by followers of Walras who are more concerned with the solvability of his system of equations. Marshall's problem was the direct result of the method he used to deal with the necessity of conditional explanations. Where followers of Walras in effect try to attain the greatest generality or scope of the explanations by maximizing the number of endogenous variables and minimizing the number of exogenous variables, Marshall deliberately adopts a different strategy by attempting to maximize the number of fixed exogenous variables at the beginning of his analysis so as to reduce the explanation to a sequence of single-variable maximizing choices. All other variables are fixed because they are exogenous givens or because they are exogenously fixed by a prior maximization process. The exogenous reason that they are fixed in any problem is the logical basis for their use in his explanation.

There is a difficulty with Marshall's approach to explanation whenever there are many variables. It is difficult to distinguish between the endogenous conditions – those which are exogenously fixed for the period of time considered (e.g. fixed capital in the 'short run') – and the truly exogenous conditions that can never be explained as outcomes of a maximization process (e.g. weather, social conditions, states of knowledge, etc.). Although exogenous variables need not be fixed, in Marshall's approach they are treated as fixed by limiting the length of the period of time to which the explanation refers.

In Marshall's view, the problem of explanation is thus one of carefully defining the fixity of the 'conditions' by defining the relevant period of time for the operation of the explanatory Principle of Substitution. Of course, what is a relevant period of time depends conversely on what are the relevant exogenous conditions for the application of the Principle of Substitution. For example, in Marshall's short period – 'a few months' [p. 314] – virtually everything but the level of output and the amount of labour employed is by definition fixed; but in his long period – 'several years' [p. 315] – everything but technology and social conditions is endogenous.

As with Walras' economics, in Marshall's economics the truly exogenous variables are the only bases for explanations. Any variable which is fixed for a period of time and which serves as a constraint on anyone's maximization process must be explained at some stage or be explicitly identified as an exogenous variable. More important, if it is not an exogenous variable, its fixity at any stage must be explained in terms of acceptable exogenous variables.[8] Even though Marshall's approach begins by maximizing the number of fixed exogenous variables, his ultimate objective is, like that of the followers of Walras, to explain as much as possible. Since by definition exogenous variables are those which are to be left unexplained, the Marshallian methodological strategy then is to reduce the number of exogenous variables in stages. Marshall obviously considered the methodological problem of explanation in economics to be solvable.

In Marshall's economics the truly exogenous variables are the only 'causes' in the strict sense. According to Marshall's view, if one is to provide a long-run explanation, 'time must be allowed for causes to produce their effects' [p. 30]. Of course, this 'is a source of great difficulty in economics [because] the causes themselves may have changed' [p. 30]. Note, however, that the changeability of 'causes', that is, the changeability of exogenous variables, is *not* the problem of explanation, but rather, it is the more narrow methodological problem of *verifying or refuting* one's explanation.[9]

Even when changes in the exogenous givens are assumed away, the fundamental problem for all explanations involving time still exists. The logic of explanation (for example, of all the co-determined endogenous variables) requires that we recognize at least one exogenous variable; and given maximization with exogenous tastes and exogenous constraints, changes in endogenous variables are explained as being caused by changes in at least one of the exogenous variables. But this means that an explanation of long-run dynamic behaviour requires at least one exogenous variable which is impervious to the amount of real time elapsed in the long run (otherwise, the explanation might be circular). For this purpose, the explanatory element of time involves the identification of at least one time-independent exogenous variable – that is, one which does not change over the defined long run.

It should be noted that Marshall's view of explanation also recognizes another aspect of the element of time. *If* the state of affairs at any point in time is to be *explained* as a consequence of someone's optimizing choice, it *must have been* possible to alter one's choices – and this possibility is both a matter of the time available and the continuity of options. Needless to say, it also presumes the ability to know what is the best *option*. Learning what is the best option takes time [p. 284]. This question of learning, I would argue, is *the* explanatory problem involving the element of time. Of course, for Marshall, the inductive scientist, time is all that is necessary for the accumulation of the needed knowledge. Unlike the classical school, Marshall sees no need to assume 'perfect knowledge' because he explicitly wishes to recognize the period of time under consideration – a period he would consider sufficiently long to obtain any 'necessary knowledge'.[10]

MARSHALL'S STRATEGY

It would be misleading to suggest that Marshall's problem of explanation is merely a matter of defining a long-run equilibrium, for it is also a matter of how the long-run equilibrium is reached. Again, in Marshall's view [p. 304], the explanatory problem is that there are too many exogenous variables in the short run during which most decisions are made. His strategy is intended to reduce the number of exogenous variables by increasing the number of variables to which the Principle of Substitution can be applied at later stages.[11] Marshall thus considers the problem of explanation to be solvable since he recognizes that there is a different degree of changeability for each variable (another application of the Principle of Continuity). In short, Marshall's strategy is to distinguish between short-run and long-run explanations. Any complete explanation must specifically *assume* which variables can be changed most quickly – that is, the variables must be ordered according to their changeability. Different orderings may yield a different path to the long-run equilibrium. Unless the assumption is very specific it may be impossible to distinguish between a long-run moving equilibrium and a short-run movement toward a new long-run equilibrium.

Although Marshall gives a prominent role to the distinction between long and short periods, it is not sufficient to solve his problem of explanation – which, as I have said, is a problem concerning the methodological choice of exogenous variables that are impervious to time. Yet most commentators seem to think that Marshall's 'statical method' – namely, the contents of Book V – constitutes his solution to the problem of explanation. This is a mistake.

The first point to be made is that Marshall's 'statical' or partial equilibrium method of analysis yields incomplete explanations. The 'statical' method is relevant only for decisions 'on the margin' or in the neighbourhood of an equilibrium position. By itself the method examines the necessary but not the sufficient conditions for equilibrium. The second point to be made is that Marshall does offer a more complete explanation which is based on the contents of Book IV. By itself, Book V deals only with the 'noise' in order at best to explain it away. A source of an explanation of an economy's true dynamics and its application of the Principle of Continuity to the element of time is to be found in Book IV. These two points will be discussed in turn.

The insufficiency of Book V

I do not think Marshall ever claims that Book V alone represents a complete explanation of an economy's behaviour. Yet, judging by modern textbooks, one could easily think that Book V is 'the principles of economics'. What we call microeconomic analysis today can all be found in Book V. Nevertheless, implicitly Book V provides only the necessary conditions for any equilibrium. That is, on the *assumption* that an economy is in long-run equilibrium at a point in time, certain necessary relationships must hold whenever that assumption is true. It is a 'statical' method because it may be relevant only for that one equilibrium position at one point in time. In effect, Book V examines the local stability properties of the *assumed* long-run equilibrium that are the logical consequences of definitions of equilibrium and of the long period. But it will be argued below that the stability properties are heavily dependent on the empirical assertions of Book IV.

To be specific, before Book V can be considered relevant for anything, that is, before it can play a role in economic analysis, a key question must be asked: why should there ever be a long-run equilibrium? Marshall approaches this question in two ways. The most familiar is in Book V where he defines an ordering of the changeability of the variables with respect to three periods of time – 'the very short period', 'the short period' and 'the long period'. The quickest variable in Marshall's world is the market-determined price. In fact, his definition of a market is not the textbook one of a *place* where buyers and sellers meet to haggle over the price. Marshall makes the existence of a market depend on whether the price clears *quickly* enough for all producers to face the *same price* regardless of their location. For Marshall then there is no market for any good whose price is either not uniform[12] or not quickly established. In effect, this axiom about market prices makes all firms price-takers since it takes longer to establish their (short-run) decisions than the price itself.

Marshall's definition of the market means that the market price (as opposed to the short-run or long-run equilibrium price) is the only *real time* observable price. This theory of market prices assumes that the supply quantity is fixed – virtually everything is fixed but the price. The remainder of the discussion in Book V is an examination of what happens to the market price over time when more and more of the fixed givens are allowed to change. For example, Marshall begins by allowing the firms to make substitutions in their quantity supplied in response to the current level of the market price (relative to costs). This 'short-run' *process* of substitution requires some time – 'a few months or a year' [p. 314].

Marshall says that he wishes to argue that demand determines the market price in one extreme – the very short run – and technology determines the market price in the other extreme – the long-run equilibrium. Implicitly the real world is somewhere in between.[13] Again, the meaning of 'determines' is only a matter of relationships made *necessary* by virtue of his defined equilibria. If at a point in time the economy is at a long-run equilibrium, it must also be at a short-run equilibrium, since if it were not there would be short-run incentives to change the givens which are the constraints in the determination of the market price. Similarly, the short-run equilibrium presumes that the market is in equilibrium. In other words, every long-run equilibrium must also be a short-run equilibrium and every short-run equilibrium must be a market-run equilibrium. This 'nesting' of the forms of equilibrium is the essence of Marshall's 'statical method'.

Although it is now very easy to list the *necessary* conditions for the existence of a long-run equilibrium, the key question still concerns the *sufficient* conditions for the existence of a long-run equilibrium, which must be consistent with both a short-run equilibrium and a market equilibrium. The question of consistency has been a major source of controversy over the last sixty years. The logical problem is that the absence of excess profits in conjunction with profit maximization in the long period implies that the production function is locally linear-homogeneous (constant returns to scale on the margin); but this implication appears to be inconsistent with a downward sloping demand curve, the ultimate constraint thought to be necessary to limit the size of the producer.[14]

Marshall's only line of defense is his other approach, which is based on the Principle of Continuity. Given the continuous operation of the Principle of Substitution, it is quite possible for the price to be above or below the long-run equilibrium price. When it is above there are positive excess profits and when it is below there are losses and, logically, there must be a (long-run equilibrium) point in between where excess profits are zero. The apparent inconsistency is due only to the discussion of the hypothetical and heuristic 'stationary state' – it is a very special type of long-run equilibrium which is supposed to hold for a specified period of time. The only inconsistency is between the previously mentioned nesting of equilibria and the stationary state. Specifically, the inconsistency is that the stability of each of the various equilibria that hold at the long-run equilibrium depends necessarily on the consideration of *different* periods or lengths of time for each whereas in the stationary state they are all supposed to refer to the *same* period of time.

Leaving the stationary state aside, there is no reason why the stability of the various forms of equilibrium has to refer to the same set of 'conditions' or variables or, equivalently, to the same period of time. Hence, the stability relations (e.g. the necessary slopes of curves) for one form of equilibrium will not be 'statically' consistent with those relations necessary for the stability of another form. If one ignores the element of time, it is only too easy to 'see' an inconsistency where otherwise there is none.

The methodology of Book V vs a complete explanation

Once one recognizes the necessary element of time it might appear that there is no logical problem with Book V. But to the contrary, there still remains the matter of explaining *why* there should ever be a long-run equilibrium,[15] and this is a question which must be tackled within an appropriate frame of reference. The essential element of the frame of reference of any behavioural explanation is the specification of exogenous and endogenous variables. All explanations must be based on something being exogenous. In Marshall's time-based view of the economy, it must be something whose exogeneity extends to a longer period of time than the 'long period' under consideration. Marshall deals with this issue first in Book IV.

Particularly relevant to Marshall's explanation of an economy is what is sometimes called his 'life-cycle' hypothesis of the firm. In its most specific form it is an empirical assertion about the history of an individual firm with a life-span of three generations [cf. Hague 1958; Loasby 1978]. In its more general form it says that at the beginning of its life the firm benefits from learning so that its ability to produce increases with its size. Implicitly Marshall is only concerned with growing firms – their size is irreversible, hence time and size go together. At the end of its life every firm suffers from diminishing returns. In either case, the life-cycle trajectory is the needed long-run exogenous variable which provides the essential frame of reference.

By itself, this hypothesis about the beginning and the end of the life of a firm does not seem very relevant. The addition of the Principle of

Continuity, however, renders the desired result. This principle allows us to conclude that, since returns change from increasing to decreasing, at some point in between there must have been 'constant' returns. This point is a *possible* long-run equilibrium. Given the life-cycle hypothesis and continuity, every firm must pass through this point. Once it is reached, the 'statical method' can be used; but it remains merely a 'snapshot', relevant only for that one point (in the history of the firm).

There is absolutely no reason why all the firms in an economy should simultaneously reach the point of constant returns – that is, reach the 'turning point,' as Marshall calls it. It might be interesting for someone to explore such a fantasy world, but nowhere does Marshall seem to be suggesting that such a state of affairs is *necessary*. Book V nevertheless explores the nature of this turning point: Book V 'is not descriptive, nor does it deal constructively with real problems' [p. 269]. However, Marshall does say Book V 'sets out the *theoretical backbone* of our knowledge of the causes which govern value' [pp. 269–70, emphasis added]. However, this statement is qualified. He says, 'it aims not so much at the attainment of knowledge [but rather] at the power to obtain and *arrange* knowledge with regard to two opposing sets of forces' [p. 270, emphasis added].

Marshall's use of the words 'theoretical' and 'arrange' differs slightly from the usual modern usage. His usage is related to Milton Friedman's *as if* approach to explanation. There is no claim that the method of analysis – of arranging the facts of business – is a true explanation. There is only the claim that the nature of the inevitable turning point can be understood to be the result *if* the world were in a state of equilibrium at a moment in time – or more properly, in a state where forces are balanced.

As in most economists' adventures in methodology, Marshall wishes to be all things to all people; thus his is not a pure example of the Instrumentalism we associate with Friedman.[16] Rather, the Introduction to Book V gives a classic example of what we now call Conventionalist methodology. We are offered *a way of looking at things*. What is offered is not claimed to be true; it can be judged only to the extent that it is *better* or *worse* than some other competing view. Book V is filled with conventions with no claim to their truth status (e.g. the representative firm, the stationary state, the market, the long period, etc.). Only in those cases where we know that he thinks a particular convention is a fiction do we have examples of the 'as if' methodology.

The methodology discussions of the *Principles* are not very interesting today but his theory of the firm should be. The point at issue is that Book IV is a foundation for a *complete* theory of the firm: the firm is always to be found somewhere on its life-cycle trajectory. Its location on the trajectory is determined completely by the time elapsed, [cf. p. 258], but the value of that position can only be determined as a relative value, relative to its past and its future. There are simply too many contingencies to be able to determine the absolute value. But remember, the Principle of Continuity is only concerned with relative values.

Book V does offer a way of seeing the absolute value as a consequence of external forces, that is, of competitive market pressures. But there is no reason why the actual, real-time values would ever be 'long-period normal' prices. The existence of long-period normal prices is merely, one might suggest, a beautiful fiction which lends itself to simple mathematical analysis having no bearing on 'real problems' [cf. p. 269].

INADEQUACIES OF MARSHALL'S METHOD VS PROBLEMS CREATED BY HIS FOLLOWERS

Over the last sixty years there have been two major problems in the application of Marshall's principles; both of them involve the element of time. The first concerns the meaning of increasing returns and the nature of the long-run equilibrium. The second concerns the artificial distinction between 'historical' and 'logical' time.

Problems with the firm's long-run equilibrium

Marshall's Victorian style lends itself easily to distortion. What he meant by certain words in one place may not have the same meaning in another. For example, the term 'increasing returns' is used in two different senses; both result from his implicit assumption that the firm is always growing; hence size and time go together. In Book V he uses the term to describe the observation that average productivity rises over time for any given input levels [p. 377]. This use is at variance with modern usage. Earlier, in Book IV, he employs the term in the limited modern sense to mean an increase in output which is proportionally greater than the increase in the size of the firm [p. 266]. A similar confusion derives from his use of the term 'margin' when discussing his 'representative firm'. By definition, the representative firm is at the 'turning point' on the life-cycle trajectory. At that point average and marginal cost both equal price; thus it is possible to use the average and marginal magnitudes interchangeably. But another use of the term 'marginal' emerges when he refers to the representative firm's contribution to its industry's output.

These confusions are merely irritants. The major problem is the one which occurs when critics ignore the element of time inherent in the 'statical method' whenever that method is applied to long-run equilibria (as noted above). Although the difficulty is primarily logical, it results from conjoining four statements whose individual truth status depends on different periods of time. They are the following:

(a) Prices are determined before the firm makes its supply choice; hence prices are given.

(b) The *Principle of Continuity* applied to all inputs (all inputs are variable) means that the production function of the firm is locally linear-homogeneous and that the level of output is always equal to the sum of the marginal productivities, each multiplied by the respective input (Euler's theorem).

(c) The *Principle of Substitution* (i.e. profit maximization) applied to all variable inputs means that the marginal productivity of each input multiplied by the product's price will always equal the price of that input.

(d) The firm is at the 'turning point', that is, its excess profits are zero.

There is no difficulty with the conjunction of these four statements if they only refer to a single point in time.[17] Moreover, even over the short run, given statement (a) any two of the remaining statements imply the other one.[18] So long as the theory of the firm is confined to the 'short period' there need not be any logical problems. The problems that are alleged to exist arise only when the theory (i.e. the Principle of Substitution) is applied in the long-run period to the short-run *constraints*.

Applications of the Principle of Substitution involve some form of maximization (or minimization) facing fixed constraints. In the short run, all the variables which (by definition) cannot be varied constitute the short-run constraints (e.g. the short run may presume capital is fixed while labour is variable). In the long run everything except the production function is supposed to be variable (by definition); but this raises a major methodological problem. Anything which is variable must logically be subjected to the Principle of Substitution. This means that the variables that served as fixed constraints in the short run become endogenous variables in the long run. But this also means that there are no constraints in the long run and this leaves the Principle of Substitution inoperable in the long run. In the long period, then, the conjunction of the assumptions of a price-taker, (a), of the changeability of all variables in the production function, (b), and of profit maximization with regard to all changeable variables, (c), seems to deny any limit to the size of the individual firm – as if size has nothing to do with time (this interpretation of Marshall's theory of the firm, by its focusing only on the internal logic of maximization, is quite contrary to the views expressed in Book IV).

The methodological problem of explaining the size of the firm (as a consequence of maximization) seems to have troubled many of Marshall's followers although it did not seem to trouble him since his Principle of Continuity discourages extreme viewpoints, such as long-run equilibria. The problem only arises when one attempts to apply the Principle of Substitution to the size of the firm *in the long run*. Today this problem is avoided (i.e. swept under the rug) by saying that one should only *explain* the size of the industry. But this tactic merely raises other questions such as What prevents any one firm from taking over the industry as a monopoly?

Although there is considerable discussion of industries in the *Principles*, Marshall's explanatory Principle of Substitution is applied only to the (short-run) decisions of the individual firm. The industry is merely an epiphenomenon – the logical consequence of what all individual firms do. This is a standard neoclassical viewpoint. However, this viewpoint has always posed certain puzzles concerning the interaction of demand and supply in the market. The difficulty is that both the market and the industry are defined for a specific good but the market is related to the individual firm only through the going price. The price by itself says nothing about quantities except that aggregate quantity demanded must equal industry supply. But, if individual firms must determine the quantity supplied independently of each other, the aggregate quantity supplied is only an epiphenomenon. In terms of Marshall's individualistic methodology, this approach to the relationship between firm and industry appears rather mysterious.

To overcome the mystery, Marshall offers the infamous heuristic fiction, the representative firm. Unfortunately, whenever one tries to use the representative firm, instead of Book IV, to explain the size of the firm as just another consequence of an application of the Principle of Substitution, another methodological problem is created. Recall that the representative firm is defined [p. 285] as a firm at the 'turning point' and it is also a firm on the margin of the industry (older firms will be making less than normal profits). As a profit maximizer at the turning point (where profits are just normal), the representative firm must face constant returns to scale (at least 'locally' [see Baumol 1977, p. 578]). On the other hand, as a representative of the industry, it must be constrained by the negatively sloped demand curve. This latter constraint means that we have a fifth statement which must be conjoined with the other four, namely:

(e) The representative firm's marginal revenue must be less than the price.

The problem is that either statements (e) and (a) are mutually contradictory or one of the other statements must be denied. With respect to any one firm it is not possible for all five statements to be true simultaneously. For example, while profit maximization implies the equality of marginal cost and marginal revenue, zero excess profits implies an equality between average cost and average revenue (the price). Thus, when marginal revenue is less than the price, the firm must be operating where there are increasing returns (since marginal cost must be less than average cost) which is contrary to statement (b). Note that a firm can still be a price-taker even when its average revenue is falling with the quantity supplied.

It could be speculated that all of the controversies surrounding the long-run theory of the individual firm are merely about which of the five statements should be dropped.[19] Moreover, most of the controversies have ignored the element of time. There is no doubt that *if* one ignores the element of time (which differs according to the statement one is considering) and, instead, views the above statements as holding at a single (static) point of time, then logically some of the statements are mutually inconsistent. As argued by Piero Sraffa [1926] and Joan Robinson [1933/69], something must give. A realistic interpretation is that the idea of a price-taker, (a), must go, but Marshall's statical method of dealing with his problem of explanation – distinguishing between very short periods and the short run – blocks that avenue. Allowing that prices may not be market-determined would lead to a conclusion that is contrary to Marshall's objective. If prices were *not* determined in a market, then demand could only play a role in the determination of the size of the *industry* – that is, given the life-cycle, demand determines the number of firms in an industry – *in the long run*. Prices are left to be determined by technical and social considerations within and between firms (e.g. without 'spoiling the market' [p. 313]).

Today, such conclusions seem to be ideologically unacceptable or mathematically inconvenient for economic theorists – hence we simply have stopped talking about Marshallian economics since what he promised (namely, a role for demand and utility maximization in the determination of prices) seems doomed. What I am suggesting here is that things may not be as desperate as everyone seems to fear. Perhaps all that is required is a proper examination of the *element of time*.

The distinction between logical and historical time

Contrary to Marshall's view, it is claimed by post-Keynesians that one must carefully distinguish between 'historical' and 'logical' time [e.g. Robinson 1974]. Historical time refers to the usual calendar or clock time within which decision processes are irreversible. In logical time decisions are reversible. For example, the life-cycle hypothesis is in historical time since it is assumed that the firm always gets older; it cannot get younger.

One might say that this is because with the passage of time the firm is learning but it cannot 'unlearn'. The stability analysis of equilibrium theory is in logical time since the analysis is always conducted in terms of questions such as What *if* the price were higher or lower than the equilibrium price? Logical time is concerned with conceivably possible alternative worlds (regardless of actual events) at any given point in time, whereas historical time may be concerned with the (necessarily) singular event occurring at that time and the accumulation of learning which has transpired up to that point.

The distinction between historical and logical time corresponds respectively to Books IV and V. But the intellectual separation of these concepts (and Books) into mutually exclusive classes is a direct contradiction of Marshall's Principle of Continuity. Marshall does not claim that these concepts or books should be separated. To the contrary, Books IV and V go together. Reality for Marshall is on the continuum *between* the two extreme concepts, that is, reality involves both Books in full measure. Any explanation of the behaviour of an enterprise must be both grounded in history (i.e. irreversible past decisions and learning) and explanatorily complete (i.e. it must at least imply a stable determination of the values of the variables to which the Principle of Substitution has been applied).

SOME CRITICAL CONSIDERATIONS

Most of modern neoclassical economic analysis concerns only the mathematics of Book V. The reason, I think, is simply that Book V is the only part of Marshall's *Principles* that is compatible with the methodological doctrine that dominates economic theory today – Conventionalism – namely, the methodology that restricts research to questions of logical validity instead of empirical truth.[20] Economists today do not wish to discuss the 'truth' of economic theories but only examine their logical validity. The reason why logical validity rather than empirical truth is the preferred object is that with the help of mathematical analysis the former can be established more quickly. Even though Marshall stressed the importance of gradual, slow change, those economists in a hurry will find the logic or mathematics of static equilibria more interesting. Logical analysis can be very quick but real change takes real time and thus may not be disposed to conveniently easy analysis.

NOTES

1. My approach is much like Negishi's [1985]. As Negishi noted, 'What is important is not whether a particular interpretation of a past theory is correct, but whether it is useful in developing a new theory in the present' [p. 2]. Thus the onus is on me and Negishi to show that we have learned something from reading Marshall.
2. For a discussion of the problem of time in neo-Walrasian and Austrian models, see Boland [1982a, Chapter 6].
3. Unless indicated otherwise, all page references enclosed in brackets are to Marshall [1920/49] which is the eighth edition of his *Principles*, reset in 1949.
4. Specifically, there must be what modern theorists might call the 'connectedness' of choice options [see Chipman 1960].
5. The entrepreneur (or manager of the firm) must always make a judgement as to whether day-to-day changes in the market will be long-lasting enough to justify investment and hiring decisions [see p. 314].
6. Remember, according to the Principle of Continuity everything is a matter of degree.
7. His reference to Cournot has often misled modern commentators to think that the mathematical conception is all that Marshall was saying – rather than the more important methodological issue of relative degrees.
8. This is one key element in the methodological 'hidden agenda' of neoclassical economics. In neoclassical economics everything explained is seen to be the consequence of the decisions made by individuals. The explained decisions are represented by the endogenous variables in the explanatory model. The acceptable exogenous variables are limited to natural givens (i.e. to things that cannot be chosen). For more about the role of so-called methodological individualism, see Boland [1982a, Chapter 2].
9. One must be careful to distinguish between the logical validity of an explanation and the verifiability of its truth status [see Boland, 1982a, pp. 102–4 and Chapter 1].
10. See note 5 of Chapter 1. For more on the role of inductivism in economics, see Boland [1982a, Chapters 1 and 4].
11. The variables to be treated later, then, are 'independent' variables.
12. Marshall allows for price differences that result from transportation costs [p. 271].
13. That is, the very short run is not realistic [p. 304], and the logical consequence of a long-run equilibrium is a stationary state [p. 315, footnote 1]; but a stationary state is alleged to be 'a fiction' [p. 305].
14. I will discuss Marshallian models of the firm which try to accommodate downward sloping demand curves in Chapter 5. For a different discussion, see Boland [1986a, pp. 25–8].
15. Book V discusses only the logical possibility of a long-run equilibrium.
16. For a discussion of the Instrumentalism associated with Friedman, see Boland [1982a, Chapter 9].
17. For a more detailed discussion of the question of time in neoclassical economic theory, see Boland [1982a, pp. 97–8].
18. I will examine this relationship between these statements much further in Chapter 5.
19. This is a speculation to be explored more fully in Chapter 5.

20 Conventionalism is the defeatist doctrine based on the recognition that an inductive proof is impossible. The Conventionalist alternative to inductive proofs is to prove something else. Rather than look for a proof of the one true theory, Conventionalism would have us choose the best theory recognizing that the best may not be true (as I noted earlier in this chapter). See further, Agassi [1963], Tarascio and Caldwell [1979] and Boland [1982a, Chapters 7 and 8].

3 Marshall's 'Principle of Continuity'

> If the book has any special character of its own, that may perhaps be said to lie in the prominence which it gives to ... applications of the Principle of Continuity.
>
> Alfred Marshall [1920/49, p. vi]

Neoclassical economics is primarily a method of analysis. It is the method of explaining all behaviour as the logical consequences of one behavioural assumption – namely, maximization subject to explicit constraints.[1] But, many critics ask, is the maximization hypothesis a sufficient basis for neoclassical economics? We saw in the previous chapter that according to Marshall the use of the neoclassical maximization hypothesis necessarily depends on what he called the Principle of Continuity. Contrary to the modern preoccupation with Marshall's Principle of Substitution (in the form of the neoclassical maximization hypothesis), in the first preface to his *Principles* Marshall clearly indicates that he gives primacy to the other principle. If the Principle of Continuity is so important, clearly it must be a fertile ground for critical study. For this reason it is important to understand what Marshall meant by his Principle of Continuity and why he thought it was so important.

The obvious reason for giving prominence to the relatively unknown Principle of Continuity is that the continuity of the domain of the maximization function is a *necessary condition* for *application* of the usual assumption of maximizing behaviour.[2] And even though continuity is necessary, too often it is taken for granted. Thus, Marshall rightfully devotes most of his *Principles* to an examination of the nature of an economy to determine when the Principle of Continuity can be applied. And for those circumstances where it is applicable, he devises an admittedly 'unrealistic', mechanical method of overcoming the problem of its necessity. This is his 'statical method' which I discussed in Chapter 2. The objective of this chapter is a critical examination of the methodological presumption of continuity. Since Marshall so strongly emphasizes continuity, it is important that his method of assuring its applicability be understood.[3]

MARSHALL'S PRINCIPLE OF CONTINUITY AND HIS BIOLOGICAL PERSPECTIVE

The non-mathematical version of the application of the Principle of Continuity was very popular at the end of the nineteenth century – especially among *aficionados* of biology. But Marshall wishes to go far beyond biology. He attempts to apply this principle to everything by showing that everything is a matter of degree. Modern axiomatic model-builders discuss a form of the Principle of Continuity which is considered a question of the 'connectedness' of choice options [e.g. see Chipman 1960]. Specifically, the range of possible choice options must be continuous even when the continuum is subdivided into finite sets of categories (with no gaps or empty categories). Discreteness of choice options does not imply a non-continuity. Even when one defines the choice set as a finite set of discrete (or lumpy) options, the discreteness of the options must have been defined over a continuous background range.[4] That is, what we call a discrete point will be defined in terms of one or more continuous dimensions such that the point is located at one distinct location on a continuum. In short, it is impossible to avoid continuity, thus the only question of applicability is whether there are external limits (constraints) on the choice set.

While the relatively unknown Book IV of Marshall's *Principles* is seldom discussed today, it is central since it is devoted almost exclusively to the question of whether one can truthfully assume the applicability of the Principle of Continuity. Marshall's objective is to establish one of the primary conditions of maximization – namely, the continuously diminishing margin. He rests the weight of his argument for continuity primarily on a foundation of biological analogies. Biology was an attractive source of analogies because in Marshall's day it was seen primarily as the study of slow, gradual and progressive change along a continuum. In many cases, Marshall's argument for continuity of a variable rests only on an observation that the variable can be changed in degrees. He refers to 'man's power of altering the character of the soil' [p. 122]; and he often discusses growth: Growth of Population [Chapter 4], and of Wealth [Chapter 7]. Although growth can be distinguished from development, development usually depends on growth, thus Marshall devotes most of Book IV to the consideration of the development of a growing enterprise. The continuum that Marshall wishes to establish concerns the 'division of labour'.

It was apparently well known that 'organization increases efficiency' [p. 200]. For nineteenth-century economists, the key to this 'biological doctrine', whenever it applies to economics, was the recognition that the growth of an organization goes hand-in-hand with an increasing division among its functions – which can be viewed as either increasing disaggregation or decentralization, so to speak, or as breaking down into smaller and more specialized functions. But the more specialized (and hence decentralized) a functional part becomes, the greater the need for organization to keep all the functional parts coordinated and cooperative. The growth of an industrial organization was seen in these terms. But Marshall recognizes that there were certain drawbacks to increasing organization.

While initially the increasing organization facilitates a division of labour and its resulting economies, eventually the size of the organization reaches a limit where, given the size of the market, further growth or development of the organization tends to reduce the effectiveness of the organization. Thus, Marshall can see a life-cycle continuum which goes from increasing returns to decreasing returns. This proposition – the inevitability of decreasing returns as size increases – is considered to be true by analogy with biological systems. Marshall's objective, however, is to establish both the continuity of (average) returns and the fact that the (average) returns must eventually diminish. Once that objective is reached, Marshall has, in effect, shown that since an average cannot go from increasing to decreasing without a fall in the margin, marginal returns must be diminishing with regard to the extent of organizational development.

A necessary condition for maximization of a function over the domain of a given variable is that the value of the first derivative (i.e. the margin) be falling at the point of the maximum. In Book IV, Marshall establishes the continuity and the necessity of a maximum by means of biological analogies. With such analogies he also establishes the necessity (the 'law') of diminishing marginal productivity in the supply of all goods. It should be noted that Marshall has little difficulty in establishing the corresponding law of diminishing marginal utility. Marshall simply asserts in Book III that there are continual 'gradations of consumers' demand' [Chapter 3] and that obviously all wants must be satiable – that is, for any good there is a quantity at which utility is maximum. Thus the result is obtained that if total utility can go continuously from zero to a positive value and back toward zero, average utility must eventually fall with increasing consumption. By the same mathematical argument that is used for productivity, whenever the average is falling the marginal must be less than the average. Thus, specifically, marginal utility must (eventually) be falling since eventually average utility must fall.

Marshall thus establishes to his satisfaction that every theory that has anything to do with demand or supply must involve 'continuous gradations'. Furthermore, by adding his life-cycle theory of the firm and his assertion that all wants are satiable, he has completed the foundation (i.e. the necessary conditions) for his programme of economic analysis.

MARSHALL'S PRINCIPLE OF SUBSTITUTION AS A RESEARCH PROGRAMME

It would appear then that, once the Principle of Continuity is applied and the appropriate diminishing margins are established, the way is clear for a direct application of the Principle of Substitution to all decisions concerning demand or supply. But as I noted in Chapter 2, Marshall claims to the contrary; there are difficulties with the 'element of Time' [pp. 92 and 274]. The difficulties, however, lie in his conception of the essence of 'scientific' explanation – namely, the notion of cause and effect relations. The problem with economic explanations, according to Marshall, is that at any point of time there are too many exogenous conditions to consider. Thus he claims that all 'scientific' explanations are conditional – in particular, they depend on the assumptions made about the relevant exogenous variables. Changes are explained only as the effects of changed conditions.

Again, unless the changeability (or fixity) of the 'conditions' is explained, the Marshallian method of explanation runs the risk of profound circularity. Circularity might be avoided by adopting the Walrasian approach, but doing so would only risk an infinite regress.[5] Moreover, the completion of the Walrasian programme of representing the economy with a set of simultaneous equations turns out to depend intimately on the mathematical form of those equations. Thus, where Marshall's programme runs the risk of circularity, Walras' programme runs the more obvious risk of arbitrariness if one does not attempt to explain one's choice of hypothesized mathematical forms.

MARSHALL'S REJECTION OF MECHANICS AND PSYCHOLOGY

Summarized this way, Marshall's research programme sounds rather mechanical. Marshall states that he wishes to avoid identifying economics with the immutable laws of physics [p. 37]. Yet he thinks economics can be more rigorous and less subjective than the 'scientific' study of history. In effect, he sees biology as an intermediate stage on a continuum between inexact, subjective historical studies at the one extreme and precise, objective physics at the other extreme. Thus he draws parallels between economics and biology by seeing them both as studies of growth and development of organisms or organizations. The mutability of the character and purpose of individuals and groups ('races') of individuals in response to changing conditions is the key to the parallels. He says the same must be true for economic analysis [pp. 30–1].

Many writers, such as G.F. Shove [1942], have noted Marshall's apparent love for biological analogies. But why was Marshall so enamoured of biological analogies? Marshall's advocacy of a biological perspective in economics appears to be due to the prevailing dissatisfaction with both the mechanics of physical analogies and the dreaded 'hedonism' implied by basing economics on the psychology of the individual.

Marshall's use of biological analogies can be better appreciated when it is contrasted with the prevailing public opinion at the time he began work on his *Principles*. Prior to the French Revolution at the end of the eighteenth century, most intellectuals on both sides of the Atlantic were convinced that the apparent success of Newtonian mechanics demonstrated the correct approach to solving all social problems. Namely, if everyone were 'rational' like the scientists, they would all see that the solution to the eighteenth century problem was the elimination of both the monarchy and the Church. This revolutionary social programme collapsed in Europe with the failures of the French Revolution. Although in many ways this programme lived on in the economic principles of the Classical School as well as in the Americans' Declaration of Independence, those intellectuals disappointed with the failures of classical Rationalism hastily retreated from the objective world of 'reasonable men' to the Romantic worlds of subjective psychology, poetry and introspection.

In this sense it is easy to see how many intellectuals identified the classical school of economics with the failure of classical rationalism and thus economic analysis was considered suspect in many circles. The shortcomings of the subsequent Romantic view were not so apparent during most of the nineteenth century. Yet Marshall rejected Jevons' Romantic theory of value (which was based on demand rather than supply) because in Marshall's eyes this was probably seen as a retreat from one extreme (namely, exclusive mechanics of supply) to another extreme (namely, exclusive mechanics of demand). Later, Keynes, dissatisfied with Marshall's neoclassical economics, was to go all the way. In order to reject the mechanics of classical economics, Keynes endorsed a psychological basis for all businessmen's decision-making.[6] But the methodological question here is whether the rejection of mechanics necessarily entails the espousal of subjective psychology. Clearly, Marshall opted for a more liberal compromise.

A psychological basis for decision-making would seem too much like the 'immoral hedonism' often identified with the Benthamite programme of explanation where all human behaviour is considered to be the consequence of utility maximization. The major problem with psychologistic explanations is that they presume an immutable 'human nature' – for example, permanently given tastes. John Stuart Mill's *Principles* came very close to being such a theory of human behaviour. As Marshall saw this, the difficulty was not maximization, but rather the view that human nature is immutable. If human nature were immutable there would be little reason for social or economic change. To a Victorian scientist, the immutability of the human character was unthinkable. In summary, Marshall saw additional significance in the support his biological analogies gave to his discussion of continuity. He embraced biology because evolutionary biological analogies were the obvious and most palatable alternative to mechanical or hedonistic theories of economics and society.

COMPREHENSIVE MAXIMIZATION MODELS

Keynes identified Marshall with the mechanistic Classical School. Disagreement would be difficult on the sole basis of Book V of the *Principles*. But Marshall insisted that mathematical models of dynamics (and hence mechanics) would be inappropriate [pp. 382 and 637]. Nevertheless, Marshall's protestations notwithstanding, it is easy to see that all economic behavioural assumptions can be reduced to maximization (or minimization).

To see how the idea of equilibrium can be reduced to one of *universal* maximization alone, consider the two most common assumptions regarding equilibrium: (1) the assumption of the existence of a specific market equilibrium and (2) the assumption of the existence of a general competitive equilibrium. It is easy to see that both can be shown to follow from the assumption of successful maximization alone.

First, let us consider the elementary idea of a market equilibrium, that is, of the existence of a price at which demand equals supply. There are two structural elements in any market: the demand curve and the supply curve. In neoclassical economics, the demand curve is the dominant logical consequence of utility maximization in the sense that the curve is the locus of price and quantity combinations for which at any given price the indicated quantity is the total demand which results when *every* consumer is maximizing utility while facing that price. Likewise, the supply curve indicates the consequence of profit maximization where for any given price the curve indicates the total supply which is achieved when *every* firm is facing that price and is maximizing its profit. To see what it means to assume the existence of a market equilibrium whenever we are also assuming universal maximization, we need only consider the contrary implications of the non-existence of a market equilibrium. Whenever there is excess demand, some of the demanders are unable to maximize due to an insufficiency of supply at the going price. Such a disequilibrium in the market would thus deny universal maximization. And thus, when it is assumed that everyone is a maximizer, disequilibria are logically precluded.[7]

The more general assumption of the existence of a competitive equilibrium meets a similar fate simply because the assumption of a competitive equilibrium implies the absence of excess profits; that is, it implies the absence of any reason to exit one industry and enter another. It is easy to show that whenever Marshall's Principle of Continuity is applicable (such that *all* relevant factors of production are variable), total revenue must equal total costs if it is also assumed that all the factors are paid their marginal product. First, whenever a price-taking firm is maximizing its profit with respect to every factor, it must be paying each factor its marginal product. Second, whenever all factors are variable, Euler's theorem is applicable: output equals the weighted sum of all the input factors, each weighted by its respective marginal product. Putting these two considerations together, we see that whenever all factors are variable there must be constant returns to scale and thus paying factors their marginal product in order to maximize profit will exhaust the output. In other words, whenever the Principle of Continuity applies, *universal* profit maximization precludes excess profit. Thus we can see that there is no need to add an assumption which asserts the existence of a competitive equilibrium if we are already assuming universal maximization as well as assuming that all factors are variable!

These considerations would seem to lend considerable support to those neoclassical economists who, by accepting that everything reduces to the mathematics of maximization, wish to consider other territories to conquer with their maximization hypothesis [e.g. Becker 1976; Stigler and Becker 1977]. Their research programme is rather straightforward. Every decision-maker faces constraints and possesses an objective (utility) function and thus every equilibrium in society or an economy can be seen to follow from universal maximization. The theorist's task is only to describe the constraints and the objective function which is consistent with the absence of any incentive for change – that is, for example, with zero excess profit and zero marginal profit. Thus, the appearance of imperfections in competition can easily be explained away as the misperception of some economic theorists who incorrectly calculate the transaction costs of encouraging additional competition. That is, even the constraints facing all short-run maximizers can supposedly be explained as the consequences of all individuals' maximization efforts by realistically assessing the cost of further substitutions in the constraints.

Such a programme has been applied to unusual questions such as those concerning an optimal amount of charity, an optimal marriage contract, an optimal capital punishment or deterrent, an optimal institutional environment, the optimality of being altruistic or even of voting, and so on. Of course, one is free to do or assume anything one likes, even to attempt to explain everything as an effect of maximization. Intellectual honesty, however, seems to require that all the necessary conditions of maximization must be fulfilled. One of them is the requirement of a continuity of options. By giving prominence to the Principle of Continuity (and the related 'element of Time') Marshall, to his great credit, recognized the limitations of applying the Principle of Substitution. In the absence of universal continuity and variability, Marshall implies that the assumption of maximization is not an appropriate method of analysis for all situations.

The major methodological question for proponents of neoclassical economics is 'Can maximization be the sole basis for the neoclassical research programme?'. I have argued above that the assumption of maximization alone is not sufficient; one must also assume or establish a minimum degree of continuity. For those who wish to extend the maximization hypothesis as a method of analysis, it is a moot point to show that the variables in question are in fact variable in both directions over a continuous range. It is all too easy to just assume that the decision-maker faces a continuum even when the choice to be made involves integer values such as when one cannot choose a half of an automobile tire or half of a radio. There are two ways to avoid this possible impasse. One could change the choice question to one involving rental time or sharing such that the choice variable more easily fits the notion of an equilibrium. Unfortunately, this type of shift in perspective usually is merely an attempt to hide the original question.[8]

Given the futility of direct criticism of the assumption of maximization behaviour, as I argued in Chapter 1, critics of the neoclassical research programme would be advised to shift their attention to the methods used (implicitly or explicitly) by neoclassical economists to establish the *applicability* of the maximization hypothesis. Surely, questions such as whether to execute a murderer or whether to vote or whether to make any irreversible decision must be a dubious territory for the method of maximization analysis. Marshall explicitly limited his analysis to those territories amenable to the Principle of Continuity. Perhaps modern 'imperialists' such as the followers of Stigler and Becker ought to learn from Marshall's avowed appreciation of the necessity of the Principle of

Continuity that neoclassical models are relevant *only* if the Principle of Continuity can be shown to apply.

NOTES

1 The systematic research programme based on the universal application of maximization is the explicit methodological agenda of neoclassical economics which I discussed in Chapter 1.
2 Note that this says that it is necessary for the sufficiency of any argument employing the maximization assumption.
3 The remainder of this chapter is based on an invited paper which appeared as Boland [1990]. The copyrighted parts are reprinted here with the permission of l'Institut de Sciences Mathématiques et Économiques Appliquées and Les Presses Universitaires de Grenoble.
4 I have discussed these notions of continuity and discreteness in more detail in Boland [1986a, Chapter 5].
5 For example, to the extent that Walrasian economics is about the allocation of given resources, the question can always be begged as to where they come from.
6 I will discuss this in more detail in Chapter 9.
7 It might be argued that the stability of the equilibrium is a separate assumption, but Samuelson [1947/65, p. 5] argues that even stability conditions are formally equivalent to maximization conditions.
8 For more on this methodological strategy, see Boland [1986a, pp. 75–8].

4 Axiomatic analysis of equilibrium states

> Often mathematical formulas are used to describe certain events without awareness of the assumptions on which the applicability of the formulas depends. Even less is there thought of an investigation to determine whether the requisite assumptions are fulfilled in the real world. Therefore it is not surprising that the results are often quite unsatisfactory.
>
> On the other hand, conclusions have often been drawn from mathematical formulas, which, strictly speaking, are not conclusions at all and which at best are valid only under restrictive assumptions. The latter may not have been formulated, not to mention efforts to discover to what extent these further assumptions are fulfilled in the real world.
>
> Thus, for a fruitful application of mathematics in economics it is essential, first, that all the assumptions on which the given mathematical representation of economic phenomena depends be enumerated completely and precisely; second, that only those conclusions be drawn which are valid in the strictest sense, i.e., that if they are valid only under further assumptions, these also be formulated explicitly and precisely.
>
> If these directions are strictly adhered to, then the only objection which can be raised against a theory is that it includes assumptions which are foreign to the real world and that, as a result, the theory lacks applicability.
>
> Abraham Wald [1936/51, pp. 368–9]

> Whenever economics is used or thought about, equilibrium is a central organising idea. Chancellors devise budgets to establish some desirable equilibrium and alter exchange rates to correct 'fundamental disequilibria'. Sometimes they allow rates to 'find their equilibrium level'. For theorists the pervasiveness of the equilibrium notion hardly needs documenting.
>
> Frank Hahn [1973, p. 1]

One common avenue for criticism of neoclassical economics is to analyze the assumptions required for a state of equilibrium. Unlike the neoclassical maximization hypothesis which is deliberately put beyond question in every neoclassical model, the assumption of equilibrium is usually open to question.[1] Some models are designed to explain phenomena as equilibrium phenomena (such as prices or resource allocations). Models which offer equilibrium explanations must at least provide logically possible equilibrium states. Clearly, such equilibrium models are open to question and thus can be critically examined to determine whether a state of equilibrium is consistent with the other behavioural assumptions made. There are some equilibrium models which are not easily criticized such as those which put the existence of equilibria beyond question (e.g. those which involve the Coase theorem or unobserved transaction costs). These necessary-equilibrium models are most often used to explain away alleged disequilibrium phenomena (e.g. involuntary unemployment or socially unacceptable levels of pollution).

In this chapter I will be concerned only with models that explicitly claim to offer explanations in which it is asserted that the phenomena in question are equilibrium phenomena. In the next chapter the focus will be models which by claiming that the phenomena are disequilibrium phenomena posit the equilibrium state as an unattainable ideal.

Equilibrium models which explain why the phenomena occur usually do so by stating a series of explicit assumptions which together logically entail statements representing the phenomena in question. Now, the most common models are ones which represent each assumption with an equation and thus show that the solution of the system of equations is a statement representing the phenomena. Where there is a solution there must be a problem (except perhaps in chemistry). In this case the problem is to find values for the endogenous variables which (given the values of the exogenous variables) allow all the assumptions to be *simultaneously* true. There may be many sets of such values. When there is just one, we call it a *unique* solution. If none is possible we say the model is unsolvable. If one could never solve the system of equations, then the model cannot explain the phenomena as equilibrium phenomena.

When do we know that we are successful in explaining something? There are two necessary conditions. The first is the easiest. Most economists seem to agree that we are successful when the theory we construct is shown to be internally *consistent* and is shown to allow for the *possibility* of the phenomena, that is, when the theory does not contradict the phenomena to be explained. If we look closer at the notion of explanation we will find that this consistency criterion for success is insufficient. The condition that causes difficulty is the second one. Specifically, if one is to explain why prices are *what they are* then for a *complete* explanation (i.e. beyond just possibilities) one must also explain why prices are not *what they are not*. In this chapter I shall examine these two necessary conditions of a successful explanation. Namely, I shall examine why we are successful in explaining any particular phenomena *only* when our theory is not only consistent but is also 'complete' with respect to those phenomena.

ANALYZING THE LOGICAL STRUCTURES IN ECONOMICS

Analyzing the success or failure of logical structures such as equilibrium models is not a new enterprise. Indeed, for a long time it has been an interest of pure mathematicians and some mathematical economists who engage in what they call axiomatic analysis or axiomatics.[2] Their efforts have been directed only at the formalistic aspects of logical structures and thus they have too often been more concerned with axioms of *language* models where the *form* of the axiomatic structure remains the same and the interpretations of the axioms differ to produce various languages [e.g. see Koopmans 1957]. I think axiomatics can also be of considerable importance for our critical understanding of economic phenomena. The primary importance of axiomatics is that it can offer a means of systematically criticizing a given theory (i.e. a given set of assumptions).

For the purpose of critical understanding, the two primary tools of axiomatics are the two necessary conditions of successful explanations. They are the inquiry into the *consistency* of a theory, and the inquiry into the *completeness* of a theory. Since these tools are the basis of any criticism of an equilibrium explanation, I briefly explain how they are used in economics.

Consistency requires that the set of assumptions (which form any particular theory) does not lead to inconsistencies such as would be the case if both a given statement *and its denial* were logically allowed by our theory. For example, the statement 'the economy at time t is on its production possibilities curve' and its denial 'the economy is not on that curve' could not both follow from a consistent theory. This requirement, however, does not rule out the possibility of a theory allowing for competing or contrary situations such as multiple equilibria. For example, all points on a production possibilities curve are potential equilibria that differ only with regard to the given price ratio. If there is a flat spot on the curve, there is a set of points (along the flat spot) all of which are potential equilibria for the same price ratio.

Thus, if our explanation of why the economy is at one particular point along the flat spot is that it is faced with the corresponding price ratio, then consistency alone will not enable us to explain why the economy is not at any other allowed point on the flat spot. Nevertheless, consistency is obviously important since we cannot tolerate contradictions or inconsistencies.

Completeness is the requirement that an explanation does not allow for the possibility of competing or contrary situations. Completeness rules out the possibility of a false explanation accidentally appearing to be true. That is, if our explanation is complete and happens to be false, we shall be able to show it to be false directly. For example, if we assume that the production possibilities curve has no flat spot and is concave (to the origin) then our explanation would be logically complete since each point on the curve is compatible (tangent) with only one price ratio and each price ratio is compatible with only one point on the curve. In other words, our equilibrium point is *unique* given any particular price ratio. Should any other equilibrium point be possible for the same price ratio, then we would also have to explain why we observe the one point rather than the other possible points. That is, our model must explain why we do not observe what we do not observe. The logical possibility of other compatible points would mean that our model is not complete.

The standard method of demonstrating the consistency of a theory is to construct a mathematical model of that theory and prove that it necessarily possesses a sensible solution – that is, demonstrate the *existence* of a sensible solution. The standard method of demonstrating the completeness of a theory is to show that the equilibrium solution of the model is *unique*. Although there is some danger of confusion, these two attributes of theories are usually analyzed separately. There are other, secondary, aspects of axiomatics such as inquiries into the independence and 'weakness' of the various assumptions that make up a theory. I will not discuss these topics here since they are questions of aesthetics rather than of the explanatory power of any equilibrium model.

Usually the question of consistency can be dealt with in a rather direct way: try to solve the system of equations constituting the model of the theory. If a sensible solution cannot *always* be obtained, it may be possible to specify additional assumptions to guarantee such a solution. Eliminating non-sensible solutions is a low-order completeness criterion – that is, the model must be complete enough to exclude them but it may not be complete enough to allow only one sensible solution.

The conditions which assure consistency are usually much less restrictive than those which assure completeness. For this reason the question of completeness can be a serious source of important fundamental criticism. One of the pioneers of axiomatic analysis in economics, Abraham Wald, offered such a criticism of Walrasian economics. A well known but minor aspect of his analysis was a simple proof that the popular condition that 'the number of equations be equal to the number of unknowns' was neither necessary nor sufficient to guarantee a solution, let alone a unique solution. Wald's 1936 axiomatic study of Walrasian general competitive equilibrium, which now may be merely of interest to historians of mathematical economics, can serve as an interesting case study to demonstrate the importance of completeness. Subsequently, I will present my theory of completeness which I think is relevant for general economists as well as for mathematically oriented theoretical economists and which I think may be the only effective means of criticizing equilibrium models.

WALD'S AXIOMATIC WALRASIAN MODEL: A CASE STUDY

Rarely will we find axiomatic studies of Marshallian economics. The reason is simple but misleading. The reason is that Marshall's statical method focuses primarily on the necessary equilibrium requirements for just one market at a time. The key notion is a *partial equilibrium* which is partial because all other markets are impounded in the *ceteris paribus* condition invoked in the determination of each individual's demand (or supply). But each individual still needs to know the prices of other goods. In other words, the individual makes substitution choices on the basis of a knowledge of relative prices. Thus, in effect, the partial equilibrium method is actually predicated on all other markets providing equilibrium prices – otherwise, the equilibrium of the market in question will not persist. The absence of such a general market equilibrium will usually lead to price changes in the other markets followed by appropriate substitution responses in the demand and supply curves of the market in question. So ultimately a complete Marshallian explanation of an equilibrium price involves a form of general equilibrium since only when there is a general market equilibrium can we be sure there is a partial equilibrium in the market in question. Thus Marshall and Walras differ only in their methodological procedures. Since the ultimate equilibrium state in one market depends on all other markets being in equilibrium, the most direct way to analyze the requirements of a general market equilibrium would be to consider all individuals simultaneously and try to determine a set of prices that would allow all individuals to be maximizing. This latter procedure is the Walrasian approach to equilibrium explanations. Although Marshall's procedure may appear to differ, any analysis of a Walrasian equilibrium state will have implications for any successful application of the statical method even when focused on just one market.

The Walrasian system of general equilibrium thus purports to explain simultaneously all (relative) prices and all (absolute) quantities of traded goods (in the system). The question of interest here is: What is the logical consequence of the assertion that Walras' system does *explain* all the (endogenous) variables? In particular, what are the logical conditions placed on the system for it to be truly 'in equilibrium'? When we say the system explains all the prices and quantities, we are saying that all the explicit and implicit (i.e. unstated) assumptions necessary for the sufficiency of the explanation are satisfied. In other words, we are claiming that the system of assumptions is complete. We know what the explicit assumptions are in Walras' system, but the question remains, what are the implicit assumptions? To conjecture what the implicit assumptions are is the task of an axiomatic analysis of the completeness of a general equilibrium system such as Walras'. However, before the search for implicit assumptions can begin, we must first show that the explicit assumptions form an incomplete system, that is, an incomplete system with respect to the task of explaining all prices and quantities of traded goods. Wald, in his famous 1936 paper, attempted to do both of these tasks, namely, to demonstrate the incompleteness of the Walrasian system (which supposedly Walras at first thought was complete merely because the number of equations equalled the number of unknowns) and to posit some possible implicit assumptions. His paper represents one of the first rigorous (axiomatic) studies of the mathematical implications of a Walrasian economic system (in general equilibrium).[3] His version of a Walrasian system is the following:

$$\left.\begin{array}{ll} r_i = a_{i1}X_1 + a_{i2}X_2 + ... + a_{in}X_n + U_i & (i=1, 2, ..., m) \\ U_iV_i = 0 & (i=1, 2, ..., m) \\ P_j = \sum_{i=1}^{m} a_{ij}V_i & (j=1, 2, ..., n) \\ P_j = f_j(X_1, X_2, ..., X_n) & (j=1, 2, ..., n) \end{array}\right\} \quad [4.1]$$

where the exogenous variables are as follows:

r_i is the quantity available of the ith resource

a_{ij} is the quantity of the ith resource needed per unit of the jth good

and the endogenous variables are as follows:

U_i is the unused portion of the available ith resource

P_j is the price of the jth good

V_i is the value of the ith resource

X_j is the output quantity of the jth good

This system of equations is the beginning of an axiomatic version of a Walrasian economic system. The first class of equations ($r_i = ...$) represents the production or resource allocation relations. The second class is a special consideration which says that if a resource is not scarce then some of it will be unused ($U_i > 0$), and thus the resource price (V_i) must be zero (i.e. it is a free good). Walras was claimed to have ignored this consideration (perhaps because he thought it would be obvious which resources are scarce). The third class of equations is the typical long-run competitive equilibrium condition where price equals unit cost. Now the fourth class is actually a set of Marshallian market demand curves. Wald's axiomatic version of the Walrasian system then differs slightly from the textbook version of Walrasian neoclassical economics. In particular, his version makes no attempt to explain the market demand curves by explaining *individual* consumer behaviour.

Wald's study involved the question 'Does the system of equations [4.1] have a unique non-negative system of solutions where r_i and a_{ij} are given numbers, $f_i(X_1, ..., X_n)$ are given functions, and the U_i, X_i, V_i and P_i are unknowns?' On the basis of his method of rationalizing his affirmative answer to this question, he formulated the following theorem which he said he proved elsewhere [Wald 1933/34, 1934/35].

Theorem. The system of equations [4.1] possesses a set of non-negative solutions for the $2m + 2n$ unknowns and a unique solution for the unknowns $X_1, ..., X_m, P_1, ..., P_n, U_1, ..., U_m$, if the following six conditions are fulfilled:[4]

(1) $r_i > 0$ ($i = 1, 2, ..., m$).

(2) $a_{ij} \geq 0$ ($i = 1, 2, ..., m; j = 1, 2, ..., n$).

(3) For each j there is at least one i such that $a_{ij} > 0$.

(4) The function $f_j(X_1, X_2, ..., X_n)$ is *non-negative* and *continuous* for all n-tuples of non-negative numbers $X_1, X_2, ..., X_n$ for which $X_j \neq 0$ ($j = 1, 2, ..., n$).

(5) If the n-tuple of non-negative numbers $X_1^k, ..., X_n^k$ ($k = 1, 2, ... \infty$) in which $X_j^k > 0$ for each k, converge to an n-tuple $X_1, ..., X_n$ in which $X_j = 0$, then
$$\lim_{k \to \infty} f_j(X_1^k, X_2^k, ..., X_n^k) = \infty \quad (j = 1, 2, ..., n).$$

(6) If $\Delta X_1, \Delta X_2, ..., \Delta X_n$ are *any* n numbers in which *at least one* < 0, and if
$$\sum_{j=1}^{n} P_j \Delta X_j \leq 0,$$
then

$$\sum_{j=1}^{n} P_j' \Delta X_j < 0,$$

where $P_j' = f_j(X_1 + \Delta X_1, ..., X_n + \Delta X_n)$ $(j=1, 2, ..., n)$.

Furthermore, he noted that if the rank of the matrix $[a_{ij}]$ is equal to m, then the solution is also unique for the variables $V_1, ..., V_m$.

Now let us try to see what Wald has imposed on the well known Walrasian economic explanation of prices and outputs. The first three conditions are the usual economic considerations. Condition (1) says that the resources must exist in positive amounts in order to be used. Condition (2) says that input requirements are not negative (i.e. they are not outputs). And condition (3) says the output of any good must require a positive amount of at least one input.

Conditions (4) and (5) are required for the *method* of proving *his* existence and uniqueness theorem. That is, in order to use calculus-based mathematics, he must simplify the mathematical aspects of the system. But, whereas condition (4) involves only the usual assumption of continuity, condition (5) is a more serious simplification. Condition (5) says that for the quantity demanded of a good to be zero, the price must be infinitely large. He says that this condition is not necessary for an existence proof but it does help by making the mathematics simple (this condition was the first to be discarded by subsequent developments in mathematical economics twenty years later).[5]

Now we reach (6), the most important condition. It is so important that it has been given a special name: the Axiom of Revealed Preference.[6] It says that the demand functions must be such that if combination A of goods is purchased rather than any other combination B that cost no more than A at the given prices then, for combination B ever to be purchased, the prices must change such that combination B costs less than combination A at the new prices. A rather reasonable assumption if we were speaking of individual consumers, but these are market demand curves! Unfortunately, it does not follow that if the axiom holds for each individual consumer's demand function, then it necessarily will hold for the market function. Similarly, when it holds for the market, it does not necessarily hold for all the individuals. One behavioural interpretation of condition (6) is that all consumers act alike and thus are effectively one. Thus condition (6) imposes constraints on the 'community indifference map' which may be difficult or impossible to satisfy.

We should thus ask (as did Wald): Do we *need* the axiom of revealed preference (in order to assure completion)? His answer was 'yes', and he demonstrated it with a simple model of system [4.1]. Note that if it is necessary for system [4.1] it is necessary for every model of the system;

56 *Principles of economics*

thus if we could show that it is unnecessary for any one model, we could refute its alleged necessity for the systems.

Conditions (1) to (5) are necessary for Wald's proof of the *consistency* of his version of the Walrasian system. Condition (6) is necessary to *complete* the system. To show this we shall specify a model which satisfies conditions (1) to (5), and then we show the necessity of condition (6) by describing a case in which condition (6) is not fulfilled and for which a unique solution does not exist. Consider Wald's special case of system [4.1] involving the unknowns X_1, X_2, P_1, P_2 and V_1:

$$\left. \begin{array}{l} r_1 = a_1 X_1 + a_2 X_2 \\ P_1 = a_1 V_1 \\ P_2 = a_2 V_1 \\ P_1 = f_1(X_1, X_2) \\ P_2 = f_2(X_1, X_2) \end{array} \right\} \quad [4.1']$$

And to satisfy conditions (1), (2) and (3), we can simply let $a_1 = a_2 = a$ where $a > 0$ and let $r_1 > 0$. To satisfy (4) we assume $f_j(X_1, X_2)$ to be continuous and positive. To satisfy (5) we assume that as X_j approaches zero, $P_j \to \infty$. The heart of the matter is the inverse demand functions, $f_j(X_1, X_2)$.

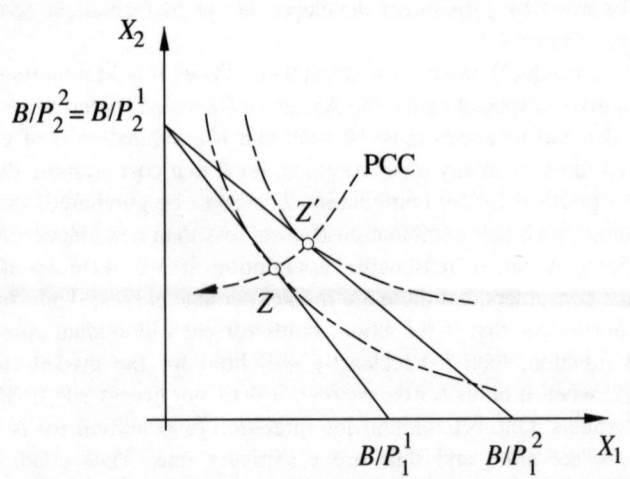

Figure 4.1 *Price–consumption curve (PCC)*

Let us therefore look more closely at them by first reviewing textbook indifference analysis, and in particular, we want to look at the nature of the set of combinations of X_1 and X_2 which give the same demand price (i.e. for P_j constant).

Axiomatic analysis of equilibrium states 57

We know that whenever we base consumer theory on indifference analysis we can derive the demand curve for a good by considering what is usually called the 'price–consumption curve'. To illustrate, consider the two goods, X_1 and X_2. Specifically, all the possible non-negative combinations of them, and let us assume that income is given. Note that in Figure 4.1, for a particular combination of goods, say point Z, there is only *one* set of prices which will be compatible with a choice of combination Z, in particular P_1^1 and P_2^1. If we were to change P_1^1 to P_1^2 without changing P_2, we should find that point Z' is the combination which is compatible with the new price(s).[7]

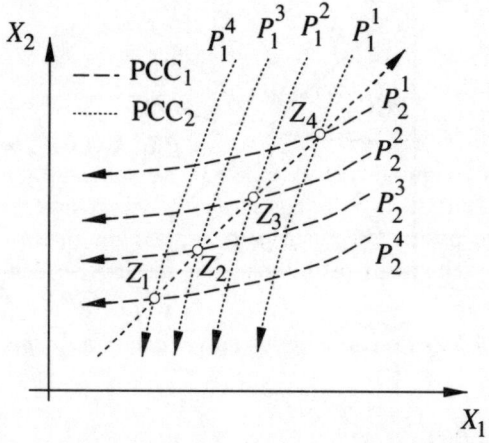

Figure 4.2 *The Z-line (income–consumption curve)*

In this manner we can trace all the combinations which are compatible with a particular P_2 (i.e. where P_2 is constant). The curve traced is simply the price–consumption curve for X_1 from which we derive the demand curve for X_1 or, in terms of model [4.1'], it is all the combinations of X_1 and X_2 such that $f_2(X_1, X_2)$ = constant. Now, instead of drawing an indifference map, we could simply draw a representative set of the possible price–consumption curves (assuming income given) and get something like Figure 4.2. In this figure each curve is labelled with the appropriate fixed level representing the fixed price of the *other* good. On this diagram we can see that point Z_1 is compatible only with given prices P_1^4 and P_2^4. If we hold P_2 constant and move outward from point Z_1, in neoclassical consumer theory we should find that P_1 *falls* along the price–consumption curve labelled with the fixed price P_2^4 (see also Figure 4.1). Similarly, if we hold P_1 constant and move outward along the other price–consumption curve from Z_1, then P_2 falls. Thus note in Figure 4.2 that the superscripts

58 Principles of economics

indicate an ordering on prices. Also we note that conditions (4) and (5) can be satisfied; for example, as we move horizontally toward the vertical axis (i.e. X_1 goes to zero) the price of X_1 rises. If we let $P_1^1 = P_2^1, P_1^2 = P_2^2, ..., P_1^k = P_2^k$, we can trace all the combinations for which $P_1 = P_2$, viz. Z_1, Z_2, Z_3, etc. The line connecting these Zs is what is usually called the 'income–consumption curve' but since the definition of price–consumption curves is based on a fixed budget or income, I will call this the Z-line.

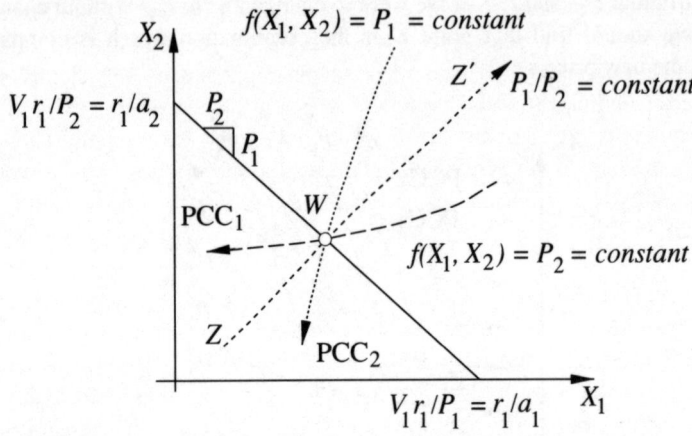

Figure 4.3 *Price–consumption curves and Wald's special case*

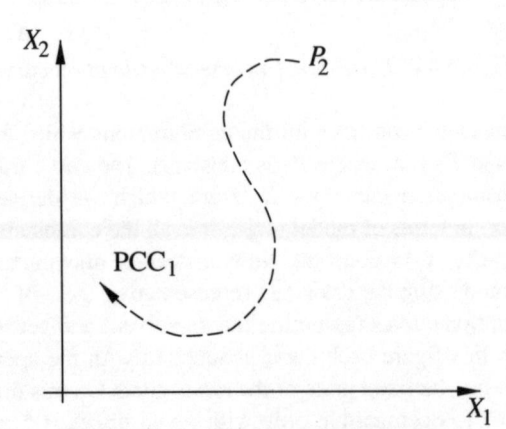

Figure 4.4 *A denial of condition (6)*

Returning to system [4.1′], we see that the first equation can be represented on the commodity–space diagram as shown in Figure 4.3. Since r_1, a_1 and a_2 are given we describe the set of combinations of X_1 and

X_2 which satisfy the first equation as a line (resembling a budget line) which satisfies conditions (1), (2) and (3). Condition (4) says that through each and every point in Figure 4.3 there is exactly one price–consumption curve for good X_1 and exactly one for good X_2. Condition (5) says that as we trace out any price–consumption curve for good X_1 in the direction indicated by the arrowhead (i.e. for a rising P_1) the price–consumption curve will never touch the X_2 axis. Condition (6) is less obvious. It says that no price–consumption curve for good X_1 will have a shape illustrated in Figure 4.4.[8] The reason for excluding such a shape is that the inverse demand function implied by such a shape might not be sufficiently well defined. Condition (6) also assures a sufficient degree of convexity of the underlying preference map (which would have to be a community's map in Wald's model). In my diagrams, this means that if you face in the direction indicated by the arrowhead on any particular Z-line, then to your left the ratio of P_1/P_2 will always be higher than the one corresponding to this Z-line.

What Wald's proof establishes is that there is at least one stable equilibrium point on the quasi-budget line through which passes the correct Z-line. The correct Z-line will be the one drawn for a P_1/P_2 ratio that equals the slope of the quasi-budget line. That is, he proves that there is at least one point like either the one on the positively sloped Z-line illustrated in Figure 4.3 or like the one on a negatively sloped Z-line which has its arrowhead outside of the feasible production points limited by quasi-budget line as illustrated in Figure 4.5.[9]

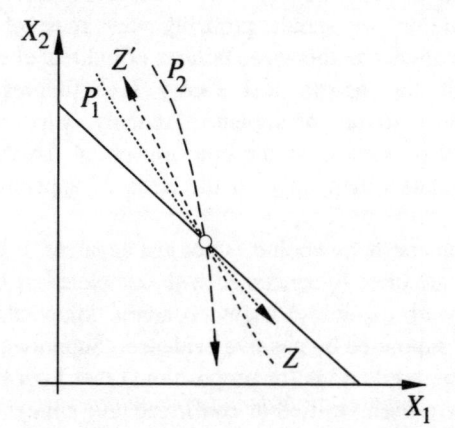

Figure 4.5 *A possible negatively sloped Z-line*

COMPLETENESS AND THEORETICAL CRITICISM

Although the inclusion of Wald's six conditions in the axiomatic structure of the Walrasian system fulfills the task of completing an explanation of prices and outputs, it does not follow that they are *necessary* for the *original* theory. As it was later shown, the existence and uniqueness of the entire Walrasian system can be proved by using either linear programming or activity analysis and these do not require such restrictive assumptions. Thus it would seem that if we are able to show that any one of Wald's conditions is not satisfied (in the 'real world') we do not necessarily refute the original incomplete theory. From a methodological position, this state of affairs is rather perplexing. We may wish to complete an axiomatic version of neoclassical price theory and then criticize it. But, if our criticism deals only with those conditions which we add (for completion purposes), then we are not really criticizing the original price theory. Some think this can be overcome by attempting to deduce testable statements from the incomplete theory and submitting these to tests. No matter how the theory is eventually completed, should any one of them be shown to be false, the theory *as a whole* will be false – otherwise, the apparent falsifying fact must be explained away! Either way, this is a very difficult task and not much has been attempted or accomplished so far.[10]

The question of testability (or criticizability in general) is above all a logical problem. And since axiomatic analysis is concerned with the logical properties of a theory, it can have something to say about empirical testability as well as being able to offer a means of theoretically testing a theory. For example, we should probably view most of the theoretical analysis of neoclassical textbooks as failures of indirect attempts to test the completeness of the neoclassical theory (i.e. failures to show the neoclassical theory to be incomplete). Actually, what we read in the textbooks should be viewed as the only aspects of the theory which are considered complete (often only on the basis of apparent, but untested, consistency).

This disagreement in viewpoints is not just apparent. It would seem that few economists are directly concerned with completeness because most of them (implicitly or explicitly) view economic knowledge as a logical system which is supported by positive evidence. 'Supported' usually means that at least some predictions (or propositions) that logically follow from their theories have been verified or confirmed. An unintended outcome of this view of knowledge is that most economists are satisfied with an argument whenever it allows for the *possibility* of the truth of their theory even though the theory at the same time may imply propositions which are false. For example, a model may have several solutions, one of which is

Axiomatic analysis of equilibrium states

true (i.e. agrees with the observed facts) but the others are false. A completed model, however, leaves no room for errors (viz. for disagreement with facts). Unfortunately, most economists would be satisfied with the incomplete model because at least one of its many solutions is true.

There are different theories of knowledge. Obviously, the one I am promoting in this book says the only way we learn is through criticism; and of course, testing is one form of criticism. Incomplete theories are very difficult to criticize because they leave so much room for conceivable contradictions. Because I want to learn, I want to be able to criticize any theory, and attempting to complete a theory is an important means of exposing a theory to decisive criticism. The unintended outcome of this view of knowledge is that when we attempt to explain an economic equilibrium (such as Walras') it is necessary to explain why all other possible equilibrium positions are not obtained. In effect, this says we must be concerned with *uniqueness*, since to be complete (and thus testable) our explanation of any alleged equilibrium must not allow for other contrary situations such as 'multiple equilibria'.[11] This view is contrary to the popular myth (all too often promoted by those economists who 'picked up mathematics on the side') that satisfying the calculus conditions of a 'stable equilibrium' is sufficient to explain the equilibrium in question. A stable equilibrium structure (such as a negatively sloped demand curve and positively sloped supply curve) is necessary, of course, but without behavioural assumptions concerning price adjustment dynamics, we still have not explained why the system is in 'equilibrium' where it is. All that the calculus stability conditions accomplish is the avoidance of confusing a possibly unstable 'balance' situation with a stable equilibrium situation. I will return to the matter of the importance of stability conditions in Chapter 14.

A THEORY OF COMPLETENESS

In spite of what economists think they are doing, they can be seen to have been indirectly concerned with completeness, and the evidence is the development of neoclassical economic theory. One way to understand this development on the basis of a theory of the development of theories is to characterize all theories as systems of assumptions where each assumption is in the logical form of an 'all-and-some' statement. As I briefly discussed in Chapter 1, an 'all-and-some' statement is one of the form 'for all x there is some y such that ...'. The 'such that ...' clause may or may not be completely specified depending on whether or not, and to what extent, the theory has been completed. Thus an attempt, such as Wald's, to complete a model of a Walrasian theory is in effect an attempt to specify the 'such that ...' clauses of the theory. Whether an 'all-and-some' statement is empirically testable is a question of *how* the 'such that ...' clause has been completed. It is always possible to complete a theory without making it testable; for example, by making it circular.[12]

The specification of the 'such that ...' clauses is almost always *ad hoc*, and so is the completion of an axiomatic system. The history of formal model-building in neoclassical economics is one of a sequence of efforts to complete systems of ideas which rationalize certain enduring propositions. The specification of the nature of indifference curves by Hicks and Allen [1934], the specification of imperfect competition by Robinson [1933/69], the specification of the idea of a market equilibrium by Samuelson [1947/65], and the attempts of Franco Modigliani [1944] and Donald Patinkin [1956] to explain Keynes, are all examples of developments in the neoclassical theory which amount to completions of 'such that ...' clauses. These are also examples of placing requirements on theories which are similar to requirements of typical axiomatic analyses.

If an axiomatic analysis of a theory manages to posit requirements which are necessary for the sufficiency of any given model of that theory, it is an important achievement which should not be left only to mathematical economists to pursue. Wald's Axiom of Revealed Preference, for example, is such a requirement. Any requirement (or 'condition') that is necessary for the completion of a theory may offer an important opportunity for critically testing that theory. However, the Axiom of Revealed Preference by itself is not an essential element in economic analysis.[13] What is essential in neoclassical economics is the notion of a state of equilibrium. In the next chapter I examine other ways to view equilibrium analysis.

NOTES

1. Of course, there are some neoclassical economists who even put the existence of a state of equilibrium beyond question.
2. This type of analysis began in the nineteenth century with studies of the axiomatic structure of Euclid's geometry [see Blanché 1965].
3. Many other axiomatic studies have been published since Wald's, for example Arrow and Debreu [1954], Arrow and Hahn [1971], Debreu [1959, 1962], Gale [1955], McKenzie [1954, 1959].
4. Note well that he does not say *only if*.
5. Specifically, by replacing it with a duality assumption [see Kuhn 1956]. It should be noted that Wald recognized the possibilities of using other mathematical techniques which did not require such a condition. See Quirk and Saposnik [1968] for a survey of the other well-known axiomatic studies of Walrasian economics.
6. Today, Wald's condition is called the *Weak* Axiom of Revealed Preference

Axiomatic analysis of equilibrium states

since it is limited to the comparison of two points. A strong version would refer to a chain of comparisons of many points [see Houthakker 1950, 1961]. None of the discussion in this book will require us to be concerned with this distinction so I will not be emphasizing the 'weakness' of this axiom.

7   The arrowhead on the price–consumption curve indicates the direction along which the changing price increases for the given income and price of the other good.
8   This interpretation of the Axiom of Revealed Preference will be the subject of Chapter 13.
9   Note Figure 4.5 can be used to represent two kinds of appropriate Z-lines simply by swapping the X_1 and X_2 labels (and the P_1 and P_2 labels).
10 Paul Samuelson has in effect attempted to deal with this in Chapter 5 of his published PhD thesis [1947/65]. I have discussed his attempt in Boland [1989, Chapter 1].
11 Whether multiple equilibria represent contrary situations depends on what we are trying to explain. For example, if we were trying to explain the price–quantity in market A and we found that it was compatible with various equilibria in market B, there would be no problem. But, if there are various possible equilibria in market A allowed by our explanation of market A, then we have an incomplete explanation.
12 To the statement 'for every rationalizable choice there is a maximizing choice ...' we might add 'such that if it is not a maximizing choice it is not rationalizable'.
13 The axiom just happens to be the one used in Wald's and others' attempts to formally analyze their invented models of neoclassical equilibrium. The *role* of this axiom in the formalization of neoclassical economics will be further explored in Chapter 13.

5 Axiomatic analysis of disequilibrium states

> The theory of stable equilibrium of normal demand and supply helps indeed to give definiteness to our ideas; and in its elementary stages it does not diverge from the actual facts of life, so far as to prevent its giving a fairly trustworthy picture of the chief methods of action of the strongest and most persistent group of economic forces. But when pushed to its more remote and intricate logical consequences, it slips away from the conditions of real life.
>
> Frank Hahn [1973, p. 1]

While the axiomatic analysis of equilibrium models can determine whether a given model is consistent and complete, little analysis has been done concerning consistency and completeness of models of disequilibrium states.[1] Obviously, we cannot expect to be able to assess solvability as a means of assuring consistency since, as discussed in Chapter 4, the solutions of the equilibrium models were sets of equilibrium prices that could be used possibly to explain existing prices. In this chapter I will offer a few elementary axiomatic analyses of models of 'disequilibrium' states. Eventually, we will need to consider how they may be used to critically assess any axiomatic analysis of disequilibrium models.

There are two ways to use disequilibrium models. One is to *explain why* disequilibrium phenomena occur and the other is to *explain away* disequilibrium phenomena as mere appearances. Both utilize underlying equilibrium models in which it is assumed that all consumers are maximizing utility (either directly or indirectly by maximizing personal wealth) subject to given equilibrium prices and all producers are maximizing their profit subject to given technology and given market equilibrium prices.

Since virtually all neoclassical equilibrium models take for granted that there are no barriers to any consumer quickly responding to changing prices, if there is a state of disequilibrium, such a state will be found by analyzing the logic of the situation facing the producers.[2] In this chapter, I will follow this tradition by focusing on the theory of the individual producer to determine how the logic of the situation facing the firm may be used to account for any state of disequilibrium.

COMPETITION BETWEEN THE SHORT AND LONG RUNS

In regard to the theory of the firm facing a general equilibrium situation, I want to examine the role played by two particular assumptions. One is the assumption that prices are *fixed givens* which in turn is based on an assumption that the firm is a 'perfect competitor' (perhaps because it is too small to be able to affect its price by altering the supply). I wish to show why dropping the fixed-price assumption would severely restrict our choice of assumptions regarding other aspects of the firm. The other assumption to be examined is one concerning the applicability of the assumption of profit maximization. In Chapter 3 I noted that Marshall defined a short run where everything but the input of labour and the level of resulting output are fixed. At the other extreme is his long run where everything but technology is variable (and thus subject to his Principle of Substitution). Here I will examine what might transpire in the shadowy area between Marshall's short and long runs, that is, in what I will call the *intermediate run*. The distinction between the Marshallian runs is solely a matter of the time available in the period under consideration and a recognition that some inputs are easier to change than others (i.e. change takes less time). In Marshallian terms (i.e. assuming just two inputs, labour and capital[3]) the question is the speed by which capital can be physically changed. While it is commonplace to define the short run as a period of time so short that there is not enough time to change capital, the long run presumes that both inputs are unrestrictedly variable. Now, the purpose of recognizing an intermediate run is to recognize that there are two ways of changing capital, internally and externally. The period of time corresponding to the intermediate run is defined to be too short to allow wholesale changes in the physical type of the capital used in the firm but long enough to allow the firm to vary internally the quantity of the existing type of capital used. In the intermediate run the firm must decide upon the *optimum quantity* of capital. In the long run, however, there is sufficient time to change to a different type of capital as is usually the case when a firm switches from one industry to another. Thus, in the long run the firm must decide upon the *optimum type* of real capital.

One reason why many theorists wish to drop either the perfect-competitor assumption or the profit-maximizer assumption is simply that these assumptions in many cases are 'unrealistic' in disequilibrium models.

Some just complain that these assumptions are plainly 'unrealistic' in the sense that it would be realistic to assume that the firm is a perfect competitor only when there are an extremely large number of firms, each of which is relatively small – for example, an economy of 'yeoman farmers' or perhaps an economy consisting of only small businesses. A small firm has to take its product's price as given only because it will go out of business if a higher price is charged since its customers can go to any of the large number of competing firms. Similarly, if it charges less than the given price when the given price is the 'long-run equilibrium price' (which equates with average cost) then it will be losing money and will still eventually go out of business. It is thus said that with a large number of small firms competition can be 'perfect'.

Would-be 'realists' argue that the modern economy consists of relatively large firms or few firms in each industry (or both) and thus, they say, in the real world there is 'imperfect' competition. Imperfect competition allows for two possible circumstances. First, it is possible for the firm to be a price-taking 'competitor' and also be one of a few producers such that changes in its output do affect the *market*-determined equilibrium price. The second is to assume that the firm is a price setter such as the usual textbook's monopolist. The first approach will be the one adopted here since it does not require the producer to know the full nature of the demand curve facing the firm. The second approach can be considered a special case of the first – namely where the firm's demand curve is the market's demand curve *and* the firm has full knowledge of the market.

THE 'PERFECT-COMPETITOR' FIRM IN THE LONG RUN: A REVIEW

In order to examine the axiomatic role of the assumptions of the Marshallian theory of the firm, we need to discuss the effect that dropping the perfect-competitor assumption would have on equilibrium models and in particular on the assumptions concerning the production function. Before we drop this assumption, however, let us review the basic logic of the perfect-competitor firm with respect to its production function.

Since by definition the intermediate run involves less time than the long run, it can be argued that a long-run equilibrium must also be an intermediate-run equilibrium and similarly it must also be a short-run equilibrium. Most important in the recognition of the intermediate run is the separation of the zero total profit idea ($TP = 0$) from the idea of *complete* profit maximization (i.e. with respect to all inputs). To do this we need to recognize the explicit conditions necessary for each of the three types of equilibria. In the short run, since only labour can be varied, an equilibrium is reached once the optimum amount of labour has been hired. The necessary condition for this is that the price of the good being produced equals its marginal cost (*MC*) or, in terms of the decision concerning labour, that the marginal physical product of labour (*MPP$_L$*) equals the real cost of one unit of labour. Specifically, the existence of a *short-run equilibrium* assures us that $MC = P_x$ or $MPP_L = W/P_x$ (where the good produced is X and the prices of X and labour are, respectively, P_x and W). Given a price of capital (P_k), an *intermediate-run equilibrium* assures that the optimum quantity of capital has been utilized such that the marginal product of capital (*MPP$_K$*) equals the real cost of capital (P_k/P_x). And since the intermediate run is longer than the short run (i.e. there is sufficient time to satisfy both sets of conditions), we can also be assured that the marginal rate of technical substitution (*MRTS*) between labour and capital equals the relative costs of those inputs (W/P_k). Except when we limit the notion of a production function to the special case of linear-homogeneous production functions, we will see that the attainment of an intermediate-run equilibrium does not assure a long-run equilibrium. Specifically, an intermediate-run equilibrium will not assure us that total profit is zero. The absence of zero total profit means that there may be an incentive for new entries or exits and thereby means that there may be incentives which deny an equilibrium state (since there is sufficient time for such reactions).

Most textbooks go straight to the long-run equilibrium from the short-run equilibrium. That is, they go from where, while $MPP_L = W/P_x$, it is possible that $MRTS \neq W/P_k$ (since not all short-run equilibria are long-run equilibria) to a long-run equilibrium where $MRTS = W/P_k$ and $TP = 0$. It is interesting to note that the long-run equilibrium is the starting point for an Adam Smith type of philosophical discussion of the virtues of competition and self-interest. That is, if every firm is making 'zero profits' with the given production functions (i.e. given technology) the only way a firm can obtain positive 'excess' profits is to develop new cost-reducing technologies. In the absence of competition such 'greed' (in this case, the pursuit of extra profits) would mean that one firm might gain at the expense of others, but if we also have 'free enterprise competition' any improvements in productive efficiency which reduce costs will eventually be shared by all the firms and thus benefit everyone through lowered prices.

All this seems to be taken for granted or ignored in most textbooks. Everyone seems to be satisfied with discussing only the necessary properties of the *long-run* equilibrium – as if there were virtue in zero profit itself! There is some virtue to having the lowest possible price for a given technology but it leaves open the question from a broader perspective of the choice of optimal production or the optimal 'quality' of capital and its associated technology.

What the recognition of an intermediate-run equilibrium allows is the discussion of situations where profit is maximized with respect to all inputs but $TP \neq 0$. The basis for this discussion is that while zero profit is due to decisions which are external to the firm, the efficiency of production ($MRTS = W/P_k$) is due to an internal decision whereby profit is maximized with respect to *all* inputs. The intermediate run is often ignored because the properties of the long-run equilibrium are considered more interesting – usually, this is because they are mathematically determinant and thus available for applications. Unfortunately, the long-run equilibrium conditions are considered so interesting that models of the firm are designed to guarantee that it is logically *impossible* to have an intermediate-run equilibrium which is not a long-run equilibrium. I shall now show how this is done and as well show how such models are also incompatible with imperfect competition.

PROFIT MAXIMIZATION WITH CONSTANT RETURNS TO SCALE

The basic ingredient of long-run models of the firm is the assumption that the production function is 'linear-homogeneous' (e.g. doubling all inputs will exactly double output) – this is usually called 'constant returns to scale'. As stated, this assumption is *not* a necessary assumption for the attainment of a long-run equilibrium since the existence of such an equilibrium only requires the existence of a point on the production function which is *locally* linear-homogeneous [see again Baumol 1977, p. 578]. However, it is not uncommon for a long-run model-builder to assume that the production function is *everywhere* linear-homogeneous.

Parenthetically, let us note that a production function will necessarily be linear-homogeneous if *all* inputs are unrestrictedly variable.[4] But, if any input is fixed (such as space, time available, technological knowledge, management talents, etc.) or cannot be duplicated, then the relationship between the other inputs and the output will not usually be everywhere linear-homogeneous.

For now, let us examine the properties of everywhere-linear-homogeneous production functions. First let us note that the homogeneity of such a function implies Euler's theorem holds, that is, for any function $X = f(L,K)$ it will be true that:

$$X = MPP_L \cdot L + MPP_K \cdot K \quad \text{at all } L, K \text{ and } X = f(L,K). \quad [5.1]$$

Now I shall show that when one adds to this assumption that the firm is in an intermediate-run equilibrium one automatically obtains the necessary conditions for a long-run equilibrium. The intermediate-run equilibrium assures that, *given* P_x (as well as W and P_k), whenever the firm is internally maximizing profit with respect to both labour and capital, the following two equations are true:

$$MPP_L = W/P_x \qquad [5.2a]$$
$$MPP_K = P_k/P_x. \qquad [5.2b]$$

Now, the combination of [5.1], [5.2a] and [5.2b] leads to the following:

$$X = (W/P_x){\cdot}L + (P_k/P_x){\cdot}K \qquad [5.3]$$

or rearranged by multiplying both sides by P_x:

$$P_x{\cdot}X = W{\cdot}L + P_k{\cdot}K. \qquad [5.3']$$

The left side of [5.3'] is total revenue (*TR*) and the right side is total cost (*TC*), hence it implies *TP* = 0. This means that in the usual long-run model, with its typical *everywhere*-linear-homogeneous production function, intermediate-run equilibrium implies all necessary conditions of long-run equilibrium. That is to say, one cannot obtain an intermediate-run equilibrium *without* obtaining the necessary conditions for a long-run equilibrium of the firm.

Given that we try to explain to students the importance of competition for the attainment of a social optimum (i.e. an efficient allocation of society's resources that allows for all parties to be maximizing), it is curious that many model-builders so glibly assume the existence of constant returns to scale. If competition is to matter, the production function *cannot* be everywhere linear-homogeneous. It is the *external* pressure of competition that eventually produces the condition of zero profit (if profits are positive there is an incentive for someone to enter the competition from outside the industry).

At this stage of the discussion,[5] an important general limitation regarding assumptions [5.1], [5.2a], [5.2b] and [5.3] should also be noted. Specifically, *whenever any three of the statements are true, the fourth must also be true*. For example, this means that even when it is impossible to vary the amount of capital used and yet the production function is everywhere linear-homogeneous, if there is enough time for a short-run equilibrium and for competition to force profits down to zero, the firm will unintentionally be maximizing profit with respect to its fixed capital.[6] Similarly, even if there is no reason for the production function to be everywhere linear-homogeneous, maximization and competition will force the firm to operate at a point where the production function is at least locally linear-homogeneous.

LINEAR HOMOGENEITY WITHOUT PERFECT COMPETITION

Note that what is accomplished with the assumption that the firm is a perfect competitor is to allow P_x to be used as it is in [5.2a]. That is, if P_x is given, P_x is both average revenue (*AR*) and marginal revenue (*MR*). Thus, [5.2a] can be rearranged according to the definition of marginal cost (*MC*)[7] to obtain:

$$P_x = MC. \qquad [5.2c]$$

Equation [5.2c] is merely a special case of the more general necessary condition of profit maximization:

$$MR = MC. \qquad [5.2c']$$

Now whenever the firm is not a perfect competitor and instead faces a demand *curve* for its product rather than just a *single* demand price, [5.2c'] is the operative rule for profit maximization. Facing a (positive-valued) *downward* sloping demand curve means that the price will not equal marginal revenue – the price will only indicate average revenue. And further, the downward slope means that average revenue is falling with rising quantity and thus at all prices

$$MR < AR \equiv P_x.$$

Given the value of the elasticity of demand relative to price changes, ε, and given a specific point on the curve with that elasticity, we can calculate the marginal revenue as

$$MR \equiv AR \cdot [1 + (1/\varepsilon)]$$

which follows from the definition of the terms.[8] If we take into account that price always equals *AR* and that for profit maximization $MC = MR$ and we recognize that a firm's not being a perfect competitor in its product market does not preclude that market from setting the output price,[9] then we can determine the relationship between price and marginal cost:

$$P_x = MC / [1 + (1/\varepsilon)]. \qquad [5.2c'']$$

And if the firm is still a perfect competitor with respect to input prices[10] then the idea expressed by [5.2a] still holds and thus the necessary conditions for profit maximization with respect to both inputs are now:

$$MPP_L = (W/P_x) / [1 + (1/\varepsilon)] \qquad [5.2a']$$
$$MPP_K = (P_k/P_x) / [1 + (1/\varepsilon)]. \qquad [5.2b']$$

Next I want to show how these last two equations affect our assumptions regarding the production function. Recall that if the production function of the firm is linear-homogeneous, then [5.1] holds, that is,

$$X = MPP_L \cdot L + MPP_K \cdot K.$$

If we assume the imperfect competitor has a linear-homogeneous production function, whenever we apply the conditions of profit maximization in the intermediate run to this, namely [5.2a'] and [5.2b'], we get:

$$X = \frac{(W/P_x) \cdot L}{1 + (1/\varepsilon)} + \frac{(P_k/P_x) \cdot K}{1 + (1/\varepsilon)}$$

or rearranging,

$$P_x \cdot X \cdot [1 + (1/\varepsilon)] = W \cdot L + P_k \cdot K$$

or further,

$$P_x \cdot X = (W \cdot L + P_k \cdot K) - (P_x \cdot X/\varepsilon).$$

Since $-\infty < \varepsilon < 0$ (because the demand curve is negatively sloped) we can conclude that whenever *MR* is positive (i.e. $\varepsilon < -1$) it must be true that:

$$P_x > (W \cdot L + P_k \cdot K)/X \equiv AC$$

or in other words there will be an excess profit of

$$TP = -(P_x \cdot X/\varepsilon) > 0.$$

Thus we can say that if the firm is not a perfect competitor but is a profit maximizer with respect to all inputs (as well as facing a linear-homogeneous production function), then total profit will be positive – that is, a long-run equilibrium is impossible.[11]

POSSIBLE ALTERNATIVE MODELS OF THE FIRM

Now let us look at all this from a more general viewpoint by recognizing the four separate propositions that have been considered.

[A] The production function is *everywhere* linear-homogeneous (i.e. [5.1]).

[B] Total profit is maximized with respect to all inputs (i.e. [5.2a'] and [5.2b']).

[C] Total profit is zero ($TP = 0$).

[D] The firm's demand curve is negatively sloped ($-\infty < \varepsilon < 0$).

We just saw at the end of the last section that a conjunction of all four of these is a contradiction – that is, if [A], [D] and [B] are true then necessarily [C] is false. We also saw before that if [A] and [B] hold, [C] also holds if [D] does *not* hold (i.e. when the price is given).

In fact, more can be said. *When any three of these propositions are true the fourth must be false.* To see this let us first note that the traditional discussion of imperfect competition with a few large firms usually considers a long-run equilibrium where total profit is forced to zero (by competition from new firms or competing industries producing close substitutes). With these traditional models, then, [C] will eventually hold. But it is usually also assumed that the firms are all profit maximizers ([B] holds) even when facing a downward sloping demand curve (i.e. even when [D] holds). All this implies that [A] does not hold, that is, the production function cannot be *everywhere* linear-homogeneous. Specifically, the firm must be at a point where there are *increasing returns to scale*.

So far I have only discussed the properties of *everywhere*-linear-homogeneous production functions. To see what it means to imply *increasing* returns to scale, let us now examine a production function which is homogeneous but not linear. If a production function is homogeneous, it is of a form that whenever the inputs are multiplied by some arbitrarily positive factor λ (i.e. we move outward along a ray through the origin of an iso-quant map), the output level will increase by some multiple of the same λ or, more generally, for $X = f(L,K)$:

[H] $$\lambda^n \cdot X = f(\lambda \cdot L, \lambda \cdot K).$$

Note that a linear-homogeneous function is then just a special case, namely where $n = 1$. When $n > 1$ the function gives *increasing returns* to outward movements along the scale line since the multiple λ^n is greater than λ. Note also that this is just one example of increasing returns – increasing returns do not require homogeneity. Nevertheless, it is often convenient to assume that the production function is homogeneous because the question of whether returns are increasing or decreasing can be reduced to the value of the single parameter n. Moreover, in this case, we can use the particular property of any continuous function that allows us to calculate the changes in output as linear combinations of the changes in inputs weighted by their respective marginal productivities. By recognizing that at any point on any continuous function it is also true that:

[E] $$dX = MPP_L \cdot dL + MPP_K \cdot dK.$$

If we also assume [H] holds, then if using [E] we set $dL = \lambda \cdot L$ and $dK = \lambda \cdot K$, it follows that

$$dX = \lambda^n \cdot X,$$

or in a rearranged equation form:

$$\lambda^{n-1} \cdot X = MPP_L \cdot L + MPP_K \cdot K. \qquad [5.1']$$

We see here again that equation [5.1] is the special case of [5.1'] where $n = 1$.

I now wish to put [5.1'] into a form which will be easier to compare with some later results and to do so I want to express λ^{n-1} differently. Since we really are only interested in the extent to which λ^{n-1} exceeds 1, let us calculate this directly. There are many ways to do this but let us calculate the fraction, $1/\beta$, which represents the portion of the multiple λ^{n-1} that exceeds 1, that is, let

Axiomatic analysis of disequilibrium states

$$\lambda^{n-1} - 1 \equiv (1/\beta)\cdot\lambda^{n-1}.$$

For later reference, note that β can be considered a 'measure' of the *closeness* to constant returns (i.e. to linearity). The greater the degree of increasing returns, the smaller will be β.

The reason why I have chosen this peculiar way of expressing λ^{n-1} will be more apparent a little later, but for further reference let me re-express [5.1′] using β rather than λ:

$$X / [1 - (1/\beta)] = MPP_L \cdot L + MPP_K \cdot K. \qquad [5.1″]$$

Let us put these considerations aside for now except to remember that a production function which gives increasing returns to scale will be expressed with $0 < \beta < \infty$ or equivalently with $(1/\beta) > 0$. A few paragraphs ago it was said that [A] is denied whenever we add [C] to [D] and [B]. Let us consider the more general case where all that we know is that [D] and [B] hold – that is, the profit-maximizing firm is facing a downward sloping demand curve in an intermediate-run equilibrium situation. First let us calculate its total cost (*TC*):

$$TC \equiv W \cdot L + P_k \cdot K.$$

Assuming [D] and [B] hold allows us to use [5.2a′] and [5.2b′] to get

$$TC = P_x \cdot [1 + (1/\varepsilon)] \cdot (MPP_L \cdot L + MPP_K \cdot K).$$

Now we can add [C]. Since total revenue is merely $P_x \cdot X$, zero profit means that

$$X = [1 + (1/\varepsilon)] \cdot (MPP_L \cdot L + MPP_K \cdot K)$$

or more conveniently,

$$X / [1 + (1/\varepsilon)] = MPP_L \cdot L + MPP_K \cdot K. \qquad [5.4]$$

Now we can make the comparison which reveals an interesting relationship between imperfect competition and increasing returns. First note that equations [5.1″] and [5.4] have the same right hand side thus their left hand sides must be the same as well. Thus whenever [B], [C] and [D] hold, we can say that

$$1 - (1/\beta) = 1 + (1/\varepsilon)$$

or more directly,

$$\beta = -\varepsilon \,! \qquad [5.5]$$

While we have obtained [5.5] by assuming that the imperfect competitor is in a long-run equilibrium (and an intermediate-run equilibrium), this is really the consequence of the mathematical relationship between the marginal and the average given the definition of elasticity.[12] Equation [5.5] shows that there is no formal difference between the returns to scale of the production function (its closeness to constant returns) and the elasticity of the firm's demand curve *in long-run equilibrium*.

Again we can see how *special* the linear-homogeneous production function is. Proposition [A] is consistent with [B] and [C] – that is, with a long-run equilibrium – but this is true only when $\varepsilon = -\infty$ (that is, when the price is given, $MR = AR \equiv$ price). Equation [5.5] shows this by noting that in this case $\beta = \infty$ or $(1/\beta) = 0$ which implies that the production function is (at least locally) linear-homogeneous.

Finally, note that the existence of 'increasing returns' is often called the case of 'excess capacity' – that is, where the firm is not exploiting the full capacity of its (fixed) plant which if it did it could lower its average cost (in other words, it is to the left of the lowest point on its AC curve). All this leads to the conclusion that when [D] holds with profit maximization, that is, with [B], either we have 'excess profits' (viz. when there are constant returns to scale) or we have 'excess capacity' (viz. when $TP = 0$).

PROFIT MAXIMIZATION [B]

Note that so far we have always assumed profit maximization. Let us now consider circumstances under which [B] does *not* hold. First let us assume that the firm is a perfect competitor, that is, that [D] does not hold. But this time we will assume the firm in the intermediate run is maximizing the 'rate of return' (r) on its capital[13] or what amounts to the same thing, is maximizing the average-net-product of capital (ANP_K) which is defined as,

$$ANP_K \equiv [X - (W/P_x) \cdot L] / K.$$

And since average productivity of capital (APP_K) is simply X/K,

$$ANP_K \equiv APP_K - (W/P_x) \cdot (L/K).$$

Moreover, when ANP_K is maximized in the intermediate run, the following holds:[14]

$$MPP_K = [X - (W/P_x) \cdot L] / K \equiv ANP_K \qquad [5.6]$$

$$MPP_L = W/P_x. \qquad [5.2a]$$

First let us see what this means if we assume [A] holds but not [C], such as when $TP > 0$. From the definition of TP, TR and TC, when $TP > 0$ we get:

$$P_x \cdot X > W \cdot L + P_k \cdot K$$

or, rearranging,

$$[X - (W/P_x) \cdot L] / K > P_k / P_x.$$

Since by [5.6] the left side of this last inequality is equal to MPP_K if the firm is maximizing ANP_K, the firm cannot also be maximizing profit with respect to capital (because $TP \neq 0$). However, had we assumed that $TP = 0$, we would get the same situation as if [5.2a] and [5.2b] were the governing rules rather than [5.2a] and [5.6]. That is to say, if we assume the firm is in

Axiomatic analysis of disequilibrium states 75

a long-run equilibrium, it does not matter whether the firm is a profit maximizer (i.e. [5.2b] holds) or thinks it is an ANP_K maximizer (i.e. [5.6] holds) with respect to capital. Now earlier we said that if [A] but not [D] holds the intermediate run implies a long-run equilibrium. Thus, if we only know that $TP > 0$, we can say that whenever [A] holds, [B] cannot hold except when [D] also holds. Alternatively, when $TP > 0$ whenever [D] does not hold, [A] cannot hold if [B] does.

ON BUILDING MORE 'REALISTIC' MODELS OF THE FIRM

Now all this leads us to an argument that we should avoid assuming linear-homogeneous production (i.e. assumption [A]) and thereby allow us to deal with the intermediate-run equilibrium with or without profit maximization. In particular, I think a realistic model of the firm will focus on the properties of an intermediate-run equilibrium which is not a long-run equilibrium, or on the excess capacity version of imperfect competition, both of which require that the firm's production function not be everywhere linear-homogeneous. Neither assumption denies the possibility that the production function can be *locally* linear-homogeneous at one or more points. This latter consideration means that the intermediate-run view of the firm offers the opportunity to explain *internally* the size of the firm in the long-run equilibrium. Size is impossible to explain if [A] holds (unless we introduce new ideas such as the financial endowments of each firm). Furthermore, it is again easy to see that competition is unimportant when [A] is assumed to hold and [D] does not. That is, the traditional argument that 'competition' is a good thing would be vacuous when [A] and [B] hold but [D] does not hold. This is because [A] and [B] alone (i.e. without the additional assumption that competition exists) imply [C] which was one of the 'good things' explicitly promised by long-time advocates of free-enterprise capitalism or more recently implicitly by advocates of the privatization of government-owned companies. So, again, if economists are to argue that competition matters, they must avoid [A].

USING MODELS OF DISEQUILIBRIUM

Now with the above elementary axiomatization of the Marshallian theory of the firm in mind, let us return to the consideration of how such a theory can be used to explain states of disequilibrium. To do this we need only consider each of the four models we will get when we decide which of the assumptions [A] to [D] we will relax (since, as I explained, the four assumptions cannot all be true simultaneously).

Model 1. Dropping assumption [D]

Dropping the notion that the firm can affect its price (by altering the quantity it supplies to the market) merely yields the old Marshallian theory of the price-taking firm (see Figure 5.1). Nevertheless, it does give us the opportunity to explain various states of disequilibrium. Let us consider various attributes of disequilibrium. If the firm is *not* at the point where the production function is locally linear-homogeneous, there can be several interpretations of the situation depending on whether or not we assume [B] or [C] holds. If [C] does not hold but [B] does, there could be either positive or negative profits. If we wish to explain the absence of zero profits, we can always claim that this is due to our not allowing sufficient time for competition to work. If [B] does not hold but [C] does, then there must be something inhibiting the firm from moving to the optimum point where price equals marginal costs. In comparative-statics terms, we can explain either type of disequilibrium state by noting that since the last state of equilibrium was reached certain exogenous givens have changed. For example, tastes may have changed in favour of one good against another, thus one firm will be making profits and another losses or the firm has not had enough time to move along its marginal cost curve. Similarly, it could be that technology has changed. Any such explanation thus would have to be specific about the time it takes to change variables such as capital as well as specify the changes in the appropriate exogenous variables. Hopefully, such an explanation would be testable.

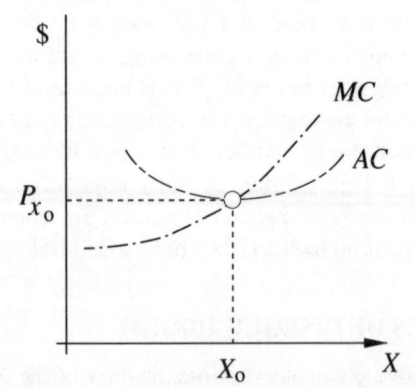

Figure 5.1 *Firm in long-run equilibrium*

Sometimes there is little difference between models which explain the occurrence of a disequilibrium phenomenon and those which explain it away. For example, models which drop assumption [D] usually explain away apparent disequilibrium phenomena as possible consequences resulting from the limited amount of time available for competition to produce either zero profit or the optimum use of all inputs. The phenomena are suboptimal only in comparison with long-run equilibrium. Once one recognizes that there has not been enough time, as long as the firm is maximizing with respect to every *variable* input, nothing more can be expected. In other words, disequilibrium phenomena may be long-run disequilibria and short-run equilibria.

Model 2. Dropping assumption [B]

Dropping assumption [B] leads us astray from ordinary neoclassical models since [B] says that the firm is a maximizer. What we need to be able to explain is the situation depicted in Figures 5.2(a) and 5.2(b), again depending on whether or not we are assuming a long-run situation. In either case it is clear that the firm is setting price equal to marginal cost[15] which means that MPP_L equals W/P_x and thus cannot be satisfying equation [5.2b'] which is the necessary condition for profit maximization when [D] holds. An exception is possible if we assume the owner of the firm is not very smart and attempts to maximize the rate of return on capital rather than profit. For a maximum ANP_K, all that would be required is that ANP_K equals MPP_K. There is nothing inconsistent since it is still possible for [D] and [A] to hold so long as ANP_L equals MPP_L and this is the case. But again, maximizing rates of return to either labour or capital is not what we would normally assume in a neoclassical explanation.

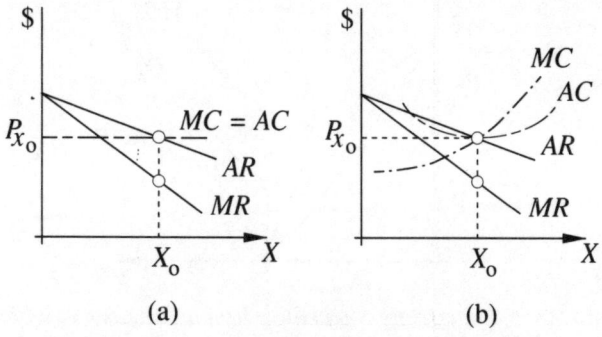

Figure 5.2   *[A] + [C] + [D] implies not-[B]*

Models which drop assumption [B] usually resort to a claim that there is some sort of unavoidable market failure or governmental interference preventing the firm from choosing the optimum amounts of inputs. Some imperfectly competitive firms are regulated to charge full-cost prices, that is, set price equal to average cost. Again, the apparent disequilibria may still be the best that is possible. Since one cannot give a neoclassical explanation without assuming [B], one must resort to non-economic considerations such as external politics or internal social structure to explain the constraints that inhibit the firm from using the optimum amounts of inputs.

Model 3. Dropping assumption [A]

The most common disequilibrium model would involve the phenomenon of 'excess capacity'. The typical model is shown in Figure 5.3. There is no literal long-run version since if all inputs were variable (the definition of the long run) then [A] would have to hold. Models which drop assumption [A] usually try either to explain why excess capacity may be an optimal social equilibrium or to explain [D] away so that [A] can be allowed to hold. When [D] holds, competition can drive profits to zero without forcing the firm to a point where it faces local linear homogeneity. To see this we need only note that [B] combined with [C] is represented by equations [5.2a′], [5.2b′] and [5.3]. And as we noted before these imply that the firm is facing a falling *AC* curve since it must be facing increasing returns. As I noted above, the common justification of [D] is to say there are transaction costs which if recognized would explain that the situation represented by Figure 5.3 is an optimum rather than a disequilibrium. It is the best *possible* world.

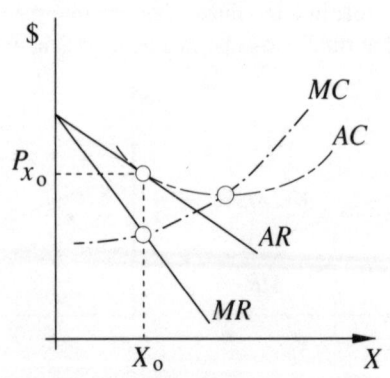

Figure 5.3 *Imperfectly competitive firm in long-run equilibrium*

Some people wish to interpret excess capacity as evidence that imperfect competition leads to inefficiencies where it is clear that the firm is not maximizing its output for the resources used (i.e. *AC* not minimum). It could equally be argued that the transaction costs needed to make decisions when there is the very large number of producers required to make everyone a perfect competitor are too high. A long-run equilibrium with zero profits and increasing returns may very well be the best we can do for society. Too often the transaction costs are invisible or imagined. The cleverest models are those which claim that the prices we see do not represent the true costs of purchase. The fact that people are willing to join a queue and wait to be served when there are few producers is interpreted as evidence that the price marked on the good is less than the price paid. The full price includes that opportunity cost of waiting (i.e. lost income). Thus, implicitly, the demand curve for the 'full' price is horizontal and the resulting 'full' cost curves if visible would look like Figure 5.1, thereby denying [D] and allowing [A] to be re-established. I think such a model may be too clever since it is difficult for me to understand what is being explained with such a model.

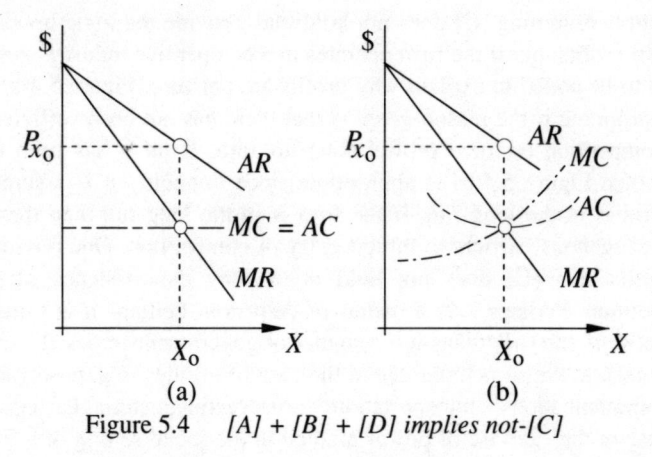

Figure 5.4   *[A] + [B] + [D] implies not-[C]*

Model 4. *Dropping assumption [C]*

One obvious way to explain the existence of profits is to simply drop [C] without dropping assumption [D]. The explanation in this case will be direct since given assumptions [A] and [B] it is logically impossible for profits to be zero or negative whenever [D] holds, hence the absence of zero profits is quite understandable. Consider Figures 5.4(a) and 5.4(b). In each figure we represent [D] by a falling demand curve (the *AR* curve) and its resulting marginal revenue curve which is necessarily always below. Assumption [B] is represented by the point where marginal revenue equals marginal cost. Assumption [A] is represented only at the point or points where average cost equals marginal cost. Which of Figures 5.4(a) or 5.4(b) is the appropriate representation depends on why [C] does not hold.

Models which initially drop assumption [C] will usually be transformed into ones where [A] or [D] does not hold so that [C] can be allowed to hold. When the objective is to explain [D] away (e.g. with the recognition of 'full' costs), then [A] will be explained or explained away using one of the strategies I noted in the discussion of Model 3 and this leads to the re-establishment of Figure 5.1. Another strategy is to try to explain the *appearance* of profit as a return to an unrecognized input factor such that, when accounted for as a cost, total profit is really zero. This latter strategy allows [D] to hold but puts [A] or [B] into question. However, if there is only one missing factor, its recognition begs the question as to whether it is being optimally used. Only if [D] is denied can it be argued that the existence of profit implies that some of the factors are not being used optimally.

Simply assuming [C] does not hold may provide the logic necessary to explain profits, but if the firm operates in a competitive industry something needs to be added to explain why profits are not zero. Figure 5.4(a) would be appropriate if the reason given is that there has not been sufficient time for competition to force profits down to zero. If there has been enough time, then Figure 5.4(b) is appropriate since implicitly it is assumed that the firm is in the long run. If the firm is in the long run then there must exist exogenous barriers to inhibit entry or competition. One obvious way to justify that [C] does not hold is to deny the existence of sincere competition. Perhaps it is a matter of collusion. Perhaps it is a matter of high cost of entry. Perhaps it is a matter of government-imposed barriers to entry such as we sometimes see in the case of utilities (e.g. power utilities, telecommunications, transportation, broadcasting, etc.). Perhaps it is because of the exercise of power granted in the social setting of a firm, so-called exploitation of workers by the owners of the firm [see Robinson 1933/69].

Whatever the reason given, least-cost production [A] combined with maximization [B] means that the existence of a falling average revenue precludes negative profits. In other words, we can never explain a disequilibrium that involves negative profits with an imperfectly competitive neoclassical model based on [A] and [B]. Moreover, we are also limited to using such a model only to explain part of the economy since it is impossible to have an economy where everyone is making profits.[16] Aggregate profit for an entire (closed) economy must be zero, hence if any firm is making profits, some other firm must be making losses. Thus, the disequilibrium state of an entire economy cannot be explained with an imperfect-competition-based neoclassical model.

UNIFORMITIES IN EXPLANATIONS OF DISEQUILIBRIA

I will consider how many of the above models can be seen as variants which use the same mathematical property inherent in disequilibrium states. In one sense I have already discussed the notion that increasing returns and imperfect competition are two ways of interpreting what is represented in Figure 5.3. And I showed that in this case the measure of distance from the perfect competition equilibrium is either a measure of closeness to constant returns or a measure of closeness to perfectly elastic demand. The measures are equivalent.

Can we do something similar for all disequilibrium models? That is, are all explanations based on positing disequilibrium phenomena (inefficiency, exploitation, suboptimal resource allocations, profits, etc.) reducible to statements about some measure from the perfectly competitive optimum equilibrium?

Interest rate as a measure of disequilibrium

Let us examine some models which are based on the presumption of a state of disequilibrium. Many years ago, Oscar Lange [1935/36] presented an elaborate model which in effect claimed that the interest rate (actually, the net internal rate of return) is implicit in a firm's or economy's misallocation of resources between the production of final goods X (by firm x) and intermediate goods K (which are machines produced by firm m).[17]

Lange's Model

Let the economy consist of two firms which are given the following production function for final goods:

$$X = F(L_x, K_x) \quad \text{[L1]}$$

and the following production function for machines which last only one production period:

$$(K_m + K_x) = \phi(K_m, L_m) \quad \text{[L2]}$$

where the subscript indicates which firm is using the machine. And we note that [L2] also indicates that it will be assumed that the supply of machines is exactly equal to the demand for machines (which are assumed to be used up in one production period). Similarly, it will be assumed that the market for labour is cleared (i.e. there is full employment):

$$L = L_x + L_m. \quad \text{[L3]}$$

Let us now assume the economy is producing with an allocation of labour between the two firms such that X is at its maximum. This assumption implies that there must be no surplus machine production on the margin (i.e. the last machine produced is used to replace the last machine used up):

$$(MPP_K)_m = 1 \qquad \text{[L4]}$$

and that there is an efficient resource allocation (i.e. $MRTS_x = MRTS_m$):

$$(MPP_L)_x / (MPP_K)_x = (MPP_L)_m / (MPP_K)_m. \qquad \text{[L5']}$$

Note that when [L4] holds with [L5'] it gives:[18]

$$(MPP_L)_x = (MPP_K)_x \cdot (MPP_L)_m. \qquad \text{[L5]}$$

If X is not maximum, either [L4] or [L5'] does not hold (or neither holds).

If we assume [L5'] holds because the two firms have somehow achieved an efficient allocation of labour between them, that is, they have achieved a Pareto optimum for the given amount of labour, L, then failure to maximize X must imply that equation [L4] does not hold. If the failure to maximize X is the result of misallocating too much labour to the production of X, then we can measure the extent to which [L4] does not hold by a scalar i as follows:

$$(MPP_K)_m = 1 + i. \qquad \text{[L17]}$$

This i is equivalent to what Lange calls a net 'rate of real interest'. Note that whenever this two-firm economy is *not* maximizing X but has reached a Pareto-optimal equilibrium in the sense that neither firm can increase its output without the other firm decreasing its output, i cannot be zero.[19] In other words, i is a measure of the distance the Pareto-optimal point is from the global optimum of a maximum X for the given amount of labour being allocated between these two firms.

We can look at Lange's real interest rate as a measure of increasing returns if we assume the machine producing firm is a profit maximizer. In effect equation [L17] can be the equivalent of my equation [5.2b'] once we recognize that the real price of capital in the production of machines is P_k/P_k thus [L17] is really:

$$(MPP_K)_m = (P_k/P_k)\cdot(1 + i). \qquad \text{[L17']}$$

Thus we can say that

$$(1 + i) = 1 / [1 + (1/\varepsilon)].$$

Since ε is in general a measure of the difference between the marginal and the average[20] (and thus equal to $-\beta$), we can determine the one-to-one correspondence between i and my measure of closeness to local linear homogeneity as follows:

$$(1 + i) = 1 / [1 - (1/\beta)]$$

or, equivalently, we can say either that

$$i = 1 / (1 - \beta)$$

or that

$$\beta = 1 - (1/i).$$

Other measures of disequilibrium

Let us now consider other, more familiar or more recent, models of disequilibrium which claim to offer measures of the extent of disequilibrium and see whether we can generalize the relationship between those measures and either my β or equivalently the elasticity of demand. We will look at Robinson's [1933/69] measure of exploitation due to monopoly power, John Roemer's [1988] more general measure of exploitation, Abba Lerner's [1934] index of monopoly power, Michal Kalecki's [1938] degree of monopoly, and Sidney Weintraub's [1949] index of less-than-optimum output.

Robinson's measure of exploitation due to monopoly power is the difference between the marginal product of labour and the price paid for the labour services. This index can be derived straight from equation [5.2a'] above. In effect her measure is merely $1/\varepsilon$ since this fraction is the measure of the difference.

Roemer's measure of exploitation is the ratio of profit to variable costs. Roemer's measure does not assume [C] holds. If we assume that his disequilibrium model has only one input, then his measure is just

$$(\text{price} - AC)/AC.$$

If we also assume Roemer is presuming maximization in the sense that price equals MC then his measure of exploitation is just $1/\beta$.[21]

Kalecki's degree of monopoly is based on an assumption that [A] and [B] hold but [C] does not. Thus his measure is the difference between AR and MR which again is $1/\varepsilon$.

Lerner's index of monopoly power is defined as the ratio of difference between the price and MC as a proportion of the price, or since AR is price:

$$(AR - MC)/AR.$$

If we assume zero profit then his index is my $1/\beta$ and if instead we assume profit maximization ($MR = MC$), then his index is the negative of $1/\varepsilon$. If we assume both conditions hold (i.e. an imperfect competition equilibrium) then his index is equivalent to both my $1/\beta$ and $1/\varepsilon$ (as I explained earlier).

Weintraub's index of less-than-optimum output is the ratio of less-than-optimum output to optimum output where the optimum is the one where [A] holds or, equivalently, where $MC = AC$. Thus his index is dependent on the specific form of the production function or, equivalently, of the cost function. To illustrate, let us assume the total cost (TC) of producing X is as follows:

$$TC = 200 + 10X + 2X^2$$
then
$$AC = (200 + 10X + 2X^2)/X$$
$$MC = 10 + 4X.$$

Now let us calculate the ratio of MC to AC using the given cost function:
$$MC/AC = X\cdot(10 + 4X)/(200 + 10X + 2X^2)$$
or
$$MC/AC = (5X + 2X^2)/(100 + 5X + X^2).$$

Note that $MC = AC$ when $X = 10$ and thus Weintraub's index (*WI*) will be $(X/10)$ for the given cost function. Since $MC = AC \cdot [1 - (1/\beta)]$, we can calculate β *for the given cost function* if we are given an X:

$$\beta = (6 + WI + 2WI^2)/(2WI^2 - 6).$$

So, again, we see that the measure of distance from a perfectly competitive equilibrium can be seen as a variant of β or ε.

A GENERAL THEORY OF DISEQUILIBRIA

In general terms, each of the models of disequilibrium I have discussed here are combinations of the axioms I have presented in this chapter. Which of the four axioms ([A] to [D]) is denied will be the basis for a clearly defined measure of disequilibriumness. The opportunities for criticism are limited to examining the reasons why the particular axiom was denied. And since any measure of disequilibrium will be determined by the denied axiom, not much will be learned by arguing over the nature of the measure presented. In general, unless the same axioms are used to build alternative models of disequilibrium, arguing over which is a better measure would seem to be fruitless. Whether the disequilibriumness is the result of assuming [D] or [A] in combination with either [B] or [C] will determine which is the appropriate index. And as we saw in the case of imperfectly competitive equilibria, either index will do. With the one exception of Kalecki's degree of monopoly which neutralized the role of the production function by assuming linear homogeneity [A], all of the other measures can be seen to depend on the extent to which the production function is not linear-homogeneous (as measured by my β).

The questions of the pervasiveness of equilibrium and maximization are fundamental and thus little of neoclassical literature seems willing or able to critically examine these fundamental ideas. Outside of neoclassical literature, however, one can find many critiques that are focused on what are claimed to be essential but neglected elements of neoclassical explanations. There are two particular exogenous elements that have received extensive critical examination. One is the question of what a decision-maker needs to know to be a subject of the maximization assumption. The other involves

Axiomatic analysis of disequilibrium states

the social institutions that are needed yet taken for granted in neoclassical explanations. The critics complain that until these two exogenous elements are made endogenous, neoclassical theories will always be incomplete. While some critics argue that such a completion is impossible, some friends of neoclassical theory willingly accept the challenge. In the next three chapters I will examine these disputes to determine the extent to which they represent serious challenges to neoclassical economics.

NOTES

1 There have been some analyses of the stability of equilibrium models which recognize the need to deal with conceivable disequilibrium states [e.g. Hahn 1970; Fisher 1981, 1983]. Also, in macroeconomics we find models which try to deal with the disequilibria caused by 'distortions' such as sticky prices or wage rates [e.g. Clower 1965; Barro and Grossman 1971]. Little of this literature approaches the way equilibrium models have been axiomatized. Besides, it is not clear what consistency and completeness mean when one sees disequilibrium as a distorted equilibrium.

2 It might appear that by assuming all consumers are maximizing we are always assuming that the only possible disequilibrium is one of excess supply, that is, for disequilibrium prices above the equilibrium level. This does not have to be the case if one adopts the Marshallian view of the producer where the given price is a demand price and marginal cost represents the supply price. In this way, prices on both sides of the equilibrium level can be considered.

3 Here 'capital' always refers to physically real capital (e.g. machines and computers, etc.).

4 If all inputs are unrestricted then it is possible to double output either through internal expansion (viz. by doubling all inputs) or through external expansion (viz. by building a duplicate plant next door). It should not matter which way. If it does matter then it follows that not all inputs are variable. By definition, a linear-homogeneous function is one where it does not matter which way output is expanded. Some of my colleagues argue that, even in the long run, some production functions cannot be linear-homogeneous. They give as an example the production of iron pipe. One can double the capacity of the pipe without doubling the amount of iron used – the perimeter of the pipe does not double when we double the area of the pipe's cross-section. Unfortunately, this example does not represent a counter-example as claimed. To test linear homogeneity one would have to restrict consideration to producing more of the *same* product and 20-inch pipe is not the same product as 10-inch pipe.

5 It should be noted that equations [5.1], [5.2a], [5.2b] and [5.3] are formalizations of the statements (b) to (d) used to discuss Marshall's method (see above, pp. 32–5).

6 That is, if [5.1], [5.2a] and [5.3] hold, [5.2b] must also hold.

7 That is, $MC \equiv W/MPP_L$.

8 The calculation follows from the definitions of these terms:
$$\varepsilon \equiv (\partial Q/Q)/(\partial P/P) \equiv (P/Q) \cdot (\partial Q/\partial P)$$
and
$$MR \equiv \partial(P \cdot Q)/\partial Q \equiv Q \cdot (\partial P/\partial Q) + P \cdot (\partial Q/\partial Q)$$

86 *Principles of economics*

$$\equiv P \cdot [1 + (Q/P) \cdot (\partial P/\partial Q)].$$

Thus,

$$MR \equiv P \cdot [1 + (1/\varepsilon)]$$

and since $P = AR$, the relationship between AR and MR follows.

9   See above, p. 66.

10 The implausibility of the firm being a perfect competitor with regard to *output* prices does not necessarily imply an implausibility of the firm being a perfect competitor with respect to *input* prices. That is, a few big firms in one industry still may compete with many other industries for labour (or capital). This, of course, assumes at least a minimum degree of homogeneity or mobility of labour — that labour could easily move from one industry to another. If for any reason this is not the case, then we will have to include the elasticity of labour supply, ξ, in the calculation of Marginal Cost. If we do this, we will get (for the short-run equilibrium):

$$MC = (W/MPP_L) \cdot [1 + (1/\xi)]$$

But since I wish to keep things as uncomplicated as possible here I will not develop this type of imperfect competition further.

11 The difficulties with combining the notion of imperfect competition with a long-run or general equilibrium model are not new. Recent discussion [e.g. Hart 1985; Bonanno 1990] have complained that most attempts to do so [e.g. Negishi 1961] usually have involved compromising assumptions that leave the end results far from being an ordinary general equilibrium model augmented with the assumption of imperfect competition. John Roberts and Hugo Sonnenschein [1977] seem to be going further by arguing that such an augmentation is impossible. In my simple-minded arguments which follow it seems that the problem is not just a question of coming up with a clever modelling technique but rather a fundamental logical obstacle.

12 That is, by analogy we can see that using equation [5.5] yields:

$$-\beta = (\partial Q/Q)/(\partial AC/AC) \equiv (AC/Q) \cdot (\partial Q/\partial AC)$$

and since $\quad MC \equiv \partial(AC \cdot Q)/\partial Q \equiv Q \cdot (\partial AC/\partial Q) + AC \cdot (\partial Q/\partial Q)$

$$\equiv AC \cdot [1 + (Q/AC) \cdot (\partial AC/\partial Q)]$$

we get $\quad MC \equiv AC \cdot [1 - (1/\beta)].$

13 Consideration of the *intermediate-run* equilibrium makes it possible to entertain an alternative assumption for the goal of the firm in the intermediate run even when the firm may wish to maximize profit in the short run. While it will be easy to show that maximizing the rate of return makes sense only when comparing equal amounts of investment (i.e. it is possible to make more profit at a lower rate of return when the amount is not fixed), it is not uncommon to find people bragging about high rates of return achieved as if this were optimal.

14 Consider the relationship between MPP_K and ANP_K. In particular, let us show that

$ANP_K = MPP_K$ whenever ANP_K is maximum (with respect to K), and

$ANP_K < MPP_K$ whenever ANP_K is rising as K increases.

By definition:

$$ANP_K \equiv [X - (W/P_x) \cdot L] / K. \qquad [\text{i}]$$

Now let us determine the slope of the ANP_K curve $(\partial ANP_K/\partial K)$ by differentiating equation [i]:

$$(\partial ANP_K/\partial K) = [(\partial X/\partial K) - 0]/K + [X - (W/P_x) \cdot L] \cdot (-1) \cdot (\partial K/\partial K)/K^2. \qquad [\text{ii}]$$

Since by [i]:

$ANP_K \cdot K \equiv X - (W/P_x) \cdot L$

we can transform [ii] into the following:

$(\partial ANP_K/\partial K) = [(\partial X/\partial K)/K] - [(ANP_K \cdot K) \cdot (\partial K/\partial K)]/K^2.$ [iii]

Since $(\partial X/\partial K) \equiv MPP_K$ and $(\partial K/\partial K) = 1$, we can further obtain:

$(\partial ANP_K/\partial K) = (MPP_K - ANP_K)/K.$ [iv]

With [iv] we can see that if the slope is positive (i.e. ANP_K rising) then $(MPP_K - ANP_K) > 0$, which implies $MPP_K > ANP_K$. And, if the slope is zero (i.e. the slope is horizontal when ANP_K is maximum) then $(MPP_K - ANP_K) = 0$, which implies $MPP_K = ANP_K$.

QED

15 Note that the marginal and average cost curves are short-run curves in Figure 5.2(b). I will not try to define an intermediate version since it will not add much to the analysis.

16 As Samuelson [1972] noted, for there to be a net profit for an entire economy begs the question of whether there is a Santa Claus [see further Boland 1986a, Chapter 2].

17 Lange uses m to represent the output of machines but here I will use K, to maintain the notation of this chapter.

18 It should be noted here that Lange does not state equation [L5'] since he derives both [L4] and [L5] using Lagrange multipliers and thus implicitly assumes [L4] and [L5] are both true. By recognizing [L5'], I am making it possible to treat [L4] and [L5'] separately while still recognizing that Lange's equation [L5] is also a necessary condition of a maximum X.

19 According to Lange, the real rate of interest is zero when X is maximum [p. 169]. It should be noted here that my representation of Lange's model is slightly different from what he explicitly states. Lange takes equation [L4] as obviously true such that any disequilibrium can *only* be the result of my equation [L5'] not being true. All of Lange's propositions still follow from my representation of his model.

20 See note 8.

21 If instead we assume the profit-maximizing firm has two inputs, L and K, then the measure $(1/\beta)$ is increased by the factor $[1 + (P_k \cdot K)/(W \cdot L)]$.

Part II

Some neglected elements

6 Knowledge in neoclassical economic theory

> the economist's advice to policy-makers must often appear crude and be misleading ... he gives the impression that investment policy is a matter only of millions spent per year, no matter on what. Efficiency is for him a matter of best mixes, not of best shapes. He seems to treat knowledge as a stuff, obtainable in measurable quantities for a known expenditure, and guaranteed to produce effects knowable in advance; he believes that we can know in advance precisely what it is, in all essentials, that we are going to find out. Better a contradiction in terms than acknowledge a chink, let alone a gaping rent, in the armour of rationality.
>
> George Shackle [1972, pp. 114–15]

> Whatever assumptions about knowledge we may attribute to it, general equilibrium does not seem to stand up well to a critical inquiry. In modern Austrian economics, by contrast, we find the problem of knowledge to be a matter of fundamental concern.
>
> Ludwig Lachmann [1976, p. 55]

Neoclassical economic theory is often criticized for neglecting an essential element of knowledge in models of economic decision-making. The most common critiques would have us reject all neoclassical models because they are claimed to be based upon 'perfect knowledge' and the like. Often it is argued that neoclassical explanations are incomplete without a formal treatment of uncertainty and information search. The distinguishing feature of such critiques is the presumption that assumptions regarding imperfections in knowledge can be recognized in the neoclassical world without, at the same time, completely undermining other desirable methodological properties of this framework, such as internally stable equilibria, consistency with 'rational' decision-making and in general an 'explicitness' regarding explanation. Other more radical critics find such a proposal for piecemeal reform untenable. Many neo-Keynesian thinkers, among others [e.g. Clower 1965; Leijonhufvud 1968; Kornai 1971], argue that any systematic programme to incorporate imperfect and incomplete knowledge into economic theory must sacrifice the traditional neoclassical concepts of (general or long-run) equilibrium. George Shackle's [1972] lengthy critique is even more uncompromising. He argues that such a programme must imply the sacrifice of all the methodologically desirable properties listed above.

Shackle's critique is perhaps the most interesting (and dangerous) of the above critiques and it is therefore of interest that the Austrian economist, Ludwig Lachmann [1976], has argued that Shackle's critique constitutes a successful and decisive challenge to neoclassical economics. Lachmann sees Shackle's results as even grounds for rehabilitating Austrian views which give a more fundamental role to knowledge and changes in knowledge, notably the Austrian theories of Hayek and Ludwig Mises.

In this chapter I will focus primarily on the arguments of Lachmann and Shackle and in particular on Lachmann's overriding view that, since the theories of Shackle and the Austrians give a more strategic role to knowledge and its limitations, they possess a clear-cut advantage over neoclassical economics in explaining economic phenomena. While one can agree with both authors that no economic theory can be methodologically complete without a careful specification of the knowledge considerations lying behind all decision-making, their arguments are insufficient for either the rejection of neoclassical economics or the resurrection of Austrian economics. Rather, what Lachmann's essay reveals is that neither the neoclassical nor the Lachmann–Shackle viewpoint under discussion is explanatorily complete with respect to knowledge. Specifically, neither provides a satisfactory solution to what might be called 'the problem of knowledge dynamics' – the problem of defining an explicit and non-trivial role for changes in knowledge to play in the explanation of the transition between short-run (temporary) equilibria and long-run (general) equilibria.

Before I begin discussing Lachmann's and Shackle's viewpoints I need to explain why these critics seem to have an excessive concern for the requirements of 'rationality' rather than the more mundane notion of maximization that I discussed in Chapter 1. Once this distinction is clarified, I will examine the failures of the neoclassical and Lachmann–Shackle viewpoints to provide a satisfactory solution to the problem of knowledge dynamics. In doing so, I will have to discuss two other important distinctions. One is the methodological distinction between exogenous and endogenous knowledge in decision-making. The other is the distinction between epistemology and methodology which will play a major role in this chapter. Using these distinctions it will be argued here that a central shortcoming of both the neoclassical and the Lachmann–Shackle viewpoints resides in their failure to permit the epistemological (as distinguished from methodological) features of a decision-making environment to play a major role in determining the decision-maker's response to knowledge 'shocks'. At the end of the chapter I will consider a possible solution to the problem of knowledge dynamics which sees theories of knowledge ('epistemologies') as an autonomous foundation for any explanation of an individual's methods or decisions which are based on historical observations or expectations.

MAXIMIZATION AS 'RATIONALITY'

It is common to find economists using the term 'maximizing' interchangeably with 'rational'. As Samuelson noted many years ago [1947/65, p. 98], what most philosophers might call 'rationality' is a much stronger concept than what is required for decision-making. For Samuelson, 'consistency' was sufficient – the Axiom of Revealed Preference is merely an expression of consistency. While in many cases one could substitute 'consistent' for 'rational', it would be misleading when the stronger notion is intended. The stronger notion of rational is often a confusion between the mechanics of giving an argument in favour of some proposition and the psychology of the person stating the argument. The psychology version is not what economists usually mean by 'rational' even though they sometimes refer to a failure of an argument as evidence of the 'irrationality' of the decision-maker. The accusation of 'irrationality' is but a left-over artifact of the eighteenth century rationalism which Voltaire parodies in *Candide*. The eighteenth century rationalists would have us believe that if one were rational one would never make a mistake and thus whenever we make a mistake (e.g. state a false argument) then we must be irrational [see further, Agassi 1963].

One does not have to take such a strong position to understand what economists mean by a rational argument. All that is intended is that whenever one states an argument – that is, specifies a set of explicit assumptions – the argument will be rational if and only if it is logically valid. Logical validity does not require that the argument be true but only that the assumptions are logically sufficient, that is, that the conclusions reached are necessarily true whenever the assumptions are *all* true. But why the concern for 'rational' arguments? One reason for the concern is the *universality* and *uniqueness* provided by rational arguments. The promise of 'rationality' is that once the assumptions are explicitly stated, *anyone* can see that the conclusions reached are true whenever the assumptions are true. That is, if the argument is rational, everyone will reach the *same* conclusions if they start with the *same* assumptions. It is this universality of rational arguments that forms the basis of our understanding behaviour or phenomena. If the behaviour or phenomena can be 'rationalized' in the form of a rational argument for which the behaviour or phenomena are logical conclusions, then anyone can understand the behaviour or phenomena if one accepts the truth of the assumptions.

In the nineteenth century this notion of universality was captured in the notion of maximization since both notions involve similar mechanics. If we can specify an appropriate objective function for a decision-maker who is a maximizer then we can understand the choice made. This is because, if the objective function (e.g. a utility function) is properly shaped so that there is a unique optimum, then everyone using this function while facing the same constraints will make the same choices. Thus, again, it is the universality and uniqueness that form the basis of our understanding. Every neoclassical theory is offered as an intentionally rational argument. The explicit assumptions include those which specify the shape of the objective function, the nature of the constraints and, of course, the assumption of maximization.

The criticisms discussed in this chapter focus on how the decision-maker *knows* his or her objective function or the constraints. The question asked by this type of criticism, which presumes that rationality is always the stronger notion, is whether there is also a rational way to acquire this essential knowledge. Many people apparently still think that one can inductively acquire knowledge by means of an inductive logic – a logic which uses singular observations as assumptions and reaches general, universally true conclusions. Trying to show how one acquires true knowledge in this way always involves what is called the 'problem of induction'. Unfortunately, this is not a solvable problem since there is no inductive logic that will meet the requirements of universality and uniqueness in every case as implied by the notion of the 'rationality' of an argument.

Whether one thinks the 'problem of induction' is solvable or not, the questions raised by Lachmann and Shackle do not require induction or rationality in the stronger sense. Maximizing decision-making does require knowledge of the objective function and of the constraints (e.g. prices) and if we are to explain the choices made we must somehow deal with the decision-maker's knowledge.[1]

THE METHODOLOGICAL PROBLEM OF KNOWLEDGE

As Lachmann notes, identifying precisely what assumptions concerning knowledge distinguish neoclassical theory 'is anything but easy' [1976, p. 55]. Nevertheless, it is still possible to identify the basic methodological flavour of the neoclassical view of knowledge and this may be conveyed by the proposition that, no matter how knowledge is characterized, knowledge in short-run models is a fixed and exogenous parameter. The assumption of exogeneity guarantees that knowledge considerations can determine short-run choices, but not vice versa. The assumption of fixity guarantees that any variation in economic choices can be fully explained by variations in objective factors (i.e. factors other than knowledge).

The assumption of fixity has often been defended on the basis of either of two propositions:

(a) That there exists unlimited 'perfect knowledge' – that is, if knowledge (of past, present and future) is perfect, then it follows trivially that it cannot change, or

(b) That the time period being considered by the theory is too short to permit any knowledge change whatsoever, the limiting case being explanation at a point in time ('statics').

Knowledge, in the sense of (b), is thus analogous to capital in the short run. But on either grounds, the assumption of fixity leads directly to Lachmann's (and Shackle's) major criticism of the theory. In a world of actual uncertainty, knowledge cannot be stable but must inevitably be volatile; thus short-run equilibria are extremely temporary. Of course, no explanation of a short-run equilibrium *per se* is sufficient for the determination of the eventual long-run equilibrium. Since a long-run equilibrium is merely a special short-run equilibrium, the attainment of a long-run equilibrium presumes the existence of the one state of knowledge appropriate for that special short-run equilibrium.

The methodological problem which neoclassical economics presumes to be solved is: How does knowledge change to that which is necessary for the long-run equilibrium state, that is, to the one state of knowledge which is appropriate for the special short-run equilibrium which holds in the long run? A complete explanation of long-run equilibrium must provide an explanation of knowledge dynamics [see Arrow 1959b; Gordon and Hynes 1970]. But, if the acquisition of the knowledge appropriate for long-run equilibrium is explained, knowledge ceases to be exogenous.[2] In the long run, knowledge is an endogenous variable (like prices or capital) hence knowledge does not play a decisive role – at least not in the sense of the role played by individuals' tastes and the current state of technology. This means that, for the purposes of determining or calculating the long-run equilibrium, (endogenous) knowledge is irrelevant.

Lachmann's and Shackle's criticisms of the above view may be seen to be more than just a plea for 'realism of assumptions'. First, if Lachmann's criticism of neoclassical theory is simply that it does not take knowledge into account in any explicit form even though we clearly know that states of knowledge do determine the properties of short-run economic choices, then it follows trivially that the neoclassical explanation must be incomplete and its predictions arbitrary (in the sense that neoclassical results must vary indeterminately with an unspecified state of knowledge). This would be an unfair representation of neoclassical economics and therefore an unfair criticism. As suggested above, a better way to characterize the neoclassical tradition is as one where, in the long run, knowledge is explanatorily irrelevant and in the short run it is specified explicitly as fixed and exogenous. We may then judge this specification against other alternatives, specifically against those of Hayek, Mises and Shackle.

Shackle's critique [1972] may be seen as an attempt to show that the assumption of fixed and exogenous knowledge is unsatisfactory primarily because it means relinquishing the explanation of economic processes over time ('economic dynamics'). Shackle reaches this conclusion in two ways. His first argument, and the one he stresses, introduces an additional proposition:

(c) That perfect knowledge is possible *only* at a single point in time [1972, p. 165].

It then follows directly that, in so far as neoclassical theory depends upon the assumption of 'perfect knowledge' to explain the 'fixity' of knowledge, neoclassical theory can only be rationalized for a point in time and not over time. It is thus only if unlimited perfect knowledge could exist over time that a neoclassical theory based on fixed knowledge could produce meaningful dynamic explanations. Would the incompatibility between neoclassical theory and dynamic explanation be removed if we settled for a view of knowledge as limited, incomplete or otherwise imperfect (i.e. 'expectational') and in turn introduced the view that this knowledge was fixed or rigid over an acceptable, yet small, duration? Shackle's second argument is that the answer to this question is 'No'. Since Shackle [1972, pp. 77, 180, 436] sees expectations as subject to moment-to-moment instability and thus as perfectly volatile, even a neoclassical theory which sacrifices the assumption of perfect knowledge is still limited to a point in time. If Shackle is suggesting that neoclassical economics faces only two alternatives, then it must choose to analyze either static situations or situations of perpetual change and instability, but not both.

One can easily agree with the general spirit of Shackle's criticism, since it is easy to see that, if one wants to explain the properties of a dynamic economy, it is methodologically much more interesting to do this within a framework where knowledge is variable. Moreover, there is little reason why knowledge needs to be fixed in neoclassical theory. Traditional arguments that deny the potential variability of knowledge in neoclassical economics can be seen to be based on the unwarranted fusion of the methodological problems connected with the fixity of knowledge and the epistemological problems connected with the perfection of knowledge. These two types of problems are easily made indistinguishable whenever one insists that perfect knowledge must have an indispensable place in the neoclassical framework – for example, when it is presumed that, without it, (complete) rationality is impossible. A commitment to a perfect knowledge assumption on these confused grounds thus constrains neoclassical theory to use an assumption involving the fixity of knowledge. Yet this constraint only exists because of the presumption that perfect knowledge is a precondition for rationality – a view which has been criticized [e.g. Tisdell 1975]. In short, if we separate rationality from perfect knowledge, the way is made clear for the introduction of 'imperfect' and thus potentially-variable knowledge into neoclassical theory. A possible key to this separation is the rejection of the Marshallian long-run vs short-run dichotomy.

Shackle does not make these arguments. His critique is essentially in an earlier tradition of showing that any explanation which requires the assumption of perfect knowledge must be inconsistent with any theory which incorporates dynamically-variable knowledge. It should also be noted that while Shackle is especially wary of the epistemological problems which are entailed by the perfect knowledge assumption, he is notably lax on developing the epistemological rationale for his own viewpoint. This will be the major critical theme of the following sections.

I discuss Shackle's version of the Austrian arguments in some detail here because, according to Lachmann [1976, p. 57], Shackle's arguments represent a convenient modern expression of much of the Austrian viewpoint and stand as a major source of criticism of neoclassical theory. And the essence of this viewpoint is that knowledge is better specified as an exogenous, yet highly volatile, item in our economic explanations. Note that from Shackle's perspective the conflict between the neoclassical and Austrian viewpoints involves only the variability of knowledge over time; it does not involve its exogeneity. While Lachmann refers to the possible 'endogeneity' of knowledge in Shackle's theory [p. 56], it is important to recognize that this concept is interesting only when it is defined relative to a dynamic process such as learning dynamics. The appropriate relation between changes in knowledge and adjustments in economic choices is that of lagged endogeneity since learning takes time and must precede decision-making. On the other hand, a concept of 'static endogeneity', that is, the proposition that knowledge and economic choices are simultaneously determined, is not relevant here since this would leave Austrian theory, let alone neoclassical theory, undetermined and thus make both theories equally incomplete or circular.

Lachmann is correct in arguing that the Austrian assumption of exogenously-variable knowledge is preferable to the short-run neoclassical assumption of exogenously-fixed knowledge. Moreover, the Austrian assumption provides a vital starting point for examining the question of how the stability of knowledge (viz. expectations) affects the stability of the aggregate economy. However, one might implicitly disagree with Lachmann over the calculation of the net benefits associated with this specificational improvement. No matter how satisfactory the methodological role one assigns to knowledge in economic models, the benefits of this will be nullified if one happens to pick, at the same time, an unsatisfactory characterization of the views of knowledge held by economic agents.

THE EPISTEMOLOGICAL PROBLEM OF KNOWLEDGE

So far nothing I have said would require a commitment to any particular views of knowledge which might be held by economic decision-makers. My concern has only been with the methodological role that knowledge, however defined, might play in the structure of economic explanations. In this section the central concern is explicitly with these alternative views and their implications for neoclassical and Austrian theory. In this light, it is interesting that nowhere in Lachmann's essay does he tell us exactly what constitutes 'knowledge'. Implicitly Lachmann must hold that there exists some 'accepted' theory of knowledge upon which all economic agents inevitably base their decisions, a theory which apparently is so well accepted that it need not be stated. The implied claims about the homogeneity of viewpoint shared by all economic decision-makers are indeed comforting. However, they do not sit well alongside the facts that, in spite of Lachmann's grouping of them, Mises is usually considered an Apriorist[3] while both Hayek and Shackle based their views of knowledge on Inductivism[4] (albeit of the sceptical kind). Lachmann is in fact prepared to play down Mises' Apriorism [p. 56] on the grounds that epistemological differences are of little consequence to the matters at hand. My point is simple. Such differences in views of knowledge are absolutely central to the matters at hand.[5]

We need not be troubled with the many questions of overriding philosophy of science implied here. We only need a few simple characterizations of theories of knowledge which 'ordinary' economic decision-makers might hold. The importance of these theories may be directly brought out by considering a problem posed frequently in Shackle's critique [1972, p. 180]. He asks, in what way do decision-makers respond to an (exogenous) change in 'the news' – the new information or data which is accumulating daily? If this were a problem in price theory, and we were to ask for the impact of a price change on an individual's consumption, it would be evident that we could produce a satisfactory answer only if we had a satisfactory characterization of the individual's underlying tastes. The same point applies to the problem at hand. If we wish to determine the impact of a change in 'the news' on an individual's expectations and thus on the pattern of his or her decisions, we must satisfactorily specify the theory of knowledge through which the changed news is fed. Lachmann and Shackle would appear to assume that all individuals respond to the news through a common theory of knowledge. It is, however, easy to conceive of at least three different epistemological viewpoints on the same change in the news and thus three different decision-making responses.

Consider first individuals who follow Mises and thereby hold an Apriorist theory of knowledge. Since, by definition, their expectations are formed quite independently of the 'data' revealed by the news, their expectations and the pattern of their decisions can only be invariant to changes in the news. Consider next people who, like many of us in the past, hold a Positivist view of knowledge. These individuals will normally only look for new positive evidence to empirically support their guesses (viz. their inductive inferences). If a change in the news reveals predominantly 'verifying facts', then these individuals' expectations (which are being verified) will change little and thus the pattern of their decisions will change little. It is only in the extreme case where the changed news reveals predominantly 'refuting facts' that these decision-makers' expectations will be appreciably affected. Consider finally people who hold a Scepticist theory of knowledge.[6] These are people who are always looking to the news for indications that they should change their expectations. Except in the case where the changing news consistently reveals only 'verifying facts' (which are irrelevant to the Sceptic), it is evident that these people rarely have uniform patterns of behaviour and the effect of new 'refuting facts' can often have a devastating impact on their expectations and decisions.

These alternative characterizations are of course most relevant in assessing Shackle's view that volatility and instability in the news imply volatility and instability of the aggregate economy in general. Clearly if all decision-makers were Apriorists or the news revealed only 'verifying facts', Shackle's argument simply could not hold. Perfect volatility in the news is consistent with perfect stability of decision-making in aggregate. In fact, it is only in the extreme case where most decision-makers are Scepticists and the news contains mostly 'refuting facts' that Shackle's instability argument may prove interesting. And emerging from this extreme case are all the criticisms of the neoclassical presumptions of rationality, economic stability and the fixity of knowledge.

The question, of course, is whether Shackle's extreme case is a 'satisfactory' characterization of the epistemological environment faced by an aggregate of individuals. If it is not, in the sense that a weighted average of the theories of knowledge held by all individuals does not reveal them to be predominantly Scepticist and a weighted average of all new 'data' does not reveal a high proportion of 'refuting facts', then criticism of the stability and fixed-knowledge presumptions of neoclassical economics are beside the point. Even if the news is perfectly volatile and unstable, this is of limited interest whenever individuals show little responsiveness to changes in the news. Moreover, the methodological comparative advantage of specifying knowledge as a variable must be largely illusory under these circumstances. However, even if Shackle's extreme case was a 'satisfactory' one, there is no way in principle in which this could challenge the rationality assumption of neoclassical economics. Scepticism is an eminently rational viewpoint for a decision-maker to hold and it would be a mistake to confuse the very high elasticity of response to a change in the news with non-rational behaviour.

THE INTERDEPENDENCE OF METHODOLOGY AND EPISTEMOLOGY

Lachmann's efforts to stress the importance of knowledge in economic theory in general are commendable. Nevertheless, neither he, nor Shackle, nor any existing economic theory has gone far enough in stressing the epistemological role of knowledge in particular. None of the viewpoints considered here can be taken as both methodologically and epistemologically complete with respect to knowledge. This is primarily due to all parties taking the answer to the question 'What is knowledge?' for granted, and this presumption may in turn be explained by the common acceptance of a very particular view of the role of 'rationality' in all decision-making and in explaining all decision-making. This view is simply that the 'adequacy' of the assumptions about the role of knowledge in economic explanations is to be judged only by whether or not they can 'rationalize' *successful* decision-making. Shackle and the Austrians are correct in noting that a theory of *successful* rational action does require some judgement as to what constitutes adequate knowledge, although one may admit to a variety of different notions of 'success' and 'adequacy'. Where Mises 'examines the elements of a logic of successful action' [Lachmann 1976, p. 56], Shackle examines what kind of success (albeit limited) is possible when we constrain rational decision-making by the limitations of necessarily-imperfect knowledge.

This general concern with only successful rational action greatly limits the role of rationality in economic theories and methodology. It is well known that logic or rationality can only tell us when we can expect our rational conclusions (predictions or expectations) to be true. It cannot help us predict whether our conclusions are false. This means that true and successful conclusions are logically possible even when one's assumptions are 'unrealistic'. This is because it is possible for one to deduce true conclusions from false assumptions even when the deductions are logically valid.[7] Thus successful actions do not prove that the decision-maker's assumptions were true. Moreover, if one follows Shackle by accepting the view that 'rational success is only possible with perfect knowledge', then one could never explain a decision-maker's successes as a necessary outcome of a rational argument. Not only because true assumptions are not necessary for successful actions, but because even if they were the decision-maker could never know for certain whether his or her assumptions were true – knowledge is always changing in response to the news. It is for this latter reason that Shackle would have us replace the rational successes of neoclassical economics (i.e. stable equilibria) with a second-best kind of success – his 'kaleido-statics' or constantly changing temporary equilibria. His concept of knowledge, he claims, is adequate for that limited purpose. On this last point he may be correct, but what would be the cost?

In this light, Shackle's critique seems to have lost sight of at least one important methodological virtue of modern neoclassical economics. That virtue is the requirement that we should be explicit concerning all our active assumptions. Any long-run equilibrium can be shown to follow logically from some specific set of exogenous givens (resources, technology, tastes, etc.). But if, as Shackle argues, one of the givens of neoclassical theory is the fixed and exogenous knowledge and it is not logically complete itself, then the explicitness of neoclassical theory turns out to be the source of its alleged downfall. Unfortunately, the insights gained through Shackle's focus on change and instability can never be a satisfactory compensation for the resultant loss of neoclassical explicitness.

CONCLUDING REMARKS ON THE LACHMANN–SHACKLE EPISTEMOLOGY

I have stressed a number of key points in the above sections. It is misleading to claim that neoclassical theory is wrong whenever it does not give an essential role to knowledge. To the contrary, as can be seen in Chapter 4, when examining the *long-run* equilibrium solution to any neoclassical model, knowledge does not play a *decisive* role. Specifically, the solution can be obtained without reference to the knowledge of the decision-makers. Thus any argument for the relevance of knowledge presumes the absence of a long-run equilibrium. But the Marshallian tradition based on the long-run vs short-run dichotomy is misleading. In the short run the decision-maker's knowledge is necessarily fixed, but as Shackle also stresses, any knowledge which is fixed is also potentially unstable. It constantly needs updating. His conclusion regarding the inevitability of instability is based unfortunately on his inductivist epistemology which presumes that all knowledge necessarily 'rests on inductive inference' [1972, p. 407]. Such an epistemology by its peculiar nature is limited since it can only comment on the *successful* acquisition of the needed knowledge.

While Shackle's views can be criticized, there is much to learn from them. One can see that almost all relevant issues concerning the role of knowledge in modern economic theory can be reduced to two key questions:

(1) What constitutes a 'satisfactory' explanation of any economic decision-making *process* if knowledge is taken to be an exogenous and/or fixed element in this explanation?
(2) What is a 'satisfactory' characterization of the theory of knowledge[8] held by any given decision-maker of our economic models?

The first question concerns the *methodological role* of knowledge and calls for judgements as to the explanatory adequacy of alternative specifications of a knowledge variable in economic models. These judgements are to be distinguished clearly from those on the second, which concern theories of what knowledge actually is (as seen by economic decision-makers) or the *epistemological role* of knowledge in economic models. The second question is irrelevant only for models where long-run equilibria are assumed to hold since such an assumption entails the (successful) acquisition of adequate knowledge (however characterized).

As Lachmann suggests, historically it is trivially true that Austrian theorists have answered the first question better than those classical and neoclassical theorists concerned only with long-run equilibrium solutions. However, like most writers on the role of knowledge, Lachmann appears to assume that the second question is of little importance or, at least, that there exists an answer to it which can be taken for granted in any case. Such a view would be acceptable only if (i) the first question could be answered independently of the second, or (ii) the assumed answer to the second was satisfactory on its own grounds. Fortunately, Lachmann argues neither point (i) nor point (ii). Moreover, both points are false. As I have argued here, in any model where knowledge or time is supposed to be relevant, the two questions cannot be regarded as independent of one another since answers to the first must constrain answers to the second and vice versa.

Epistemology considerations should not be taken for granted. An inductivist epistemology will always be an inadequate foundation for discussions of knowledge dynamics. Logically, the complete success of induction requires an infinity of time.[9] This requirement raises an important problem. For a short-run equilibrium to be also a long-run equilibrium, the appropriate knowledge must have been acquired. But if the attainment of a long-run equilibrium is to be presumed, successful inductive inference must entail a sufficient amount of time. Such sufficiency is at least problematic; and this problem is the keystone of Shackle's critique of neoclassical economics. He argues that in order to maintain the relevance of knowledge real time must matter. Specifically, the amount of time necessary for the attainment of the long-run equilibrium must be denied. But this critique works only for an inductivist epistemology. One could just as easily argue for the irrelevance of (successful) inductive inference in decision-making, even in the short run. Thus without an argument for the necessity of inductive inference, Shackle's inductivist epistemology will necessarily be an inadequate explanation of both short-run knowledge and the role of knowledge or knowledge change.

In summary, it is only by attributing a questionable theory of knowledge (viz. Inductivism) to the economic decision-makers of neoclassical economics that Lachmann and Shackle can successfully reach their critical conclusions. Once the importance of real time and the resulting interdependence between the methodological and epistemological roles of knowledge are recognized, in conjunction with alternative views of the epistemological role in particular, the supposed comparative advantage of Austrian theory over neoclassical economics disappears.

In so far as neither neoclassical nor Austrian theory provides a 'satisfactory' characterization of such epistemological foundations, both theories share a common defect. A most important part of this failure is the common assumption that the objective of any economic theory is to explain only rationally-successful action, which then constrains all epistemological theories to explain universal (rational) success or universal (non-rational) lack of success. While Lachmann wishes to establish a clear-cut comparative advantage for Shackle's Austrian economic theory over neoclassical theory, there would seem to be little point in elevating the former simply on the grounds that it is less optimistic about rational success or that it suggests an extreme characterization of an epistemological environment which leads to this conclusion. Any proof of the ultimate superiority of Shackle's foundations must be clearly demonstrated for any and all epistemological specifications and it is indeed fortunate that such global proofs are themselves largely precluded by their own scepticism.

NOTES

1 The remainder of this chapter is adapted from Boland and Newman [1979] which I co-authored with my friend and former student Geoffrey Newman. I thank the editors of the *Australian Economic Papers* for giving me permission to do so.
2 I have discussed the role of exogeneity in Boland [1989, Chapter 6]. Elsewhere [in Boland 1982a, Chapters 2 and 6], I explained that in long-run models, where appropriate knowledge is simply assumed to exist, any question about the time needed to acquire that knowledge is beyond consideration.
3 Apriorism is usually of the form that knowledge is based on introspection and in particular all knowledge is founded first on *a priori* assumptions such that observations always are secondary.
4 Recall that Inductivism is a methodological doctrine that limits all claims to knowledge to inductive proofs. I have explained this doctrine more fully in note 5 of Chapter 1.
5 It is thus ironic that Lachmann defends the view that expectations may be divergent among economic decision-makers [1976, p. 58] without admitting that epistemologies that decision-makers endorse could also be divergent by the same arguments.
6 Scepticism is the rationalist view of knowledge that says that all attempts to prove knowledge to be true will lead to an infinite regress. Thus, according to Scepticism, all knowledge that is claimed to be true will always be questionable.
7 Philosophers call this the 'fallacy of denying the antecedent' [see further Bear and Orr 1967; Boland 1982a, Chapter 9].
8 For example, is it Apriorism, Positivism, Inductivism, etc.?
9 One might say that this is the only way to 'solve' the problem of induction – of course, if by 'infinity' we mean an impossibly long period of time, then the problem is not solved [see further, Boland 1982a, Chapters 2 and 6].

7 A naive theory of technology and change

> Sometimes it may be natural to think of 'technology' as a separate *input* element, an extra variable in the production function... Suppose we have a change that could be described, roughly, as an increase in the productivity of labor. This could mean that there has been a change in certain conditions upon which the productive effect of a certain specified standard input of labor depends. But it could also mean that the units of labor have changed their quality in a way which is not reflected in the kind of measure we use for labor input. The same could be true for the input of capital... Changes in the kind of capital used would be a time-requiring process. A change in technology would permit a larger potential of capital accumulation.
>
> Trygve Haavelmo [1960, pp. 147–8]

There is one aspect of knowledge that has always been explicitly recognized in Marshallian economics, namely technical knowledge. However, the knowledge recognized in Marshallian economics is about production technology. While technology is thereby not a neglected element in neoclassical models, it can be argued that changes in technology have been ignored. Recall that Marshall defines the long run as the period during which knowledge is fixed [1920/49, pp. 291 and 315]. Since long-run prices are determined mostly by production costs, I think Marshall is saying that *technical* knowledge is fixed. In this regard, consideration of the problem of knowledge dynamics discussed in Chapter 6 might lead us to question the adequacy of neoclassical models to deal with questions involving changing technology and particularly their adequacy when it comes to questions of economic history.

In Marshall's day, technical knowledge was variable only over very long periods such as between generations. Of course, historians are more concerned with the big picture which involves inter-generational comparisons. To the extent that history does involve inter-generational comparisons historians must deal with changes in technology. But while knowledge can be acquired by anyone, technology is usually embodied in machinery. Without the capital or machinery which embodies the current technology, one cannot benefit from the current state of knowledge. So it would seem that to study economic history one ought to examine neoclassical capital theory. But unfortunately, neoclassical capital theory is more concerned with adjustments of capital within the long-run period where technology is fixed. When a firm changes from one industry to another in the long run, it changes the quality or type of capital from what was appropriate in one industry to that which is appropriate in the next. The choice of industry is based on a given menu of technologies in Marshall's long run.

When, as a new PhD, I first considered the matter of technology and change I had an idea which I naively thought would be rather easy to work out. That idea was that since a firm (i.e. a business enterprise) is fundamentally a social institution, it would be possible to apply the standard theory of social change to the analysis of the technology of a firm with respect to changes in an economy. That was a nice idea, but it would have failed for the lack of a standard theory of social change that could be applied. This forced me to deal with social change as I dealt with technology. It is my view now that this can be done by viewing them both as interrelated aspects of social learning. This chapter presents my early attempts to demonstrate just this view.[1] In the last section of this chapter I will briefly outline my conclusions regarding the simple theory of social institutions developed between the lines, so to speak. In the next chapter I will further develop this simple theory to deal with more general questions of institutions in economic history.

The evidence of learning by an economic institution, such as a firm, is any accumulation of (new) technology and any improvements in efficiency. This suggests a view of social learning whereby there are two ways a social institution can learn: (1) through *changes* in the institution, and (2) through institutional *reforms*. And, while an *institution* might not learn through a revolution, a *society* can learn by overturning some institutions. By institutional changes in the case of a firm I mean the acquisition of new or different machinery or personnel. By institutional reforms I mean improvements in the methods of using existing machinery and personnel. In each case the learning process takes time. The major learning process, the accumulation of technology, is limited both by the *discovery* of new ideas and by the *implementation* of them. One can stoically accept the lack of discovery, but the lack of implementation of a known improvement can be very frustrating. There is necessarily a disparity between the growth of knowledge and the growth of technology, that is, between availability and implementation. This disparity exists because *all* economic technology can be seen to be embodied in capital and the accumulation of capital takes time. This would seem to mean that there can be no significant change in our productive capabilities (i.e. our economic technology) until we have changed our capital stock (physical or human). It also would seem that changes in capital cannot be explained by changes in technology and that changes in output of an economy can only be explained by changes in capital (physical or human).

NON-AUTONOMY OF TECHNOLOGY

I now present my argument for why I think economic technology does not exist by itself but must be manifested in the capital used by a firm or industry. It is common knowledge that we have on many occasions known how to do something but it was not until much later that we acquired the technical capability to do it. In other words, knowledge is not the same thing as technology. For example, technology may depend on knowledge but knowledge need not depend on technology [see Agassi 1966]. What is it that stands between our knowing how and our acquiring the ability? When after acquiring knowledge are we able? This would seem to be a fundamental question for the historian of economic technology. Today in this age of specialization I think the answer is that we are able to accomplish a technically difficult feat, or to produce a new product, only *after* we have accumulated the specialized capital in terms of either sophisticated machinery or technical personnel. By itself, all the research and development of a firm adds little to the economic technology of that firm. The fruits of the research or development become part of the firm's technology only when the firm invests in (or acquires) the *necessary* machinery and personnel that are specifically designed or trained to do the new job. In other words, all technology exists only by being built into the economic institutions, that is, by embodying it in the capital either through specialized design or through specialized training.[2]

To say we cannot obtain new technology without a change in capital (mechanical or human) is to say that technology is not autonomous. Since technology may not be autonomous, we need not expect the growth of technology to appear to be continuous. Technology necessarily grows in discrete jumps because before a new technological capability appears, institutional changes are required, that is, new specialized machinery must be designed and constructed, and/or (new or old) personnel must be trained. In either case, the process of introducing a new technology takes time; the greater the change, the longer the time. We should not, of course, rule out improvements in productive capabilities that arise through improving efficiency. These improvements also take time but they would not account for the substantial changes in productive capabilities. Parenthetically, I should point out that this latter kind of improvement, or institutional reform, is assumed automatically in neoclassical economic theory. Not quickly seeking and finding the most efficient means of producing a *given* quantity of output would be considered irrational. The neoclassical problem has always been to find the most 'efficient' level of output of all those that are technologically possible.[3] And institutional changes, such as increasing productive possibilities, is considered an outside question for neoclassical capital theory – but not for the reasons I have laid out here. In neoclassical capital theory it is merely a matter of having *more* of the *same* type cr quality of capital rather than choosing a different type or quality of capital. In terms of Chapter 5, neoclassical capital theory is concerned with the achievement of an intermediate-run equilibrium.

CAPITAL AS EMBODIED TECHNOLOGY

A further extension of the idea of embodied technology is that future (as well as current) advances in technology are limited by the *quality* as well as the growth of capital. For example, the exploration of space which made new research and development possible was itself limited by the development of technical capabilities. In other words, not only is the growth of technology limited by the changes in capital, but so is the growth of knowledge limited. This idea was employed by Arrow in his famous [1962] capital theory article about the economic implications of learning by doing.

I have said that changes in capital cannot be explained by changes in technology. Stated another way, if we ask, 'Why has the capital stock of a large firm, an industry, or an economy changed?' we *cannot* answer 'Because there was a *prior* change in the technology of that firm, industry, or economy, respectively.'[4] It might be asked, if we exclude changes in technology as bases for explaining changes in capital, what does it leave? Of course, neoclassical theory offers another explanation. The direct reason why capital would be changed is that the entrepreneur or manager of a firm seeks to increase profits. The assumption of profit maximization leads to another question. Why should changing capital be more profitable? The answer to this question can be that the output which only the new capital can produce may now be more desirable. Increased desirability might be indicated by contracts, by market research, or by rising market prices. In any case, these would be the *reasons* for profitability and ultimately the reasons for changing capital, that is, for institutional changes.

CAPITAL AND CHANGE

Recognizing capital as embodied technology leads to a consideration of whether changes in output of an economy can be explained *only* by changes in capital. I am speaking here of the *ex post* realization of a change in output which would clearly be the case when there is a substantial intergenerational change in the type of output – such as might occur when the automobile industry changes from gasoline engines to electric motors. We already know about the substantial retooling necessary to bring out a new model of the present type of automobile output.[5] To advance the argument for a capital-based explanation of secular changes in output, we should ask: Are there any other bases for the accomplishment of a change in output? Clearly, we could say that desirability of a different output should affect its being produced. Unfortunately, desirability would not be an adequate explanation because desirability is neither necessary nor sufficient even when it may appear that we have the theoretical capability. Clearly, desirability is not sufficient when we do not have even the theoretical capabilities of a different output. To see that it may not be sufficient we need only observe one occasion where it is not, although we have the 'know-how'. As long as one is willing to recognize real time, it is easy to find such examples. The usual problem is not how to produce a desirable good but how to mass-produce it. The American space shuttle programme is replete with examples of goods that are produced as one-only items that would be useful if mass-produced. Today, the most important is the fuel cell that can produce electrical energy with virtually no pollution and a very low cost of operation. The fact that such items can be produced (albeit at an extremely high cost) only makes it frustrating that the means of massproducing them has not been found. Sometimes it takes decades before such one-only items in the space programme see their way to the mass consumer market. This is a problem of implementation rather than knowledge.

TOWARDS A THEORY OF SOCIAL CHANGE

To many anti-neoclassical economists my naive arguments in this chapter would not seem to be very amazing since much of it goes against the neoclassical theory of the textbooks. Technology is always assumed to be 'given' in Marshallian models. The questions of capital theory are always in terms of the *quantity* of homogeneous capital, and technology is always something independent and exogenous. The role of capital in the growth of technology and the development of new and different goods is central to both economic theory and economic history.

On the basis of what I have said here it could be argued that capital theory should be the foundation for all future improvements in economic theory and perhaps even economic history. This is simply because the growth of technology today is probably the most important aspect of the modern economic decisions of economic institutions such as firms. As many already agree, technology can no longer be considered exogenous; it must be endogenous, that is, any theory of the firm, as an economic institution, must also explain the growth of technology.

Most neoclassical theorists are unlikely to heed the call for a rethinking of neoclassical capital theory. It is all too easy to retreat to the view that capital is merely a commodity like any other and thus it is subject to Marshall's Principle of Substitution (i.e. to the neoclassical maximization hypothesis) and thus explainable as discussed in Chapters 2 and 3. So what can be learned from this elementary exercise in dealing with Marshall's secular or inter-generational run? What I have said so far can be generalized into a simple theory of social institutions. This simple theory says that society's institutions are, like the firm's capital, embodiments of society's social technology. Social institutions are social capital. The evidence of learning in society is the changing of social institutions through simple change, more elaborate reforms, or even through revolution. Although a revolution in the case of a firm means going out of business, it need not mean that for the case of the society as a whole. Since technology can always be viewed as merely accepted solutions, it follows that social institutions are merely accepted solutions to standard social problems. Without *new* problems there need not be any social change. Even though the problems solved by the current institutions are no longer interesting, we may still have solutions for them.

This chapter constitutes the results of my early study of institutions and technological change. In retrospect, it does seem rather naive. Nevertheless, it suggests some interesting ideas concerning an analogy between the neoclassical theory of capital and a more general theory of institutional change. And the awkwardness of my naive early views did prompt me to learn more about social change and social institutions in general. In the next chapter I present the results of my later explorations into a more substantial view of the role of institutions in neoclassical economic theory.

NOTES

1 The remainder of this chapter is based on a paper I delivered to the Society for the History of Technology meetings in 1967 [see Boland 1971].
2 One could easily see supporting evidence in the high degree of specialization prevailing in today's economy.
3 This is considered a low-level criterion of efficiency and requires only that the firm find its optimum point *on* its production function – that is, it is not wasting inputs.
4 Except in the case where to produce the new capital the technology of the production of capital itself may have changed.
5 Until recently, every time there was an energy crisis, automotive executives would point out that it takes at least four years to introduce a new model. Executives of the Chrysler Corporation are now claiming that the lead time can be reduced to less than two years.

8 Knowledge and institutions in economic theory

> Though economic analysis and general reasoning are of wide application, yet every age and every country has its own problems; and every change in social conditions is likely to require a new development of economic doctrines.
>
> Alfred Marshall [1920/49, pp. 30–1]

> The failure of economists to appreciate the transitory character of the assumed constraints and to understand the source and direction of these changing constraints is a fundamental handicap to further development of economic theory.
>
> Douglass North [1978, p. 963]

For more than six decades, neoclassical economics has been criticized for neglecting the social institutions that form the framework in which the neoclassical economy functions. In North America the criticisms have come from those economists who huddle under the banner of 'institutional economics' and focus on the problem of explaining institutional change. This chapter discusses the role of institutions in neoclassical economics. Whether there is a problem with how neoclassical economics explains the evolution of institutions is a question open to debate. Proponents of neoclassical economics argue that since one can explain any institutional setting and its evolution as merely the consequences of the logic of choice (i.e. of optimization facing given constraints), our understanding of institutions is merely another example of neoclassical analysis (e.g. James Buchanan, Gordon Tullock and Douglass North).

The primary concern of some opponents of the neoclassical economics has been to show that the pro-neoclassical view is simply false. In particular, they have seen that advocates of the neoclassical view presume that neoclassical choice theory can easily be made dynamic. Some opponents go so far as to argue explicitly that this presumption is completely unfounded [Shackle 1972; Hicks 1976]. The question of dynamics is even sometimes alleged to be the 'fatal flaw' of neoclassical theory [Robinson 1974].

So much has been made of this criticism over the last two decades that those institutionalists among the anti-neoclassical group have turned their attention from a study of the nature of institutions to the study of the evolutionary aspects of any economy. So far, the institutionalists' critical programme of study – called 'evolutionary economics' – has failed to persuade neoclassical economists to drop their 'paradigm'. To the contrary, many neoclassical theorists believe that the evolution of an economy's institutional setting can be explained *within* the neoclassical paradigm [e.g. Buchanan and Tullock 1962]. However, it would be misleading to suggest that this is only a methodological dispute over the ability to 'explain within'. Underlying this question is a more fundamental theoretical issue concerning the nature and role of institutions in neoclassical theory.

Here I will argue that the essence of the methodological dispute lies not in the depths of sterile philosophy, but in the apparently contradictory roles played by institutions in economic theory. On one hand (viz. in neoclassical theory), institutions are tacit or given static *constraints* which ultimately define various equilibrium positions. On the other hand (viz. in economic policy analysis), institutions are explicitly dynamic or active *instruments* used either to facilitate or to prevent change. Both aspects of institutions are explicitly recognized in Lance Davis and Douglass North [1971]. Following Buchanan and Tullock, Davis and North distinguish between the *institutional environment*, which includes the 'legal ground rules' that constrain on-going political and economic business, and the *institutional arrangement*, which provides a workable mechanism either for operating *within* the ground rules or for changing them. It will be shown that any appearance of contradiction here can easily be overcome with an explicit recognition of the relationship between institutions and knowledge.

I will argue here that since the neoclassical conception of an institution (i.e. a short-run constraint) is inherently static, all attempts to promote and defend the pro-neoclassical view will necessarily result in methodological failures. Moreover, if neoclassical economics is ever going to be able to explain the evolution of institutions then a broader view of institutions will have to be developed. I think such a broader view is possible within neoclassical economics. But, unless the dynamic nature of institutions is properly explained, no explanation (neoclassical or institutional) of evolutionary economics can ever succeed.

I will begin by presenting the neoclassical view of institutions, namely, the one where institutions are merely some of the constraints facing the optimizer. Specific attention will again be given to the Marshallian method of dealing with the dynamics of constraints. Next, I will summarize from

Chapter 7 my criticism of the adequacy of any neoclassical programme for dealing with questions of dynamics. Then I will present a theory of the nature and role of institutions designed to overcome the inadequacy of the neoclassical approach to institutional dynamics.[1] It will be based on an explicit recognition of the relevant epistemological questions involved as well as the instrumental aspects of institutions. Finally, I will explain the essential relationships among time, knowledge and institutions.

THE NEOCLASSICAL VIEW OF INSTITUTIONS

Within neoclassical theory, all *endogenous* variables are explained as the logical consequences of self-interested rational choice, whereby one's choice may be limited by the similarly motivated rational choices of others through any activity in the market. This form of rational choice involves maximization (or minimization) of some objective function while facing some *given* constraints. The nature of the constraints facing any *individual's* choice may or may not be explained as a matter of his or her past or irreversible decisions or those of other individuals. Those constraints which are not considered a matter of choice cannot be *explained* within neoclassical theory. Operative constraints which limit individuals' choices (e.g. anything which is naturally given or beyond control, such as the availability of resources, technology, and so forth) are by definition the *exogenous* variables of neoclassical theory.[2] Also by definition, any fixed or exogenous variable can be seen to play a determining role (viz. in the determination of the values of the endogenous variables) *only if* changes in that variable necessarily result in changes in the endogenous variables.[3]

Neoclassical theory, of course, recognizes many exogenous variables, including institutional or socially determined constraints such as legal limits and property rights. The constraints facing any *individual's* choice include some 'endogenous givens' which are determined in concert with the rational choices of other individuals; for example, the givens of consumer theory include market-determined prices. In this sense, some of *any* individual's *constraints* are explained as the consequences of (the equilibrium or concert of) *all* individuals' choices. Moreover, any constraint the establishment of which requires the (implicit) participation of many individuals is in some sense an institution. For this reason, some economists might consider a system of all market-determined prices to be an institution whose function is to provide the decision-maker with a 'summary of information about the production possibilities, resource availabilities and preferences of all other decision-makers' [see Koopmans 1957, p. 53]. However, the view that a price system is a social institution is true (if at all) *only* in long-run equilibrium, the attainment of which may take an unrealistic amount of time. More important, it would be very misleading to focus on prices as the *only* institutional constraint. The tendency to do so persists because many neoclassical economists rely on the *normative* view that price *should* be the only institutional constraint. As a matter of positive economics, dealing with real-time phenomena – which must exist in the short run – there are other institutions which constrain individual choices (see Coase's theorem). Whether or not the existing institutions can be explained away by assuming there are no incentives to change them, because they are optimum, is the moot point discussed in this chapter. Given any neoclassical model of the economy, if there are many exogenous variables involved in the explanation of one or more endogenous variables, then formally there are many possible causal explanations for observed changes in the endogenous variables. The explanations formally differ only to the extent to which changes in different exogenous variables are recognized as the causes.

In these terms one can identify many types of neoclassical explanations which are distinguishable in terms of the method used in each to deal with the multiplicity of 'causes'. At one extreme, we find the approach which follows Walras and William Stanley Jevons in being concerned only with the logical and mathematical adequacy of the neoclassical model.[4] At the other extreme is Marshall's approach, which is the foundation for virtually all neoclassical theories of institutions.

When there are many possible causes, (causal) explanation becomes a very difficult methodological problem. And as I discussed in Chapters 2 and 3, solving this problem was the central purpose of Marshall's *Principles of Economics*. His solution was based on an explicit recognition of 'the element of Time' and its relationship with what he called the Principle of Continuity. As I explained before, the latter presumes that anything that can be varied in the given amount of time must yield to the Principle of Substitution, that is, can be explained as a matter of optimizing choice. His solution is built on two assumptions. First, he assumes away changes in all variables which are impossible to control (such as weather) or for which there is not enough time to change them (such as cultural traditions). Such variables cannot be explained with his Principle of Substitution hence they are unexplained givens or exogenous variables. Note again, such 'exogeneity' may depend on the amount of time under consideration. The second assumption is that it is possible to rank-order the changeability of variables such that those that can be changed more quickly are explained before those that are more rigid. Specifically, Marshall's method of duration-ordered periods depends on an assumption about dynamics, namely, about the rate at which the given variables could be expected to change. The rigidity of capital stock relative to the variability of labour is, of course, the hypothetical and only basis for the distinction between the long and short periods.

Although many variables are to be objects of choice in Marshall's long period, that period is not without some givens. He specifically noted that 'there are very gradual ... movements of long-run equilibrium prices caused by the gradual growth of knowledge, of population and of [available] capital, and the changing conditions of demand and supply' as well as changing social conditions 'from one generation to another' [Marshall 1920/49, p. 315]. There is nothing in Marshall's *method* which prevents any neoclassical economist from attempting to explain inter-generational changes in such variables as long-run prices or the long-run distribution of resources.[5] But, if the changes in the long-run variables are to be explained as the results of changes in institutions (as elements of the 'social conditions'), the question is begged as to whether changes in the institutions are themselves the result of additional applications of Marshall's Principle of Substitution, that is, have the existing institutions been chosen in the way that other endogenous variables are chosen (as objects of optimization)? In other words, by including social conditions among the *endogenous* variables (i.e. among the objects of choice), neoclassical economists are merely modifying Marshall's concept of a long period without changing his neoclassical method. Whereas institutions (as 'social conditions') are among the exogenous givens in Marshall's long period, they are considered endogenous variables in the modified long-period analysis. In this manner, the modified long run forms the starting point for the neoclassical view of institutions.

In all neoclassical analyses of endogenous institutions, the prevailing institutional constraints are viewed as the outcomes of attempts to minimize costs or maximize benefits for those individuals or groups who are in a position to alter the institutions in the modified long run. Once the institutional arrangement (or environment) has been established, it becomes the set of ruling constraints on individual choices – at least in the short run. In terms of the logic of choice, institutions are like capital, which by definition is fixed in the short run and is the basis of the cost functions facing the decision-maker. In the modified long run, when equilibrium has been reached, the optimum institutional constraints as well as the optimum amount of capital must have been chosen. The ultimate modified long-run equilibrium values of all endogenous variables, including the institutional constraints, are logically determined (for any given set of behavioural assumptions) by the values of the *recognized* exogenous variables that cannot be considered the results of optimization (either because they are difficult to change or their changes are beyond control).[6]

As implied early in Marshall's book, every explanation requires the recognition of something exogenous [1920/49, Book I, Chapter 3]. Since Marshall's long-run explanation (of prices) assumes that institutions (as 'social conditions') are exogenously given, any approach which makes them endogenous requires the recognition of something else as an exogenous variable. For example, the primary exogenous variable in Douglass North's neoclassical theory of institutional change is what he calls 'ideology'. In particular, the evolution of institutions is to be explained as the result of 'a fundamental change in ideological perspective' [1978, p. 974]. North adds that he sees 'no way to account for this transformation without the systematic study of the sociology of knowledge' [p. 974]. Although I can agree with this courageous statement, it would create methodological problems for the pro-neoclassical view, to which I now turn.

A CRITIQUE OF NEOCLASSICAL THEORIES OF INSTITUTIONAL CHANGE

Marshall cannot be blamed for the more recent tendency among neoclassical economists to take institutions for granted. In his theory of market prices, he did allow for the role of changing social conditions (including institutions) in the explanation of the history of an economy, that is, of the inter-generational changes of long-run prices and allocations. However, it must be recognized that to explain the dynamics of prices or allocations, one must explain *why* the social conditions have changed. This is because when changes in social conditions are considered exogenous (as in the Marshallian long run), they are thereby deemed unexplainable *within* the economic model. However, if the only reason the long-run endogenous variables (such as long-run prices) change is *because* social conditions changed, then the *changes* in the long-run endogenous variables remain unexplained.[7] It would seem, then, that for an adequate explanation of long-run prices, the evolution of institutional constraints (on short-run optimization) must be explained. In other words, the recent concern for institutions among neoclassical economists is not merely idle curiosity (nor more neoclassical 'imperialism'). It is a fundamental methodological requirement for a complete explanation of the dynamics of long-run prices and allocations.

There are two methodological aspects of neoclassical theories of the evolution of institutions which deserve critical examination.[8] First, as noted in Chapter 6, every neoclassical explanation presumes that (subject to constraints) individuals always get what they want, that is, all individual decision-makers are *successful*. As North observes, 'Neoclassical theory simply ignores the losers.' Although the presumption of successful decision-making may seem plausible in most neoclassical analyses, it should be recognized that it implies that the individual decision-maker's knowledge is always correct (or otherwise, how the required true knowledge was acquired must be explained as well [see Hayek 1937/48]). In Chapter 1 and elsewhere I noted that, since there is no inductive logic, there is no way to guarantee that the knowledge which is essential for successful decision-making is always true. Moreover, an induction-based knowledge involves a very static (since it is timeless) concept of knowledge, one which begs the question as to why there should ever be a change in *long-run* variables. This methodological problem can be overcome by explicitly recognizing the role of the decision-maker's knowledge and by recognizing that changes are usually the result of systematic failures due to reliance on false knowledge, rather than of systematic successes based on necessarily true knowledge.

Second, if the ultimate basis for any explanation of the changes of the institutional constraints is *outside* the neoclassical explanation, then the pro-neoclassical view cannot be sustained. As noted before, to avoid circularity every explanation of any set of variables requires the recognition of one or more exogenous variables. It should be obvious, then, that without a change in at least one exogenous variable (e.g. in an ideological perspective in North's theory), the long-run neoclassical economy is static, since there is no reason for a change in the endogenous variables (such as institutional constraints) once the optimum values of the institutional 'constraints' have been successfully established. If, for example, the optimizing changes in the endogenous constraint variables are to be explained as the result of changes in the exogenous ideology variable, then by definition of 'exogenous' (not explained *within*), that change in ideology must be explained *outside* the neoclassical explanation of institutions – an exogenous ideology cannot be an object of optimizing choice. But even worse, if one wishes to make ideology an endogenous variable in a neoclassical model, then another new exogenous variable must be invented. Of course, having to invent a stream of new exogenous variables as the neoclassical programme progresses merely means that one is marching down the long road of the infinite regress.

These methodological considerations reveal, I think, the inherent poverty of every neoclassical programme for explaining the *evolution* of the organizational structure (institutions) of an economy as the dynamic consequences of constrained optimization. Specifically, these considerations call into question the adequacy of the decision-maker's knowledge by questioning the presumed success of the intended optimization. They also question the neoclassical view of the nature of institutions which, for methodological reasons, views them as *static constraints* facing the short-run optimizer.

A SIMPLE THEORY OF SOCIAL INSTITUTIONS

Although I can agree with the view of North and others that the evolution of institutions can be explained, I cannot agree that a neoclassical programme by itself is methodologically sufficient. An adequate explanation of dynamics must recognize all limitations on successful decision-making as well as the essential role of knowledge. More important, an adequate explanation of the evolution of institutions must be based on a theory which explicitly gives institutions a broader role than is allowed by seeing them as merely static constraints on the choices of any individual decision-maker. I will outline a theory of institutions which will form a basis for an adequate explanation of institutional dynamics. Although my theory will not necessitate giving up the fundamental assumption of rational decision-making, it will show that all neoclassical theories of institutional *change* are very special cases.

To begin, I would like to note that the critical issues of the adequacy of the knowledge available to a decision-maker and the methodological role of institutions are not independent. The reason is simple. One of the roles that institutions play is to create knowledge and information for the individual decision-maker. In particular, institutions provide social knowledge which may be needed for *interaction* with other individual decision-makers.[9] Thus, the following theory of institutions emphasizes the primary role of social institutions, namely, to institutionalize social knowledge. However, for an adequate dynamic theory, I will avoid the presumption of successful decision-making; thus, in particular, I will not assume that the social knowledge is correct, even though it may be durable. But I go too fast. Let me proceed very deliberately by putting my theory in the form of explicit propositions.

> *Proposition 1.* All sociological acts are based on expectations of expectations. Specifically, all interactive decision-making involves the actor's knowledge of the other individuals' knowledge.[10]

The significance of this proposition lies primarily in the conceivable alternatives, such as the actor's direct questioning of the other individuals.[11]

> *Proposition 2.* All social problems result from conflicts over expectations (or knowledge), which in turn result from the lack of acceptable limits on the range of expectations (at either source).

The significance of this proposition is dependent on the first and would mean little without it. Since most of our everyday experience involves previously *solved* social problems, it would be fairly difficult to give a pure description of any social problem apart from its assumed solution. Thus, I turn directly to solved social problems.

It should be clear that, based on the second proposition, all solutions to social problems involve the limits on expectations. There are basically two different ways of limiting expectations: (1) narrowing the range of possible options (with prohibitions, taboos, and so forth), and (2) increasing the likelihood of particular possible options (with norms, standards, guides, conventions, and so forth). This brings me to my third, fourth and fifth propositions.

Proposition 3. All social institutions exist to solve social problems.

Proposition 4. All social institutions can be divided into two categories: *consensus institutions*, which exist as socially accepted solutions to specific problems (or to a set of problems), and *concrete institutions*, which exist to solve social problems resulting from relying on consensus institutions (e.g. common agreements) to solve problems.

Proposition 5. All concrete institutions are attempts to manifest the extent of a society's learning, that is, they are a society's social knowledge.

And, as a corollary of the fifth proposition, I note:

Proposition 5a. The sole job of a concrete institution is to represent a given particular consensus institution (or system of institutions).

There are many examples of concrete institutions; the American Constitution is the most obvious, and legal contracts are the most common. Consensus institutions are much less obvious, but one can identify all 'unwritten laws' and 'gentlemen's agreements' as common examples.[12]

Propositions 1, 2 and 3 form a static theory of institutions. That is, one can explain the existence of an institution by explaining the problem for which the institution was intended to be (or accepted as) a solution.[13] Such problems include those discussed by North and others. One can also explain the continuance of the institutions by explaining the current problem for which the members of the society *think* the institution is a solution. In both cases the individual members may be mistaken, either in terms of the competence of the solution (as it may not do the job) or in terms of the realities of the problem (it may be a false problem or an impossible one to solve).

The addition of Propositions 4, 5 and 5a allows for a dynamic theory of institutions. More technically, these propositions form what has been called 'institutional individualism' [see Agassi 1974; Boland 1982a, Chapter 2]. If all institutions are considered to be *essentially* of the consensus type, it would lead to the view which Agassi called 'psychologistic individualism'.

Knowledge and institutions in economic theory 121

If all institutions were viewed as *essentially* concrete, it would lead to the view called 'institutional holism' (sometimes called 'collectivism').[14]

The theory formed here views institutions as social conventions which can be influenced by individual members of the society but which also extend (in terms of time or space) beyond the individuals and thereby can influence the individuals either as constraints or as instruments of change. *How* the institutions can be influenced depends on the institutions designed to deal with that problem (such as election rules). This theory can best be understood in terms of a sequence of events or steps.

Step 1. A society faces a problem for which there is at least one conceivable solution.

Step 2. A consensus is formed around one particular solution, thereby establishing a consensus institution.

The establishment of the consensus may depend on a political process. In the modern urban world, a consensus is virtually impossible to achieve. One can easily see that the institutions of political parties and platforms are parts of a solution to the problem of forming a consensus. Specifically, a platform ties together a set of problems for each of which a consensus for a particular solution cannot be obtained. To construct a consensus, every party member agrees to support all planks in the platform, even though he or she may not be interested in every plank.

Step 3. It is recognized that the solution of Step 2 has inherent methodological difficulties because a consensus institution is limited in terms of space and time.

In particular, the solution of Step 2 will be limited to the members that form the consensus in terms of both their life-span and their number. For example, in this semester's seminar, everyone may know what to expect of one another in terms of operating rules, but next semester (or in any other seminar at the same time) there will be a new set of students who may not know what to expect. Thus, every semester a new consensus will have to be reached. The fact that there is no carry-over from one period (or place) to another is in effect another social problem for which some form of *durability* is the only solution.

Step 4. The society establishes a concrete institution to represent the consensus of Step 2; however, the durability or concreteness of the institution is merely another consensus institution.

Durability is the essential ingredient for a truly dynamic model, even if the durability is not exogenous.

Step 5. In the future, the succeeding consensus is formed partly as a result of the existing concrete institutions and partly as a result of the existing social problems, and so forth.

In other words, when Step 4 has been reached, the succeeding generations are taught how to solve *their* social problems by teaching them about the existing (concrete) institutions. Of course, the process involves to a great extent teaching them what their problems 'are'. Note that concreteness may present other social problems, which in turn are solved by a higher level of concrete institutions (e.g. an ombudsman). Some societies may wish to prevent any further changes. Others may design their institutions so that they can be easily altered in order to be able to adapt to changing circumstances. Whether a concrete institution actually possesses the intended durability is an important question of dynamics, but the form of concreteness is still only a consensus institution. In other words, concrete institutions continue to exist only because we allow them to exist. As individuals, we can choose to ignore them or persuade others to ignore them. There may be certain social or personal costs involved in such a stance, but it clearly is an option open to every member of a society.

Clearly, with this theory the question of social change becomes very delicate because of the seemingly indeterminate nature of the structural relationship between problems and solutions at both static and dynamic levels. The structural relationship at issue is an instance of 'circular causation'. Simultaneously, in the process of teaching (or socializing) new members of a society, the prior existence of an institutionalized solution is used as evidence of the importance of certain social problems, but the existence of the solution is in turn justified on the basis of the prior existence of the social problem. Such a symbiotic relationship may lead to a very static society if the 'elders' are skilled at socializing. It also raises certain difficulties with regard to the concept of a change in 'social conditions', including the existing institutions. My presentation of a hypothetical sequence which would lead to a concrete institution presumed the existence of a consensus institution. But, given the symbiotic relationship, can the consensus institution be changed *without* a change in the concrete institution?

This methodological problem for the explanation of social change is usually avoided, but not solved, in one of two ways. The first way to avoid 'circular causation' is to view all concrete institutions (such as the laws that constrain individual choices) as the *only real* institutions. Although this view has the advantage of being clear-cut and more appealing to common sense, it also has the methodological disadvantage of leading its proponents to view all matters of social change as matters of *only* power politics. But

Knowledge and institutions in economic theory 123

more important, this view of institutions is inherently static. Once the institutions have been established, there can be no real institutional change, hence changes in other endogenous variables cannot be explained within the given institutional structure. This view's static nature, combined with its emphasis on power politics, leads its proponents to make political mistakes. For example, this view's proponents often oppose the establishment of an undesirable (concrete) institution because they fear the rigidity of its concreteness even though it can usually be shown that a concrete institution (such as a written rule) is easier to change than a consensus institution (an unwritten rule).[15]

The second way to avoid the problem of 'circular causation' is to say that consensus institutions (which underlie any concrete institutions) are the *only real* institutions. Moreover, there may be more than one way to represent a consensus institution; thus, changes in concrete institutions do not imply changes in consensus institutions or social conditions. This alternative has the advantage of avoiding collectivist dogma, but the disadvantage of viewing all social change entirely as a matter of persuasion (such as 'Madison Avenue' advertising techniques). Of course, with this view, changes in social conditions are very slow whenever communication is very controlled (e.g. 'one should not talk about such things'). But there is a more serious methodological problem. It is virtually impossible to know when a consensus institution has changed, and thus an operational explanation of social change becomes impossible. Any theory (such as Marshall's) which explains long-run changes in prices as the consequences of changes in social conditions (consensus institutions) is inherently untestable!

Neoclassical theories of institutional change can be seen to be variants of the theory represented by Propositions 1 through 5a. But being basically concerned with the individual decision-maker, every neoclassical theory would have to view real changes as those in consensus institutions; however, such changes may (have to) be brought about by changes in concrete institutions. It should be clear that most modern societies provide specific institutions which make orderly changes or the creation of other institutions possible. The legislative bodies of most Western democracies are an example. In fact, the changeability of any institution is a problem for which the rigidity of other institutions provides the solution. It should be noted that those institutions whose role is to provide information (such as norms, guidelines and legal limits) are effective only to the extent that they are stable. Thus, the changeability of such institutions compromises their knowledge role [see further, Newman 1976].

The critical issue with any neoclassical variant, as noted earlier, is whether a chosen concrete institution is, in fact, a successful representation of a given consensus institution (e.g. whether it adequately represents the given ideology). Kenneth Arrow's (im)possibility theorem [1951/63] might easily be seen as an argument against the possibility of (complete) success in every social situation. Specifically, one cannot guarantee a successful social decision mechanism (a concrete institution) which will always represent the society's welfare function (a consensus institution).

Similarly, there is the critical issue of the adequacy of the solution over which the consensus is formed. Does the given ideology, for example, solve the social problems that exist? People may *think* the market system can solve all social problems, but that does not prove that it can. It is only a conjecture, the truth of which is neither proven nor provable. For example, Arrow [1974] has argued that one essential ingredient for social interaction (which includes doing business in the market as well as within the firm) is simple trust but the existence of a market for trust would be a virtual contradiction.

TIME, KNOWLEDGE AND SUCCESSFUL INSTITUTIONS

The neoclassical programme for explaining the evolution of an economy's institutions is quite compatible with my simple theory of the epistemological role of institutions. However, once one recognizes that neoclassical programmes (Marshallian or otherwise) presume *successful* decision-making and hence, for continuing success over time, that every individual must possess correct knowledge (which includes accurate representations of relevant consensus institutions), it becomes clear that a neoclassical theory is a special case of my version of institutionalism presented here. That is, in my theory, when the consensus institutions do succeed in accurately representing those solutions, then (and only then) are my theory and a neoclassical theory of institutional change completely compatible.

Neoclassical theories are incompatible with my theory whenever any individual's knowledge is not correct (i.e. not true). But, incompatibility is not the important issue here. As has been argued elsewhere [e.g. Hayek 1937/48; Hicks 1976], the existence of false knowledge is an essential ingredient in any dynamic theory of economic decision-making. If all knowledge were true (including knowledge about the future), then there would be no reason for (disequilibrium) change without changes in one or more exogenous givens. If one is going to explain change, the source of the change cannot be exogenous. Thus, it has been argued, dynamic theories must recognize false knowledge (and explain why it might be false). Furthermore, a theory of dynamic behaviour must specify the *systematic* way each individual responds to the discovery that his or her knowledge is false. Stochastic theories, their popularity notwithstanding, do not *explain* response variations but only cover up the failure systematically to explain them accurately.[16]

In this chapter I have extended this dynamic issue of false knowledge to the question of institutions. I have argued that institutions provide essential knowledge to individual decision-makers. If that institutional knowledge is false, there is another reason for change. The only difference between institutional knowledge and knowledge in general is that the former (like capital) takes longer to change. In other words, institutional knowledge may be durable, and its durability may create problems. Even though an institution may successfully represent social knowledge that is true for one period of time, its durability may extend to a period for which it is false. Thus, since institutional knowledge is durable, it is likely to be false. Moreover, the existence of false institutional knowledge is a reason for change and, because change takes time, false knowledge is a continuing reason why the success assumption of neoclassical explanations is often unrealistic.

In this part I have discussed three widely recognized but allegedly neglected elements in neoclassical economics. To the extent that these elements are essential, proper consideration of them can surely improve neoclassical explanations. In the next three chapters I will discuss additional ways by which new elements might be included. Each of them represents a major departure from neoclassical methodology but it will remain an open question whether they represent impossible avenues for the possible repair of neoclassical theory. I will argue that Keynes clearly wished to recognize missing elements in Marshall's economics which would make long-run equilibrium explanations rather precarious. And as always one can find lurking about proponents of the alleged necessity to give neoclassical economics a transfusion of psychology to make it realistic. Into these murky waters I will venture the need to address the methodology of the individual decision-maker on the grounds which were introduced in Chapter 6. Each chapter involves a claim that there is one or more missing elements in every neoclassical explanation.

NOTES

1 This theory of institutions was developed in an undergraduate sociology class that I taught in 1968. It was subsequently reported in Boland [1979b] and is partially reprinted here by special permission of the copyright holder, the Association for Evolutionary Economics.
2 Exogeneity is, of course, defined as the purported intrinsic property of certain variables of a model *within which they cannot be explained* (i.e. they are not influenced by changes in endogenous or other exogenous variables of the model).

126 *Principles of economics*

3 For a more detailed discussion of the methodological role of exogeneity and the requirements of determinant explanations, see Boland [1989, Chapter 6].
4 Consequently, in terms of the logic of solvability, it does not matter whether a formal constraint is socially given or is a parameter of nature (e.g. available resources).
5 To avoid circularity, it must be remembered that there still have to be some givens which do not endogenously change within or with the generation.
6 For the given values of the exogenous variables, if the current choices of values for the endogenous variables are such that there exist incentives for changes in any endogenous variables, then the (modified) long-run equilibrium has not been reached.
7 For more on the methodological question of explaining dynamics, see Boland [1982a, Chapter 6] and for a discussion of the technical requirements of explanation as distinguished from description, see Boland [1989, Chapter 6].
8 I say 'methodological aspects' to distinguish them from empirical aspects, such as the truth of the assumptions about the relative variability of the givens used to distinguish the short run from the long run.
9 The equilibrium price system is one instance of such a social institution; other institutions include the laws governing trade and advertising practices and tax laws. The extent to which the social knowledge provided (such as norms, guidelines and legal limits) is necessary is directly related to the power of the institution.
10 Such a situation was recognized by Plato in his dialogue 'Laches'. It is observed at the beginning that 'some laugh at the very notion of consulting others, and when they are asked will not say what they think. They guess at the wishes of the person who asks them, and answer according to his, and not according to their own, opinion.'
11 Clearly, it does not attempt to be relevant for the explanation of the observed behaviour of a hermit or anyone else who opts out of a society (although it would apply to a group that opts out). In other words, it does not attempt to apply to an asocial situation.
12 In correspondence, Ludwig Lachmann noted to me that he offered a similar theory of social institutions in his 1970 book. His illustration of the differences between consensus and concrete institutions is the difference between 'the market' and the stock exchange.
13 Of course, not all solutions are invented or designed – some may be 'discovered'.
14 Let me define these two different views of the *explanatory* relationship between institutions and individuals. Psychologistic individualism is the methodological requirement that says all explanations of institutions must recognize that only individuals can make decisions and that the only exogenous variables allowed are nature-given, including the psychological states of the decision-makers. Institutional holism would allow other exogenous variables such as the 'destiny of the nation', class interest, etc. In the extreme, institutional holism would deny a role for the individual in determining the social outcomes [e.g. Sraffa 1960].

It is commonly thought that if an explanation is not psychologistic-individualist then it is 'holist' (or 'collectivist'). This is a mistake. The distinctions to be drawn are between individualism and holism and between psychologism and institutionalism. This means that there are four distinct views. Economists since

Schumpeter use the term 'methodological individualism' to actually mean the stronger psychologistic individualism. It would be best to reserve the term 'institutional individualism' to indicate the form of individualism that allows exogenous variables beyond the limits of natural givens and psychological states of the individual.

15 Similarly, when in power, this view's proponents waste much time or many resources on superficial changes, that is, on those which change (concrete) appearances without altering the underlying consensus.

16 For a more elaborate discussion of the methodological problems with stochasticism in economic models, see Boland [1982a, Chapter 7; 1989, Chapters 1, 7 and 8].

Part III

Some missing elements

9 The foundations of Keynes' methodology

> By 'uncertain' knowledge ... I do not mean merely to distinguish what is known for certain from what is only probable... Even the weather is only moderately uncertain. The sense in which I am using the term is that in which the prospect of a European war is uncertain, or the price of copper ... twenty years hence... About these matters there is no scientific basis on which to form any calculable probability whatever. We simply do not know...
> I accuse the classical economic theory of being itself one of these pretty, polite techniques which tries to deal with the present by abstracting from the fact that we know very little about the future.
>
> John Maynard Keynes [1937, pp. 214–15]

> Liquidity is freedom. When a firm takes action that diminishes its liquidity, it diminishes its freedom; for it exposes itself to the risk that it will have diminished, or retarded, its ability to respond to future opportunities. This applies both within the financial sphere and outside. I have myself become convinced that it is outside the financial sphere (very inadequately considered, in relation to liquidity, by Keynes) that liquidity is potentially of the greater importance... Liquidity preference, for the financial firm, is a matter of marginal adjustments, as Keynes very rightly saw. But the liquidity problem of the non-financial firm is not, as a rule, a matter of marginal adjustments.
>
> John Hicks [1979, pp. 94–5]

> Generality pursued too avidly leads to emptiness. As scientists we must be willing to live dangerously. What we must seek is no inadmissible specialisations and no unnecessary generality.
>
> Paul Samuelson [1950, p. 374]

Keynes said that the readers of his book would have to endure a 'struggle of escape' if his critical assault upon them was to be successful. This chapter is about his 'assault' strategy, its comportment relative to common views of what Keynes was trying to do, and its logical possibilities of

132 *Principles of economics*

success. Since Keynes was arguing against the then predominant Marshallian neoclassical method of economic analysis, we will have to also give some more time to considering the essentials of Marshall's methods in order to determine where Keynes might have thought he was placing the most telling blows.[1]

GENERAL VS SPECIAL CASES

The claimed thrust of Keynes' assault was to show that 'classical' economic theory was merely one special case on a more general continuum of possible cases. Unfortunately, this way of presenting his assault can be very misleading. Whenever we are dealing with formal models we are always dealing with arbitrary frameworks defined in terms of specified sets of variables. What may be a special case in one framework of given exogenous and endogenous variables can often be seen as the general case in another merely by rearranging the allocation of those variables between being considered endogenous or exogenous. I think the arguments of 'Keynesian' economists such as Patinkin [1956] demonstrate this. As long as the only variables allowed are natural givens and the aims of individuals (i.e. no social variables are allowed if they are not reducible to the logical consequences of individual choices), their interpretation of Keynes' 'general vs special' case argument will always see Keynes' assault as a failure.

For Keynes, generality refers to a methodological-cum-historical continuum. On this continuum any current state of equilibrium is a special case, as it is merely one point on a historical-time continuum. Similarly, any realistic state of disequilibrium is also just a specific point on that continuum. A state of disequilibrium is more general in the sense that there are many more possible states of disequilibrium than there are possible states of equilibrium.

In the other camp, which includes followers of Marshall and the so-called Keynesian Counter-revolutionaries [see Clower 1965], generality is seen differently because they are referring to a different continuum. It is different because Marshall's method of explanation uses a logical continuum of time periods which runs from a zero point at the left end representing an infinitely small instant to a point at the right end representing an infinitely long period of time. In between the extremes are his various temporal perspectives – 'market periods', 'short periods', 'long periods' and the inter-generational 'secular' periods. For Marshallian advocates of neoclassical economics, whenever one is considering points further to the right one is automatically considering periods of time which allow more and more variability – that is, which allow for more time for all

The foundations of Keynes' methodology 133

variables to change. When we are discussing Keynes' assault it is important for us to keep the Marshallian logical continuum in mind since it is directly relevant to the significance of the 'general vs special case' debate and it is indirectly but more fundamentally relevant to the intellectual background against which Keynes was directing his assault.

Since a longer time period is being considered whenever one adopts a methodological perspective further to the right on Marshall's continuum, more and more variables can be made endogenous instead of exogenous – that is, more variables can be considered to have been chosen by maximizing individuals whenever there has been enough time allowed to make any needed adjustments or 'substitutions' (to use Marshall's term).

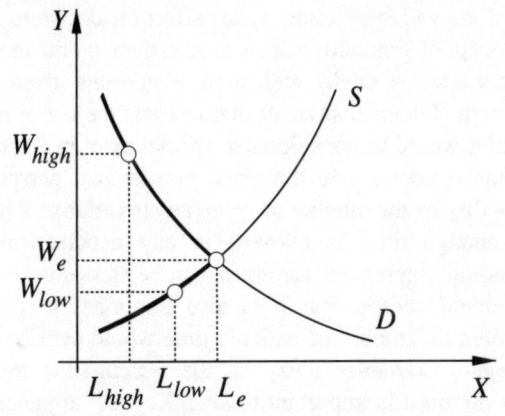

Figure 9.1 *Observable levels of employment*

If we leave aside the long-run temporal aspects of Marshall's continuum, and instead maintain a market-run perspective, then we can appreciate a different continuum. Specifically, the typical labour market can be seen to form a continuum of prices (see Figure 9.1). At any point in time a wage-rate and a level of employment will be observed. Observable points (i.e. points representing levels of actual employment at the going wage rate) will be located on the demand curve whenever the wage rate is above the equilibrium rate and they will be on the supply curve when it is below that rate. Along the continuum of observable levels of employment, the maximum observable level of employment (without exploitation) will be that one point where demand equals supply. Thus, there is then a continuum running from high wage rates to low rates with just one rate being the equilibrium rate.

GENERALITY FROM KEYNES' VIEWPOINT

Keynes' argument was more than a petty dispute over historical vs logical time-continuum viewpoints. He argued that there are important non-individualist, non-natural givens facing the real-time individual decision-maker. A main thrust of Keynes' argument is that these short-run 'macro' variables are necessary for adequate explanations even in the usual neoclassical micro model. In particular, there are 'aggregate' variables such as GNP, the general price level and expectations which do not depend on any specific individual's psychological state but on the behaviour and expectations of all other individuals. At any point of time these are contemporaneously determined variables which the individual cannot choose, yet they are variables whose states affect the decisions made.

Keynes' concept of generality seems to rest, then, on the methodological position that considers a model with more *exogenous* givens to be more general. Any methodological strategy that restricts the list of permitted exogenous variables would be considered a 'special case' in Keynes' classical framework. This is contrary to the usual neoclassical perspective which measures generality by the number of *endogenous* variables explained.

Whenever enough time is allowed in any neoclassical model, all variables, including 'aggregate' variables, can be shown to be the ultimate result of individual choice. But it is also important to realize that in Keynes' argument no amount of realistic time would ever be sufficient to explain 'aggregate' variables away as the neoclassical methodologists would have us do. So it is important to keep Keynes' arguments restricted to the Marshallian 'short run' since the definition of that time period requires the needed exogeneity of variables.

NEOCLASSICAL METHODOLOGY AND PSYCHOLOGISTIC INDIVIDUALISM

It is a central methodological feature of any neoclassical theory that the only exogenous variables allowed are those natural constraints such as resource availability and naturally given psychological states of individuals such as their tastes or preferences. This limitation on acceptable exogenous variables is much stronger than mere 'methodological individualism' which requires only that neoclassical explanations be individualist – that is, be based on the notion that only individuals make decisions. As I noted in Chapter 8, the stronger version, which is called 'psychologistic individualism', should not be confused with individualism *per se*. Individualism *per se* does not require any commitment to reduce all economic explanations to matters of psychology as John Stuart Mill [1843] would have us do.[2]

Neoclassical economics can accommodate psychologistic individualism only in long-run explanations. In the neoclassical short run, according to psychologistic individualism, all non-natural variables may be considered 'exogenous' only temporarily as an arbitrary matter of methodological perspective. For example, in a short-run model one will see many variables that cannot be changed in the short run (e.g. available capital, technical knowledge, the income distribution, the interest rate, the market structure, etc.) and that are thus exogenous constraints for the individual decision-maker. Such a short-run perspective can never be an adequate neoclassical explanation since neoclassical methodology requires that all such temporary, non-individualist variables be transformed into endogenous variables by simply broadening one's logical-time horizons. As a consequence, the only acceptable neoclassical explanation will be a long-run model in which it is logically possible to reduce all endogenous variables to matters of individual choice guided by psychologically given aims [e.g. Lucas 1980].

In any Marshallian long-run model everything will be in equilibrium because there will not be any non-natural constraints artificially preventing the individual from adjusting his or her situation to its optimum. Often any short-run constraints that are neither non-natural nor non-individualist will be explained away as being the results of past (optimizing) choices. In neoclassical methodology, disequilibria caused by intervening constraints are either temporary states of affairs or they are illusions [see further, Archibald and Lipsey 1958]. In any neoclassical model, a disequilibrium is temporary merely because enough time has not been allowed to pass for the relaxation of the intervening non-natural constraints.[3] As I discussed in Chapter 5, a disequilibrium will be an illusion in Coase's sense whenever one can show that it is really an equilibrium and that its reality would be apparent if we were to properly perceive that the intervening constraints are the logical consequences of the natural givens (viz. of externalities).

It is unfortunate that most neoclassical economists confuse psychologistic individualism with methodological individualism and the situation is not helped by Keynes' reliance on such things as subjective probabilities. Referring to his theory of the consumption function, he says, 'This psychological law was of the utmost importance in the development of my own thought' [1937, p. 220]. But perhaps Keynes' insistence on taking a psychologistic view of decision-making is only because he wants his criticism accepted. In particular, he wants to avoid its being automatically rejected by proponents of neoclassical economics. He surely realized that it is all too easy for them to think his view might entail the abandonment of neoclassical theory.

KEYNES' MACRO-VARIABLES VS NEOCLASSICAL INDIVIDUALISM

Keynes implicit insistence on a necessary role for macro-variables in the explanation of individual decision-makers could create methodological problems for any 'counter-revolutionary' Keynesian model. Macroeconomic variables (those whose values depend on the behaviour of all individuals in the economy) do not present a problem if we restrict our analysis to long-run equilibria. But this requirement supposedly leads to highly unrealistic models ('in the long run we are all dead') and thus the need to look at short-run models. The important question here is whether restricting economics to short-run models necessarily violates the requirements of methodological individualism.

To say that Keynes insists on a short-run perspective for economic explanations is not to criticize Keynes for not being individualistic. In a very important way he was more individualistic than typical neoclassical economists. As Spiro Latsis [1972] has argued, the neoclassical maximization model suffers from not truly allowing free choice by the individual decision-makers in question. If an individual in the long-run equilibrium is given a utility function by nature and the constraints are also given by nature, the choice option which maximizes utility is mathematically predetermined and only needs to be found by the individual. There is no free choice in long-run equilibrium. The only question is whether the individual is smart enough to know when his or her utility is maximum. Of course, the concept of 'constrained maximization' has always had its methodological problems.[4]

THE MARSHALLIAN BACKGROUND OF CONSTRAINED-OPTIMIZATION METHODOLOGY

Latsis' view of neoclassical methodology may be too severe. Nevertheless, there is a difficulty with any neoclassical framework which makes 'constrained maximization' the keystone, and this difficulty is a concern of Keynes' assault. The difficulty is that with a neoclassical model one cannot explain the existence of 'liquidity'. In neoclassical maximization models all optima are necessarily points on a boundary formed by the natural constraints, much as the textbook Production Possibilities Curve (PPC) forms the upper bound on the possible mixes of output combinations limited only by the available resources and technologies (see Figure 9.2). We are to explain the state of an economy by showing that the economy is at a point *on* such a boundary (point R) and that the *shape* of that boundary (viz. its slope) at the chosen point explains prices. Why would anyone want to be on the boundary of their capabilities? This question, we shall see, reveals the importance of Keynes' idea of 'liquidity'. What if an individual chose some degree of 'liquidity'? By choosing to have liquidity individuals deliberately choose not to operate on the boundary of production possibilities. But, most important, there is no way to rationalize the choice of liquidity in a neoclassical framework since the existence of liquidity itself is inconsistent with maximization (as maximization requires being on the boundary).

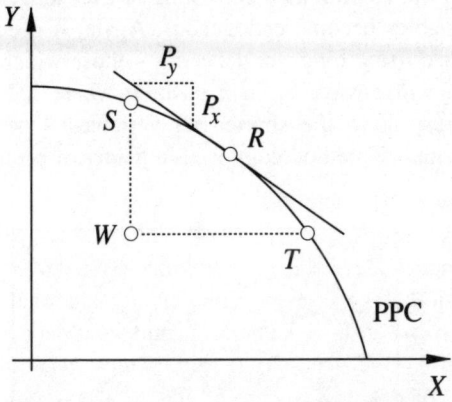

Figure 9.2 *Production possibilities curve*

Before I examine the idea of liquidity I need to reconsider Marshall's world without the phenomenon of liquidity – namely, the textbook world of Marshallian-neoclassical maximization where all predictions and explanations are based on one or more boundary functions. I will do so by briefly looking at the object of Keynes' assault: Marshall's methodological approach to economic explanations. As I discussed in Chapters 2 and 3, Marshall's methodology is quite straightforward and involves the application of the Principle of Substitution subject to the requirements of the Principle of Continuity in his economic explanations. Recall again that the Principle of Substitution merely says that every individual makes a choice between options by selecting the one option which maximizes a given objective function. The Principle of Continuity is co-requisite with the other principle because deliberate maximization presumes that the options lie on a continuum. Any finite endpoint usually represents one of the constraints facing the individual decision-maker. The chosen option must not be at one of the endpoints of that continuum – that is, the chosen (maximizing) option must be somewhere between the endpoints. If the optimum were at an endpoint it would not be clear whether the chosen option was the most desirable or simply accepted.

While Marshall's methodology of explanation can easily be based on his two principles, the task of using it runs into some procedural difficulties. One cannot explain everything in the universe all at once. Every maximization situation involves constraints of which some are irrelevant endpoints and others merely define the situation. For example, in the consumer maximization model, the budget line is a constraint but is not always an exogenous variable. Given enough time, the individual consumer chooses it, too [cf. Clower 1965]. So, as I have noted before, Marshall's strategy is to lay out a continuum consisting of ever longer time periods in which more variables become endogenous. Again, it needs to be pointed out that when discussing long-run decisions – those which require a lot of time – the firm will always be in a position where it has been able to optimize with respect to the shorter-run variables. One might say that Marshall's explanatory methodology is all a matter of peeling the temporal onion.

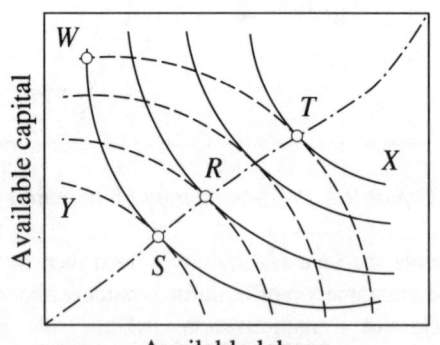

Figure 9.3 *Edgeworth–Bowley box*

The Marshallian Principle of Substitution methodology always considers the decision-maker to be facing something like a short-run production possibilities curve. The curve forms a continuum and its position is limited by given constraints. Note that the PPC represents the Pareto-optimal allocations of fixed resources which can be represented in a two-factor world by the height and width of an Edgeworth–Bowley box (see Figure 9.3). Specifically, it is a one-to-one mapping between the points on a locus of tangency points between two opposing production iso-quant maps and points on the PPC representing the (maximum) output levels indicated by the two iso-quants that are tangent. The correspondence between Figures 9.2 and 9.3 shows that the position of the PPC is limited by the available amounts of the two factors. If the size of the box is increased, then the PPC will be located further from the origin.[5] To be at a point on the PPC, the corresponding point on the locus of tangencies in the Edgeworth–Bowley box must have been chosen. To be an optimum point on the PPC, the slope of the PPC must equal the ratio of the prices for the two goods illustrated and at the point on the tangency locus in the Edgeworth–Bowley box the slopes of the respective iso-quants must both equal the given ratio of factor prices. These are all necessary conditions for an equilibrium allocation.[6]

Now, if a point interior to the PPC were chosen, the relationship between prices and marginal productivities would break down since the shape of the boundary will be irrelevant. If an interior point is chosen, all of the neoclassical marginal productivity theories of income distribution would be in serious jeopardy if not completely lost if the individuals did not operate on their respective boundaries. I shall argue below that this breakdown is the importance of Keynes' introduction of 'liquidity'. The usual neoclassical assumptions and results cannot be maintained if 'liquidity' is to be accommodated.

THE KEYNES–HICKS METHODOLOGY OF OPTIMUM 'LIQUIDITY'

Let us now turn to the matter of Keynes' concept of liquidity. As a student I was once taught that 'liquidity' was the key contribution of Keynes. Later I was taught that liquidity was only important in terms of the effectiveness of monetary policy. In these terms, Keynes would seem to have little to say except in a severe depression where interest rates were so low that further monetary stimulation of investment would not be possible. These views of Keynes' liquidity are quite unsatisfactory. Nevertheless, the concept of liquidity is the source of all the alternative views which say that Keynes introduced one particular variable or another. For example, there is the claim that all that matters is Keynes' assumption that the labour market is not in equilibrium (and hence the employment is less than maximum – see Figure 9.1). It was sometimes claimed that all that matters is the 'liquidity trap'. And, of course, many still claim it is just the recognition of 'expectations'. All of these can be seen to be merely instances of what Hicks now recognizes as a general form of liquidity,[7] as I will try to show.

Hicks' theory of Keynes' liquidity concept

A more general view of the concept of liquidity is the key to the methodological strategy of Keynes. In his 1979 book, *Causality in Economics*, Professor Hicks has carefully explained his view of the concept of 'liquidity'. While Hicks is more concerned with the quasi-Austrian aspects of real-time decision-making, he reveals the importance of why there may be good reasons for an individual to be choosing an amount of liquidity. Here the importance of an individual's choosing an amount of liquidity would be that the individual is choosing to be inside his or her possibilities boundary.

The point raised by Hicks is that in a world that is either static or moves in a sequential fashion (step-by-step, as in Marshall's world of comparative statics where there is always enough time allowed to make any adjustments), there really is no need for liquidity. However, in a world where many things are happening simultaneously, the presumption of optimization is usually misleading. Every decision involves an actual decision situation (a set of relevant givens – income, prices, technology, availability, etc.) and a time lag. Since every decision takes time to implement, during that time the original givens (which depend on the actions of other people) might have changed and thus the implemented choice decision might not actually be the optimum for the new givens.[8]

For example, if one thinks the future will favour large fuel-inefficient personal automobiles and that there will be an unlimited amount of fuel, then specializing in the production and marketing of such autos might be the optimum choice regarding one's production technology. If the market should suddenly shift in favour of small efficient autos or if the availability of cheap fuel disappears, then one's profit potential would be drastically altered. The same would be true in the less dramatic case where a certain size of market is anticipated but there is a sudden increase in demand due to a strike at a competing firm. If the previous level of output was the usual neoclassical long-run optimum (price equals average cost) then the firm would not be able to respond competitively by producing more unless there was more production capacity. To increase capacity would take time and might not even be the optimum after the strike is over. It would seem that zero excess capacity for the firm in the Marshallian short run – that is, no liquidity in the non-financial sense – would not be an optimum situation. However, the appropriate optimum (with regard to excess capacity or liquidity) may not be knowable by the firm since knowledge of it depends on unknown contemporaneous actions of other people as well as on the unknown future.

Keynes' use of liquidity

Allowing for liquidity as a deliberate choice variable is central to Keynes' assault. From Keynes' viewpoint, such liquidity is simply good business. For example, usually, whenever the labour market is in a state of 'disequilibrium' where the current real wage is above the one which would clear the market, there is excess supply. Such excess supply may very well represent a desirable state from the standpoint of the employer. For some it is always desirable to be able to expand production immediately whenever necessary. Similarly, whenever the wage is below the market-clearing wage, a thirty-five-hour work week may be optimum for an individual even though he or she could work a sixty-hour week. Having some free time to pick up some emergency side money when it is needed may be more desirable than working to one's limits according to an inflexible contract.

Good business may also require the ability to choose one's speed of adjustment to changing conditions. Sometimes a quick response is better than a slow response and at other times it is the reverse. Flexibility is the key here. But it is not a variable that can be chosen in the same way one would choose a quantity of food or a quantity of capital to achieve a given current objective. The reason is that one's choice of liquidity, be it financial as Keynes discussed or non-financial as Hicks noted, always depends on variables which cannot be easily determined. However, knowledge of them would be essential for the usual neoclassical explanation.

THE CONSEQUENCES OF 'LIQUIDITY IN GENERAL'

While Keynes focuses his idea of liquidity on the narrower concept of financial liquidity, it is easy to see that the idea of liquidity can be extended to all situations where the decision-maker is placed inside the boundary of his or her capabilities. The classic example is that of 'excess capacity' which is a position where the firm has enough capital to increase production without raising unit costs (i.e. it is within the infinitely rising cost limit at the absolute boundary of production capabilities). Whenever the firm operates with 'excess capacity' the economy must be inside the PPC and, being inside, small adjustments in the chosen point may not affect the costs or productivities.

To understand the significance of stressing the desirability of liquidity we need also to see why it is not part of the usual neoclassical model. Consider again the textbook PPC of Figure 9.2. For the sake of discussion, let us think of a firm producing two different goods, X and Y, with two factors, L and K, such that the firm's production decisions include deciding on an allocation of the available factors between the two production processes and thereby a point within the production possibilities set. The boundary of this set is the PPC.[9] So long as more is always better, any individual facing the limitations represented by such a curve will want to be producing on the boundary of possibilities as represented by the curve. To produce on that boundary, all available resources will need to be fully employed by definition of the PPC. If one does not use all resources fully then necessarily the chosen point will be inside the boundary.

Whenever the firm is producing on its PPC optimally (i.e. maximizing its 'profit' or net revenue) we know that the relative marginal productivities of those resources in the production of X will just equal the relative marginal productivities of those resources in the production of Y since both ratios must be equal to given relative prices of those inputs. Similarly, for any resource, the ratio of its marginal productivity in the production of X to that in the production of Y must just equal the same ratio for any other input since these ratios will all equal the given relative price for the two products. What is significant about all this is not that these well-known equalities are achieved but that the individual's decisions must be responsive to changes in the given prices. Note that this is why the issue of 'stickiness' of wages is so important since whenever any price is artificially restricted from changing in response to different market conditions, that price no longer provides useful information for any decision-maker. Generally speaking, prices are easier to change than quantities. A fixed price only slows down any adjustment process. Although it may take much longer, in the usual neoclassical model it is at least logically possible to find values for the quantities such that all of the equations can be restored as equalities.

What is most important here is that whenever the given prices change there is an explainable shift from one point on the boundary to another on that boundary since we can calculate the point on the boundary at which all the equalities are satisfied. And almost always there will be a shift whenever one of the prices changes. The whole importance of the competitive market is that everyone should take prices as the appropriate signal concerning what to produce or buy. That the price of fuel-inefficient autos should be falling relative to efficient autos is important social information. In responding to such a price change by reducing the output of inefficient autos, the firm is doing what society wants – just as indicated by the change in relative prices.

Let us now consider a firm that is not on the PPC defined by its amounts available of the two factors. Note that there are two ways to be at an interior point. One way is by not maximizing with respect to all the givens – such would be the case if the allocation point W in Figure 9.3 were chosen since the slope of at least one of the two iso-quants cannot be equal to the given ratio of factor prices. The other way is by not using all of the available factors, perhaps for the purpose of providing flexibility (i.e. room to maneuver).

Now what happens when the firm is not operating on its possibilities boundary – that is, when, for example, it is deliberately providing liquidity in the form of excess capacity? For one thing, except by accident, not all of the above equalities between relative prices and relative marginal productivities will be satisfied. Point *W* in Figures 9.2 and 9.3 represents the misallocation of fully employed factors. If we wish to consider a case where not all of the available factors are being employed then we need to determine a different PPC for the under-employed case. So, I have reproduced the PPC of Figure 9.2 in Figure 9.4 such that the under-employment PPC (PPC$_{ue}$) will be inside the full-employment PPC of Figure 9.2. I illustrate the relationship in Figure 9.4 where *W* is an interior point for both PPCs and may correspond to a misallocation of the employed factors in each case. Point *V* represents an output mix that is optimum for the given prices but still implies an under-employment of factors. At point *W* profit (or net revenue) is not being maximized with respect to all inputs (see Figure 9.3). As a result the income distribution will not likely reflect the indirect demand for productive services. Since there is more than one way to be at an interior point (e.g. excess capital, excess labour or any combination of these), and since by being there the firm may not be maximizing profit with respect to at least one of the inputs, predicting where the firm will be if it has chosen to respond to any change in the prices would be difficult. Similarly, if the firm has chosen a point inside the boundary, restricting any input may not have immediate effects on the individual firm's output level. For these reasons not only is there no guarantee that individual firms (or individual consumers) will be doing what society wants, but any attempt by government to alter their behaviour by changing tax rates or by manipulating interest rates may prove to be quite ineffective in the short run.[10]

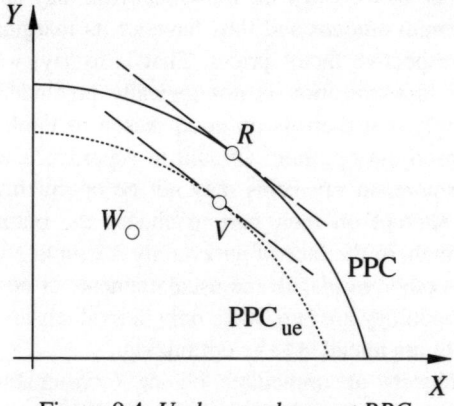

Figure 9.4 *Under-employment PPC*

Keynes' discussion of expectations (when expressed in terms of methodological and epistemological questions) raises similar issues. In his

1937 *QJE* article about the *General Theory* he explicitly identifies decision processes which are not optimizing. Collecting all the available information to make an investment decision may be uneconomical even if it is logically possible. Simple rules-of-thumb ('conventional judgement') may be adequate but may not be optimizing even for the state of limited knowledge. Follow-the-leader behaviour may be easier to justify than maximization. Since all investment decisions involve estimations about future states of affairs, relying on the going interest rate as an indicator about the appropriate relative price for future-vs-present consumption decisions (following Irving Fisher) presumes that it has been determined in a free market of buyers and sellers with perfect foresight. If buyers and sellers are, instead, using information from sub-optimizing decisions, what does the market interest rate indicate to an individual decision-maker? High interest rates may only reflect the current state of optimism rather than known investment possibilities.

ON EFFECTIVE CRITICISM

It is unfortunate that the so-called Post-Keynesians as well as the counter-revolutionaries consider the *General Theory* to be a 'blueprint' for an alternative to neoclassical economics. Such a viewpoint leads readers to miss the sophisticated criticism and challenge that Keynes offers neoclassical believers. Despite what many critics of neoclassical economics might like to believe, the introduction of liquidity or excess capacity into an otherwise neoclassical model does not always conflict with the usual assumption of maximization. For all we know the individual firm may have inadvertently chosen the optimum amount and thus have all its marginal productivities equal to their respective factor prices. That is to say, whenever there is excess capacity, maximization is not logically precluded. What Keynes argued was simply that there is no good reason to think that firms have consciously chosen the optimum amount in accordance with neoclassical models. Furthermore, to say firms may not be optimizing does not deny any conscious attempt on their part to choose the optimum amount of liquidity – although, in the face of uncertainty it is unlikely that they could ever succeed. In other words, all the usual elements of neoclassical choice theory and methodology are here since only individuals are making choices and those choices are intended to be optimizing.

For many objects of immediate choice (consumable goods, direct services, etc.) there is no good reason to doubt neoclassical maximization. However, for objects of choice involving judgements about the future state of the economy (such as investments, capacity, etc.), it is difficult or impossible to see the decision process as that of straightforward maximization. In the face of uncertainty, liquidity is a means of avoiding the difficult determination of maximizing choices. Thus, when it comes to liquidity (which, in the face of uncertainty, is offered as a necessary short-run endogenous variable in the *General Theory*), there may not be any good reason to doubt the presumption that liquidity has been chosen optimally – except one. If liquidity could be chosen like any other variable there would be no need for liquidity! So, I am arguing that Keynes' primary assault lies in the empirical claim that in any individualist model of an economy liquidity (or excess capacity) is a necessary object of choice and thus all long-run models must be empirically false. The reason why it is necessary is that so many of any individual's decisions depend on the status of what we might now call 'macro-variables' – variables which depend on the contemporaneous actions of many other individuals. Stressing the aggregate or macro aspect of the variables only emphasizes this dependence.

The point of Keynes' assault is that he wishes to challenge the advocates of neoclassical economics *on their own terms* – namely, in a world where *only* individuals make decisions. If he were to try to criticize them on radically different terms, his views could too easily be dismissed as being irrelevant for questions addressed by neoclassical economics. In this case it is not clear that Keynes was successful; the only apparent change in mainstream economics since the publication of the *General Theory* has been the introduction into the curriculum of a course called macroeconomics and with it the implicit claim that Keynes was dealing with questions that are different from those addressed by microeconomics. Keynes is entirely to blame for this means of avoiding his criticism. He is the one who stresses the necessary role of macro-variables in the theory of the individual decision-maker. Perhaps he only introduced 'macro-variables' because he accepted the psychologistic version of individualism that underlies all of neoclassical methodology, yet the introduction of such variables was against the neoclassical methodological individualist rules. Had he avoided psychologistic individualism he would not have had to stress the 'aggregate' variables – that is, had to emphasize the active role of variables which cannot be explained as being reflections of only the aims of individuals in real time.[11] But of course, this conjecture is silly. Had he not followed psychologistic individualism, as most neoclassical theorists do, he would have been dismissed on these grounds alone – without ever dealing with his criticism. Until mainstream neoclassical economics drops its dependence on narrow psychologistic individualism, Keynes' assault will not be much of a struggle for neoclassical economic theorists.

NOTES

1 The arguments presented here were those I gave in a conference at Cambridge University in 1983. Most of the proceedings of that conference were subsequently published in Lawson and Pesaran [1985].
2 As a form of individualism, institutional individualism still maintains the view that only individuals make decisions yet allows Keynesian-type macro-variables to play a role in the individual's decision process.
3 All other variables are just 'independent' endogenous variables with respect to the individual decision-maker but 'dependent' endogenous for the system as a whole [see Chapters 2 and 3 above]. Note also that in a broader sense (e.g. general equilibrium theory) only the variables which are exogenous in the long-run models are truly exogenous [see Hicks 1979].
4 But not all of the problems are usually discussed [see Chapter 1 above].
5 For an explanation of the relationship between PPCs and the Edgeworth–Bowley box, see Samuelson [1950].
6 In the special case of the price-taking individual consumer with no market power, the possibilities 'curve' will always be a straight budget line since that individual does not affect the given prices. The location of the curve is determined or constrained by the limited available resources or income. The constraints may not be naturally given but only difficult to change in the time period under consideration. But what is most important here is that the chosen option must be a point on the boundary formed by the 'curve'. In a set-theoretic sense, a possibilities curve is the positive boundary of a convex set of available options.
7 Specifically, he refers to 'financial' and 'non-financial' liquidity [Hicks 1979, 94ff].
8 This may not have been what Hayek [1933/39] intended but one can certainly find it a plausible interpretation, see further, Boland [1986a, Chapter 6].
9 The convexity of the possibilities set is logically provided in the usual Marshallian model by simply assuming that the two production functions are different and exhibit diminishing marginal returns to all factors and that there are no increasing returns to scale in any production process.
10 Note that this is a very different alternative from the current arguments against governmental intervention of the Rational Expectations school. Their argument is that if you allow for a sufficiently long time period, the government could not really change any givens by fooling everyone. In the long run, supposedly, everyone can learn the true nature of the world [see further, Boland 1982a, Chapter 4].
11 An alternative would be to recognize non-individualist, non-natural exogenous variables [see Boland 1982a, Chapter 11].

10 Individualism without psychology

> [*Mathematical Psychics* involved] considerations so abstract it would of course be ridiculous to fling upon the floodtide of practical politics. But they are not perhaps out of place when we remount to the little rills of sentiment and secret springs of motive where every course of action must be originated.
> Francis Edgeworth [1881/1961, p. 128]

> All human conduct is psychological and, from that standpoint, not only the study of economics but the study of every other branch of human activity is a psychological study and the facts of all such branches are psychological facts.
> Vilfredo Pareto [1916/35, sec. 2078]

Neoclassical economics is often thought to need an infusion of social psychology. There are two reasons for this. One is that economics should be able to recognize the social interaction between individual decision-makers; the other is that economics should recognize that the nature of an individual's utility function is essentially psychological. Both of these reasons involve the methodological requirements of the individualism that is at the foundations of neoclassical economics. In this short chapter I wish to explain why the requirements of individualism do not necessitate an infusion of social psychology.[1]

INDIVIDUALISM VS PSYCHOLOGISM

As I have been insisting in the previous chapters, it is important to avoid confusing methodological individualism with psychologism. Individualism is the methodological view that all social events must be explained as the consequences of choices made by individuals – things do not choose, only individuals do. Psychologism is the view that in any explanation (individualist or otherwise) the *only* exogenous givens other than natural constraints allowed are those representing psychological states of either individuals or groups. As I noted above,[2] individualism is distinguished from holism and psychologism is distinguished from institutionalism. This means that in addition to psychologistic individualism and institutional individualism, which I discussed previously, there are two versions of holism: psychologistic holism and institutional holism. Explaining an event as a case of 'mass psychology' would be an instance of psychologistic holism. Explanations based on such things as 'class interest' are examples of institutional holism.

Individualism as a methodological view or doctrine about how social events and situations are to be explained does not require us to base individualism on psychology. Before I can discuss the social and psychological aspects of an individual's choice situation, I need to present the explanatory problem confronting any methodological individualist.

INDIVIDUALISM AND THE LEGACY OF EIGHTEENTH CENTURY RATIONALISM

There is more to (methodological) individualism than an explicit commitment to individualist explanations. Since the eighteenth century, for any explanation to be acceptable it must be 'rational' and thus, as I explained in Chapter 6, it must be universal. Being rational means that the explanation forms a logically valid argument such that if the premises of the argument are all true then the conclusions logically derived will also be true. By universal, we mean that *anyone* who accepts the truth of the premises of a logically valid argument will also accept the truth of its conclusions. The tradition of compounding rationality with individualism is problematic in two ways which together represent the classic intellectual dilemma between unity and diversity [see Agassi 1969]. On the one hand the universality of rationality undermines individualism by making all individuals identical in a significant way. On the other hand, the nineteenth-century tendency to view rationality as a psychological process also undermines individualism by making individuality exogenous and thus beyond explanation.

To illustrate these methodological problems, consider the following hypothetical situation. Our closest friend has been caught robbing a bank. Demanding an explanation, we ask, 'Why did you rob the bank?' Before we allow our friend to answer, we must recall that, to be an acceptable explanation, any explanation given either by us or by our friend must be rational and conform to the requirements of methodological individualism. Individualism only precludes choices being made by things. Rationality is established by examining the logic of the situation facing our friend, the

Individualism without psychology

bank robber. By asking our friend for an explanation we are asking him to give a description of the logic of his situation. Specifically, we ask him to give reasons which represent (1) his aims and (2) the constraints that restrict the achievement of his aims. If he can describe the logic of his situation such that we would agree that anyone who exactly faced that same situation (aims and constraints) would also rob the bank, then we would say that we *understand* why he robbed the bank. For example, he may tell us that his child needs a very expensive operation and he wants his child to have that operation but there is no legal way he could afford it before it would be too late. Robbing the bank was the only way to achieve his aim. If his description of the situation is true (i.e. there really is no other way possible), then given his aim (to save his child) it would be rational for him to rob the bank – in fact, it might be considered rational for *anyone* with that aim and those constraints.

The logical requirements of an explanation of individual behaviour are the same whether we are discussing our friend the bank robber or the individual consumer choosing to spend his or her money on tomatoes and cucumbers. In the case of the individual consumer, the aim is supposedly the maximization of utility obtained from consuming what one has purchased while facing the constraints of given prices, given purchasing power (one's budget or income) and a given utility function. Such utility-maximizing behaviour is rational in the sense that any two individuals with the same utility function and same income facing the same prices will choose to consume the same quantities of goods so long as each individual aims to maximize his or her utility.

Rationality assures such universality and uniqueness of choice. The idea that rationality assures universality is characteristic of eighteenth-century 'Rationalism' and thus is fundamental to the origins of economic theory. The identification of rationality with utility maximization is a late-nineteenth-century perspective and the foundation of neoclassical economics. In terms of modern economics, the quantities of goods the individual consumes are considered endogenous variables. Only the utility function is unambiguously exogenous. Income and prices are treated as constraints for the individual but not for the economy as a whole, so whether they are endogenous or exogenous depends on the situation we choose to model. In neoclassical economics our task is to explain individual choices in order to explain how prices affect demand so that we can explain how demand influences prices in the market; in other words, prices and incomes (which depend on factor prices) are endogenous.

From a logical point of view (and contrary to what some people think [e.g. Mason 1988]), a single individual's choice is easier to explain than a market's demand curve. This is because in consumer theory we can treat

150 *Principles of economics*

the prices and income facing the individual as exogenous variables, leaving only the consumer's choice as the endogenous variable to explain. Any explanation of a market's demand curve requires us to explain all consumers' choices as well as all the other market prices that these consumers face. Of course, we would also have to explain the supply curve in every market in question.

UNITY VS DIVERSITY IN METHODOLOGICAL INDIVIDUALISM

Neoclassical economics, nevertheless, claims to explain all prices and the allocation of all fixed resources. How is it possible for one theory to explain so much? The particular value of prices (or state of resource allocation) depends, of course, on the nature of each individual's utility function. In this context methodological individualism allows both diversity and unity. Diversity is promoted by recognizing that some people will spend more of their income on tomatoes than other people do. Unity is promoted by the claim that all individuals are maximizers. This means that all people face falling marginal utility curves (a necessary calculus condition for maximization). Does this mean all people are identical and thus deny individuality? No; so long as everyone faces downward sloping marginal utility curves, the absolute position of that curve (relative to other goods) need not be the same for all individuals. For the same amounts of tomatoes and cucumbers, some may get more satisfaction from tomatoes, others get more from cucumbers. Also, some people may have steeper marginal utility curves than other people do. We see that on the one hand individuality is preserved since, even facing the same prices and incomes, two maximizing individuals may choose different quantities if their exogenously given utility functions are different. On the other hand, universality is provided by the common nature of utility functions if it can be shown that as a matter of human nature all utility functions exhibit diminishing marginal utility.

This is the methodological dilemma of individualist-cum-rationalist economics. If the (equilibrium) values of prices depend only on the different utility functions which are exogenously given, then prices are actually determined outside of economics. Whatever determines the nature of the given utility functions ultimately determines prices. Does this mean that economics must surrender to psychology as has often been suggested [e.g. Scitovsky 1976]?

Identifying the individual with his or her psychologically given utility function is a rather sophisticated and subtle type of psychologism. A more blunt and obvious use of psychology would be for us (or our friend the bank robber) to explain the event by claiming that our friend has a 'criminal mentality'. But such a crude psychologism would seem to be our only recourse if we are to avoid the moral dilemmas involved in the explanation based on the logic of the situation. If the robber's choice to rob the bank was a rational one, how can we object?

Crude psychologism also avoids an intellectual dilemma. When our friend (as a bank robber or a consumer) provides an 'acceptable' explanation, one which says that anyone facing that position would choose to do the same thing, the individuality of the situation is revealed to be empty. If any individual would do the same, then there is nothing individualistic about the choice made. Crude psychologism (i.e. the view that behaviour is predetermined by exogenously given mentalities) as an explanation of individual choices may seem to be a way to promote psychology. It is not – it only begs more questions. What determines who gets which mentality? How many different mentalities are there? In the extreme, crude psychologism may even lead us to discard psychology in favour of sociobiology.

If we thus reject crude psychologism, we are then left with our two dilemmas. The moral dilemma (the rationality of one's choice to commit a crime) is not easy to overcome and in the end is more a question of philosophy than of psychology. The intellectual dilemma is the foundation of attempts to promote psychology in the development of economic explanations of individual behaviour. If we allow ourselves to assume that psychologically all individuals are given different exogenous utility functions, then individuality will seem to be preserved in our explanations of rational choice. However, whenever psychologism is adopted as a means of promoting individualism, it is a defeatist methodological stance.

Individualism is in trouble here only because neoclassical economics misleadingly identifies the individual's aims with the individual's psychologically given utility function. Two individuals facing the same prices and with the same income will usually choose different consumption bundles if they have different utility functions. If our problem as economists is to explain a wide diversity of choices made by people in the same income class, then the psychological reasons for why people have different given utility functions would certainly seem to be a promising line of inquiry. But it is not a necessary line of inquiry since one may just as easily presume that the individual's utility function is socially determined.

The traditional emphasis on individualism seems to force an excessive concern for diversity to the point that economists (as opposed to sociologists) tend to overlook obvious social circumstances where diversity is more conspicuous by its absence. Specifically, the problem that should be of concern to individualist economists is to explain widespread conformity whenever considering consumption patterns. In most cultures, each social role is closely associated with a specific consumption pattern. Accountants or lawyers in similar income brackets will usually have consumption patterns much like their colleagues'. Non-conforming individualism is more the exception than the rule in organized society. For example, corporate lawyers tend to dress alike, belong to the same social clubs, acquire the same ostentatious goods such as expensive automobiles, houses, etc. Moreover, their conspicuous consumption is not a psychological phenomenon but rather it shows how profoundly one's preference ordering is dependent on social structure [cf. Veblen 1899/1934]. In short, one's consumption choices may be determined more by one's social position than by one's personal tastes [see Newman 1972; Hayakawa and Venieris 1977].

UNNECESSARY PSYCHOLOGISM

I do not wish anyone to think from my recognizing that utility functions (or, more generally, personal aims) are matters of sociological inquiry that I am thereby rejecting individualism. Such is not the case. As I have already argued in Chapter 8, social situations and institutions are the consequences of individual choices. All that I am arguing here is that there is no necessity to see deviations from narrow-minded neoclassical economics as expressions of irrationality and hence a demonstration of a need to study the psychology of the individual. Irrationality is easily interpreted as merely an expression of the incompleteness of the description of the logic of the situation facing the individual [*pace* Stigler and Becker 1977]. Perhaps a more complete description might involve psychology but psychology is not a necessity here. An individual whose utility function is completely determined by social conventions is no less capable of making a rational decision than the individual whose utility function is psychologically given. In summary, a successful methodological individualist explanation of the behaviour of a rational decision-maker is a matter of establishing the logical completeness of the decision-maker's objective situation. It is not necessarily a matter requiring the recognition of a possible role for the decision-maker's psychological predisposition.

NOTES

1. Peter Earl invited my comment on some papers he was publishing about 'psychological economics' [Earl 1988]. This chapter is based on my contribution [Boland 1988]. Those parts repeated here are copyrighted by Kluwer Academic Publishers and reprinted with their permission.
2. See Chapter 8, note 14.

11 Methodology and the individual decision-maker

> if a man had sufficient ability to know everything about the market for his labour, he would have too much to remain long in a low grade. The older economists, in constant contact as they were with the actual facts of business life, must have known this well enough; but partly for brevity and simplicity, partly because the term 'free competition' had become almost a catchword, partly because they had not sufficiently classified and conditioned their doctrines, they often seemed to imply that they did assume this perfect knowledge.
> It is therefore specially important to insist that we do not assume the members of any industrial group to be endowed with more ability and forethought, or to be governed by motives other than those which are in fact normal to, and would be attributed by every well-informed person to, the members of that group; account being taken of the general conditions of time and place.
> Alfred Marshall [1920/49, p. 449]

> there is something fundamentally wrong with an approach which habitually disregards an essential part of the phenomena with which we have to deal: the unavoidable imperfection of man's knowledge and the consequent need for a process by which knowledge is constantly communicated and acquired.
> Friedrich Hayek [1945/48, p. 91]

While it is one thing to recognize the role of knowledge in a neoclassical explanation, those few who do will usually fail to deal with how the knowledge is acquired. Unfortunately, almost all neoclassical models which do recognize the state of the decision-maker's knowledge either ignore the decision-maker's methodology or implicitly adopt Inductivism, a methodology that was refuted two centuries ago. What is missing in neoclassical models which do recognize the state of the decision-maker's knowledge is an explicit discussion of the decision-maker's methodology for learning or otherwise acquiring knowledge.

Traditionally, methodology has been of interest primarily to historians of economic thought or to those few economic theorists who view methodology as an instrument to help them explain their theories to other economists. In effect, we might say that methodology has always been 'meta-theoretical'. This instrumental view is in contrast to that which I wish to present in this chapter. Here I argue for a necessary *theoretical* role for methodology, a role implied to a certain extent in some of Hayek's papers. To be more general, we could say that any economic theory which recognizes a need for knowledge in decision-making must in some way imply a role for methodology because, as Hayek explicitly said, to explain any decision the economist must also explain the 'acquisition' of the knowledge needed to make that decision. In my 1982 book and elsewhere I have argued that while we must recognize the importance of knowledge acquisition, or learning, we must also avoid predisposing our conception of knowledge and its acquisition in favour of only one view of learning methodology – namely, inductive learning.[1] My plan for this chapter is to begin by presenting Hayek's views, which, though they are often employed in recent literature, are frequently misunderstood. I will end by presenting my alternative view.[2]

EPISTEMICS IN HAYEK'S ECONOMICS

Ludwig Lachmann [1982] has argued that one of the neglected contributions of the Austrian School was their view that 'the dissemination of knowledge plays a prominent part in the process of competition' [p. 636]. Hayek's [1937/48] argument in favour of capitalist competition depended on the assertion that this competition only requires a minimum amount of knowledge consisting primarily of easily available private knowledge (of one's personal aims and limitations) and augmented only by the public knowledge disseminated by the market. This view later led Hayek [1945/48] to argue that adequate private knowledge is obtainable in practice; but 'scientific' knowledge, even if available, is usually inadequate without the individual decision-makers' private knowledge. Specifically, the virtue of making decisions based on market-disseminated information arises because even though the day-to-day information from the market can be wrong (e.g. disequilibrium prices), the process that leads to an equilibrium *necessarily* generates the correct information. Hayek thus distinguished between possibly false practical knowledge (Lachmann's 'knowledge how') and true 'scientific knowledge' (Lachmann's 'knowledge that' or 'propositional knowledge').

Hayek complained that practical knowledge has always been considered inferior relative to scientific knowledge. More important, Hayek implied that if scientific knowledge were actually true and certain it would still play no significant role in the economic process because this economic process is concerned with economic problems which arise from changes in such things as tastes. If tastes continue as before, there are no allocation problems to be solved. In the absence of new problems, there would be no need to make new decisions or thus to learn anything new. For Hayek, scientific knowledge is knowledge of general rules and thus is inherently static. In effect, scientific knowledge is irrelevant – particularly when it is considered true and certain. Thus, the recognition of possibly false practical knowledge is essential if we want to understand the competitive market process.

This leads Lachmann to conclude that, if knowledge is to play an explicit role, Hayek's two types of knowledge must be clearly recognized. Moreover, we need to see that what the Austrians were saying is that 'practical knowledge' (or 'knowledge how') is what must be explicitly recognized in the explanation of an individual's decision process. According to Lachmann, logicians only recognize knowledge when it is certain. Thus, he argues, whenever 'strict logicians' analyze the decision-making of market participants they miss the point because, according to Hayek, the market overcomes the problems of (potentially) uncertain practical knowledge.

The importance of the Hayek–Lachmann knowledge distinction

Recognition that any individual's knowledge can be false is central to Hayek's argument in favour of focusing on market-disseminated knowledge that is potentially uncertain rather than on certain scientific knowledge. For Hayek, scientific knowledge is irrelevant to our understanding of the market economy. Whenever an individual's knowledge is false, the empirical evidence generated in the market by actions based on false knowledge actually leads towards the truth about the market. For example, over-estimating market supply at the current price leads to some individuals having to bid the price up and thereby inadvertently to reduce the shortage. That is, acting upon false ('disequilibrium') prices unintentionally leads to the creation of true (equilibrium) prices which can be the basis for realizable plans to maximize profits or utility. A competitive market economy thus creates its own adequate practical knowledge. Still, this view of the adequacy of market-generated information presumes that all markets are inherently stable. I shall argue that it is the presumption of stability as well as the presumption of the necessity of induction for certain knowledge that gives 'scientific' knowledge a less significant role than practical knowledge.

To understand the importance of Hayek's claim consider two possible states of one market from the perspective of contrasting the acquisition of 'certain' knowledge with the process of 'learning by doing' which, as Lachmann notes, underlies Hayek's viewpoint. Let the market be characterized by quantity discount selling. That is, both the supply and the demand curves are downward sloping. Following the traditional assumption of Walrasian market behaviour, excess demand at a quoted price always leads at least one buyer either to offer a higher price to attract more of the scarce supply or to give up trying to maximize his or her utility for the quoted price. Whenever the supply curve is steeper than the demand curve, the usual conception of the competitive process logically leads to the elimination of the false (disequilibrium) quoted prices. In this Walrasian stable world, Hayek's practical knowledge is provided coincidentally with the convergence to an equilibrium. However, whenever the demand curve is steeper than the supply curve, Walrasian price competition would only aggravate the situation. Whenever there is excess demand, raising the price causes an even greater excess demand. Nevertheless, if an auctioneer in charge of the market could 'scientifically' calculate the respective demand and supply curves and thereby 'scientifically' calculate the price at which they intersect, then he or she could simply start the transactions at the intersection where demand equals supply. Thus, even though the market might embody an inherently unstable Walrasian competitive process, all plans would still be realized – that is, everyone could maximize their utility or their profit whenever the price was correctly set *in advance*. (Note that I could have presented all this with upward sloping demand and supply curves or with excess supply situations.)

This example suggests that Hayek's [1945/48] view meant that true scientific knowledge (when attainable) was like the knowledge that the successful Walrasian auctioneer would require. While capable of achieving an equilibrium, true and certain scientific knowledge is unnecessary if the market is stable. In a stable market, piecemeal or trial-and-error bidding will always tend towards the equilibrium and never away from it. That is, if the market is stable, then the participants will always learn correctly from their mistakes. As my example shows, Hayek must be presuming the market to be stable – which it would be whenever the demand curve is downward sloping and the supply curve is upward sloping. Furthermore, given the common presupposition that the only method for acquiring the certain knowledge which the auctioneer needs to set the correct price would involve induction, such certainty requires too many observations to be a realistic view of any economy whenever there is the potential of an unstable market. In short, either the market is inherently stable, in which case in Hayek's view adequate practical knowledge is provided in the progress of the competitive process, or the market is inherently unstable and thus a viable (equilibrium) price will be provided *only if* someone (such as an auctioneer) can acquire certain knowledge.

The methodological problem of the Hayek–Lachmann distinction

It is all too easy to criticize neoclassical economics for confusing practical with propositional knowledge. Nevertheless, we still need to appreciate a major difficulty with this Hayek–Lachmann distinction. This distinction is based on a mistake about 'scientific' or propositional knowledge. This type of knowledge cannot be distinguished from everyday practical knowledge. Both 'types of knowledge' can be true or false. It is necessary to recognize the role of methodology in decision-making precisely because the knowledge of the individual decision-maker – whether it is scientific or otherwise – can be false.

If one is not careful, the Hayek–Lachmann distinction between practical and propositional knowledge can be used to perpetuate reliance on a false theory of knowledge – Inductivism.[3] For example, Hayek's claim that certain scientific knowledge will always be unattainable (or be otherwise inadequate) presumes that for anyone's knowledge to be true it must have been acquired by some inductive process. That is, there is the presumption that since the knowledge needed by an individual decision-maker is more intimate and less general, it can be more certain. Both Hayek and Lachmann have implicitly recognized that, simply stated, knowledge can be false and that, in the absence of induction, there is no need to consider 'scientific knowledge' any more reliable than private knowledge. But such a recognition need not imply an endorsement of Inductivism.

Today, few would so easily espouse any obvious uses of induction. Rather, most would argue that we can make do with a watered-down approach that replaces inductive proofs or inductive learning with knowledge based on convenient acceptability criteria such as those found in econometric practice. The problem of knowledge acquisition which Hayek discussed in 1937 can be too easily transformed into a standard Conventionalist theory-choice problem.[4] Specifically, it is tempting to think that all individuals participating in the market are Conventionalists who are able to participate simply through adopting adequate criteria to determine the equilibrium price so that they can proceed to maximize as usual. That is, even with insufficient evidence all successful decision-makers have supposedly employed adequate criteria to choose correctly between imperfect theories. This Conventionalist theory of knowledge is only a marginal improvement over the older Inductivism. Appealing as choice-theory may be to economists, it would be a mistake to think that only one theory of knowledge would ever be chosen at any point in time

158 *Principles of economics*

and hence that the decision-maker's theory of knowledge and methodology can be taken for granted.

THE METHODOLOGY OF DECISION-MAKERS

Economic theorists must recognize many different views of knowledge and methodology since the decisions based on them will usually lead to different patterns of behaviour. I will try to demonstrate this proposition in the narrow context of the typical neoclassical theory of decision-making.

Demand depends on the demander's theories

Consider textbook ordinal demand theory. According to the textbooks, the demand curve for any individual is merely the locus of all price–quantity combinations at which the individual's utility is maximized for the given income and prices as well as the given utility function. How does the individual know all the givens? Prices and income may be sufficiently objective that it does no harm to argue that the individual knows them, at least momentarily, when making planned purchases. On the other hand, assuming that the individual knows his or her private utility function begs far too much. A particular bundle of quantities of goods actually can be said to be better than any other (in order to explain the choice of that bundle) only if the individual is presumed to compare that bundle with all other conceivable bundles. Of course, given a typical utility function and a little calculus such a choice can be justified. But knowledge of the utility function is equivalent to comparing all pairs of bundles. Like any other universal statement, this one cannot be shown to be true in real time since such a demonstration would require an infinity of evidence (and time). But, of course, such an inductive proof is actually unnecessary.

In ordinal demand theory all that the individual needs is an assumption about the nature of his or her utility function. Like any other assumption, we assume that it is true only because we do not know whether it is actually true. In the case of the consumer, the plans for purchases must be made on the assumption of a particular utility function. The assumed utility function can be true or false. How does the individual actually know that he or she is maximizing utility with his or her latest purchase? That is, how does the individual learn what the true nature of his or her utility function is except by making purchases? It is precisely the 'learning by doing' situation that Lachmann mentions [1982]. The individual's pattern of purchases must over time reflect his or her approach to learning the true utility function. Thus, methodology must play an integral part in our explanation of demand.

Market demand depends on the consumers' methods of learning

Several alternative methodologies might be employed in the process of interacting in the market. In addition to the methodological doctrines identified in Chapter 6, namely Apriorism, Inductivism and Scepticism, I will now include the Conventionalist methodology mentioned above and the well-known methodology of Milton Friedman which I have elsewhere called Instrumentalism.[5] Using these alternative methodologies, let us now consider various types of consumers facing the same static market situations (in which all exogenous variables are fixed). Assume that all consumers have identical incomes and identical true utility functions. However, let us also assume consumers neither know these functions *a priori* nor do they share the same opinions about their utility functions.

An inductivist consumer. If one has to learn whether one is actually maximizing utility by comparing actual bundles consumed, how does one decide the issue? Some believe that you should not jump to conclusions and thus that you never know the correct utility function until you provide an inductive proof – all done without ever making any assumptions. Such a consumer will always be forced to keep trying new bundles. Although facing a static situation, an inductivist consumer would appear never to be satisfied.

A sophisticated inductivist consumer. Few would think today that anyone just collects the facts without thinking ahead. But, even if one arbitrarily adopts a theory of the nature of one's utility function, one can still never be satisfied until that theory is proven true. This approach can also lead to the appearance of unstable buying patterns. Nevertheless, if the theory is true, over time we should expect to see the buying pattern converging to a stable point.

An Apriorist consumer. Since Apriorists begin 'knowing' the true utility function (either by assumption or introspection), no market evidence could ever cause them to change their mind. The pattern is not only stable but invariant.

A conventionalist consumer. Given the many conceivable utility functions, how does one pick one to start with? If one gives up the requirement of a complete proof, various criteria can be adopted to appraise one's theory of one's utility function. In effect, the consumer need only be a good econometrician. No claim is made that the true utility function is found, but only the best available according to the evidence and the adopted criteria. The pattern of consumption behaviour will depend on the method used to process data. For example, how many tests of current theory are required before concluding one knows or does not know the

160 Principles of economics

true utility function? Competent conventionalist consumers might test their theory every third trip to the market and still be able to explain away numerous refuting observations before being forced to change their pattern of behaviour.

A scepticist consumer. At the other extreme there are consumers who are always sceptical about proving any theory true. These consumers will change their mind about their personal utility functions the first time some purchased bundle does not meet their expectations. While the conventionalist consumers can tolerate occasional disappointments and thus seldom alter their consumption patterns, the scepticist consumers will be jumping all over the map.

An instrumentalist consumer. It is not always clear what instrumentalist consumers might do since the truth of their theories of their utility functions supposedly does not matter. They might act *as if* they liked their purchases when indeed they detested them. As long as their social role does not change, one could predict that the instrumentalist consumers might continue to buy the bundle of goods that is most useful for their chosen careers. Any change in career will be accompanied by a change in the consumption pattern [see again pp. 150–2].

These crude examples should be sufficient to demonstrate the potential role for methodology in the explanation of decisions within the domain of neoclassical theory. When it is recognized that one's utility function is not known *a priori* and must be learned, it must also be understood that an appreciation of methodology is necessary to explain the pattern of behaviour in the competitive process of Hayek and Lachmann. In the typical neoclassical model two individuals with identical utility functions, identical incomes, and facing the same prices, would choose the same bundles of goods. The examples above show that this conclusion fails to hold if they try to learn their (identical) utility functions using *different* learning methodologies.

The methodology of stable markets and convex preferences

If it is now recognized that Hayek's view of the competitive process gets to the heart of the neoclassical market then it should also be easy to see that his view runs parallel with my alternative view of the decision-maker. Hayek's view, unlike neoclassical economics, does not depend on the actual achievement of an equilibrium. It depends on the progressive learning that must take place by virtue of the presumed stability of the market in question. Hayek did not actually try to explain how individuals learn what is necessary to make a market decision. Instead, he took inductive learning for granted. The same thing could be said for the traditional neoclassical theory of the consumer. While convexity of preferences is usually explicitly asserted or assumed, no discussion is provided to indicate how the individual learns which bundle will actually maximize his or her utility. If the individual's preferences are actually convex, then I would suggest that the individual's learning process is taken for granted because neoclassical theorists also take inductive learning for granted. If they do not, then there is no reason to believe that the individual will ever be maximizing his or her utility. If my claims are correct then we can safely predict that much methodological work still must be done even within the otherwise successful neoclassical theory of decision-making.

NOTES

1 The view that people learn inductively is a variant of the doctrine of Inductivism which I discussed in Chapter 1, note 5. According to this view whenever one collects any fact needed to obtain the required inductive proof, one is learning. Over three centuries ago this view of knowledge and learning was considered the essence of enlightenment since it countered those who required religious authority for knowledge claims. Unfortunately, the logical foundation for the enlightened view was undermined by the late-eighteenth-century arguments of David Hume and others who noted that such a view of learning leads to an infinite regress. If all knowledge must be based only on the facts, then it calls into question how we learned that knowledge must be inductively proven. Whatever our answer, it begs a question of methodology which must also be inductively proven but this leads to a further question requiring an inductive meta-methodology, and so on. But worse, given this infinite regress, even when the knowledge is true, there may be no way to prove it true. Failure to prove its truth, inductively or otherwise, does not prove the knowledge is false [see further Boland 1982a, Chapter 11].

2 Israel Kirzner invited me to contribute to a book of essays honouring Professor Lachmann [Kirzner 1986]. The remainder of this chapter is based on my contribution, parts of which are reprinted here by permission of New York University Press.

3 See again the discussion of Inductivism in note 5 of Chapter 1.

4 I discussed this view of knowledge in note 20 of Chapter 2.

5 Instrumentalism, as it is practiced in neoclassical economics, views theories as *useful instruments* either for understanding the economy or for assisting policy-makers. The key element of Instrumentalism is the view that theories should not be judged on whether they are true or false but on whether they are useful for the purposes at hand. Policy-makers are only required to act *as if* their theories are true. See further Boland [1979a; 1982a, Chapter 9].

Part IV

Some technical questions

12 Lexicographic orderings

> [Economics] should have that delicacy and sensitiveness of touch which are required for enabling it to adapt itself closely to the real phenomena of the world ...
> Alfred Marshall [1920/49, p. 635]

The questions of the pervasiveness of equilibrium and maximization are fundamental and thus little of neoclassical literature seems willing or able to critically examine these fundamental ideas. This does not mean that neoclassical writers do not venture criticisms. There are many critiques but they are almost always about technical modelling questions such as what way to formally represent the consumer's utility function. As I noted in Chapter 1, the question of whether to assume a consumer is a maximizer is never put into question, only the assumptions about the nature of the function. I now turn to an examination of some of the technical disputes surrounding neoclassical theory to see if they are worth while criticizing. In the next three chapters I will examine key ideas employed in neoclassical demand theory that have acquired a status that puts them beyond criticism even though that status is unwarranted.

While it may be reasonable to put maximization beyond question along the lines discussed in Chapter 1, it is not obvious that the *form* of the utility function should be limited *a priori*. Nor is it obvious why the infamous Giffen good (i.e. the case of an upward sloping demand curve) should be acceptable in any demand theory which is used in conjunction with supply curves to explain price determination in the market. While a 'generalized' demand theory might be more convenient for mathematical model-builders, those neoclassical economists who wish to use their theory to deal with practical problems will not find such models very helpful. For example, economists who try to evaluate public policies by calculating net gains or losses in terms of 'consumer surplus' (which is represented by the area under the demand curve but above the horizontal line representing the price) will be stymied by an upward sloping demand curve. Similarly, economists who see merit in a government's ordering its priorities before ordering alternative projects of a similar priority will find it difficult to form a sensible social utility function over all conceivable projects. That is, some economists consider lexicographic orderings to be a reasonable approach to public policy decision-making [see Encarnacion 1964] but, unfortunately, most neoclassical demand theorists are taught to believe that the concept of a lexicographic ordering is not plausible. The purpose of this chapter is to examine the issue in demand theory concerning the difficulty of using lexicographic orderings (*L*-orderings) in *lieu* of ordinary monotonic utility functions. In the next two chapters I will examine the issue of whether demand theory can or should preclude the possibility of upward sloping demand curves.

L-ORDERINGS

A formal preference ordering represents how a given consumer would rank-order two or more bundles of goods (where a 'bundle' specifies a quantity for each good being considered). A monotonic utility function can form the basis for such a preference ordering in a direct way. Obviously, when comparing any two bundles, the preferred bundle yields the most utility according to the utility function. The process whereby the individual goes about determining the utility for any bundles is seldom considered. The lexicographic ordering seems to appeal to those who think the *process* of ranking or assigning utility should be apparent.

The paradigm of an *L*-ordering is the dictionary and its ordering of words. It says that the order in which words are listed in the dictionary is alphabetical. And those words with the same first letter are sub-ordered according to their second letter, and so on. The *L*-ordering in the case of bundles of goods might say that the preferred bundles are those which give the most nutrition. And of those bundles which give the same nutrition, those which give the least calories are the most preferred; and so on.

Years ago, any advocacy of *L*-orderings was commonly criticized since such orderings cannot be represented by a utility function [see Georgescu-Roegen 1954; Newman 1965; Quirk and Saposnik 1968, Chapter 1]. Rarely today are such orderings mentioned and this, of course, is quite apart from the lingering suspicion of some economists that the consumer's *process* of deciding on an optimum choice is better presented by an *L*-ordering. The commonplace rejection of *L*-orderings on purely methodological grounds may be a mistake based on a confusion concerning what *L*-orderings are and how they differ from the existence of multiple criteria. If there is a confusion here it needs to be cleared up and a good starting place would be a clear understanding of the concept of an *L*-ordering.

One way to understand the concept of an *L*-ordering is to consider it to be a solution to the methodological problem created by the recognition of a multiplicity of relevant criteria for comparing goods. To the extent to which *L*-orderings solve a problem they must necessarily be *ad hoc* in the sense that they are invented to do the intended job. If we attempt to eliminate the 'ad hocery', we merely create the same (methodological) problem at a 'higher level', which means that the use of *L*-orderings as a means of explaining any consumer's choice can lead to an infinite regress. But this is not a sufficient reason for rejecting *L*-orderings since to the extent that they represent the reasons why an individual chose one particular bundle over any other affordable bundle, every form of ordering is *ad hoc* and if questioned would lead to an infinite regress.

THE DISCONTINUITY PROBLEM

If there are good reasons for rejecting the use of the *L*-ordering in demand theory, perhaps we will find them by examining how *L*-orderings might be used. There is one classic problem where it is clear that there are *formal* problems with the notion of an *L*-ordering. This classic problem (not to be confused with the methodological problems below) arises directly whenever it is assumed that the consumer is using goods themselves as an index in his or her *L*-ordering. Namely, if a person always prefers a commodity

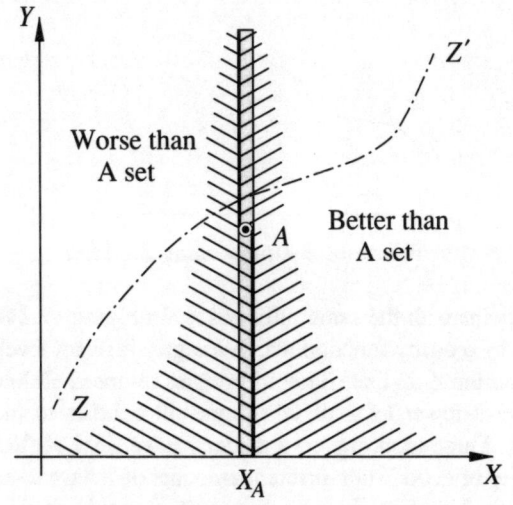

Figure 12.1 *A lexicographic ordering*

168 *Principles of economics*

bundle with more of good X to any bundle with less X regardless of the quantity of Y in either bundle, and if (and only if) the two bundles being compared have the same quantity of X, then those bundles which have more Y will be preferred. For purposes of illustration let us assume points have thickness such that the consumer's ordering looks like Figure 12.1. Here there is only one point on the boundary between the 'worse than' and the 'better than' set, namely A, the point in question. One problem is that for a continuous set represented by any positively sloped line which does *not* pass through point A, such as Z–Z' in Figure 12.1, whenever we attempt to represent the consumer's preference ordering with an ordinary utility function there is a jump in the utility index as we 'move' along Z–Z' across the boundary between bundles with less and more X than point A. This is because all bundles with the same amount of X but with a different amount of Y will have a different utility index value. Those points on the vertical line above A have a higher index than those below A. The result is such that

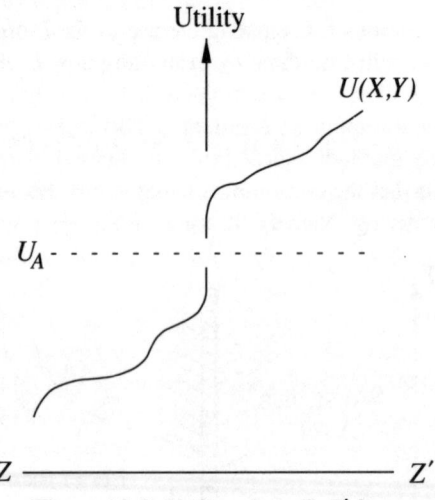

Figure 12.2 *Utility along Z–Z' line*

there is no point with the same utility as A. In Figure 12.2 this situation is represented by a utility function which assigns different levels of utility for each point on the Z–Z' line. Here all bundles on the Z–Z' line to the left of point A have a lower level of utility and all bundles to the right have a higher level. There is, however, a discontinuity since all bundles with the same quantity of good X but different amounts of Y have to have a different level of utility. This discontinuity may not be considered a serious problem but the following type of discontinuity always is.

When we directly use the quantity of good X as a proxy for the index of the utility, the real numbers used for the *index* of the utility (or of the implied ranking) turns out to be insufficient. If we assign a real number for every point in the X–Y space, there will not be enough numbers. For example, all those bundles which have the same quantity of X as point A, that is, X_A, will be represented by the same number, namely X_A, even though the consumer has ranked a sub-set of them according to the quantity of Y. That is, there exist an infinity of points for which there does in fact exist an ordering, but they all appear to be of equal rank since they have X_A as the index of utility.[1] This 'discontinuity' problem can also arise for more sophisticated L-orderings [see Georgescu-Roegen 1954]. The formal problem here is that we can never use one of the multiple criteria of any L-ordering as an index for the effect of the *entire* ordering on the space which represents all conceivable bundles of goods.

Neoclassical theorists reject L-orderings as a *form* of the utility function typically assumed in the theory of demand. This rejection of L-orderings does not seem to recognize the question of the *process* by which a consumer determines the best bundle and it is not clear that the neoclassical concept of a utility function is adequate for that purpose.

ORDERINGS AND CONSTRAINED MAXIMIZATION

Before considering multiple criteria as a basis for an explanation of the choice *process*, let us examine the only accepted way to use multiple criteria in neoclassical demand theory. In the case of constrained maximization, the choice of a best bundle involves two orderings: the unobservable preference ordering that is usually represented by an indifference map and the observable expense ordering as represented by the family of parallel budget lines where each budget line represents a different dollar value. Clearly an expense ordering by itself is insufficient to explain a consumer's unique choice since there are many points along the budget line which (by definition of that line) are ranked equally (i.e. they cost the same). Why does the consumer choose one rather than another? The consumer is thus thought to use these two orderings in a two-step manner. The consumer is thought to narrow the choice to the chosen bundle by *first* excluding all those points which he or she cannot afford (i.e. points beyond the given budget line) and *second* picking the best point among those that are affordable according to the preference ordering.[2] This is not really a choice process since it is more a 'static' choice which only requires that the individual be able to find the optimum bundle by correctly calculating utility levels for each point along the budget line.

Whether we can correctly represent the consumer's choice this way depends on what we assume about the unobservable preference ordering.

170 Principles of economics

We could assume that within the consumer's affordable set of points there is a conceivable 'bliss point', that is, a point where the consumer is satiated, as illustrated with point M in Figure 12.3. If the consumer has a relatively large budget or income (e.g. the budget line furthest from the origin in Figure 12.3), then the consumer's choice is immediately narrowed to point M since the consumer will not want more of either good even though he or she can afford more of both. While assuming that the individual can afford his or her bliss point would allow us to narrow the choice it does so by making the prices irrelevant. Since one reason for developing a theory of the consumer's demand is to explain how prices are determined in the market, a theory of the consumer which makes prices irrelevant will not be very useful. For this reason, orderings which allow 'bliss points' are usually ruled out.[3] A more common assumption is that the consumer faces a 'strictly convex' preference ordering. Technically speaking, a strictly convex ordering is one for which, if we draw a straight line between any two points of equivalent rank, all other points on that line will be preferred to the end points. In Figure 12.3 there are two indifference curves that would be ruled out by an assumption of a *strictly* convex preference ordering, namely, the indifference curve through point B and the one through point C.[4]

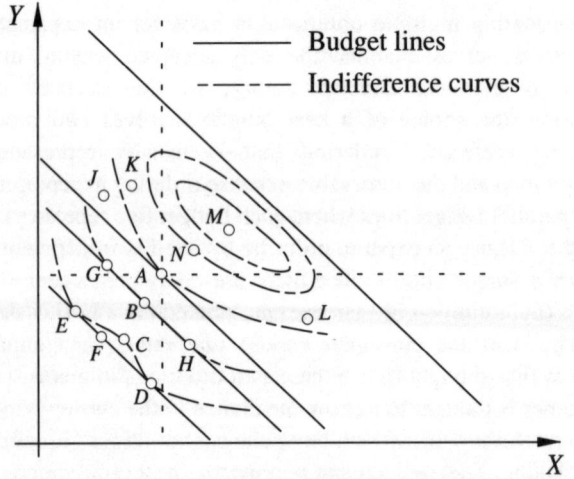

Figure 12.3 *Alternative budget lines and indifference curves*

Since neoclassical consumer theory claims to be able to explain why an observed point on the budget line was chosen, the assumption that there exists a strictly convex ordering may merely be *ad hoc* (since it is sufficient for the intended job – to explain a *unique* point). But of course, ad hocness in this sense is not considered a problem. Instead, the assumption of strictness is criticized for being 'too strong' because it is felt that we do not need 'uniqueness proofs'. For example, we may be able to narrow the choice to a set of points on the flat portion of the highest indifference curve but the choice within that set is quite arbitrary (see points between G and H in Figure 12.3). Accepting arbitrariness (so as to avoid 'strong' assumptions) may be a helpful method for avoiding arguments over the 'realism of assumptions', but it certainly will not help us to explain why the *one* point was chosen over all others.[5] Such willingness to avoid strong assumptions merely leads to arbitrariness without explanation. Since the consumer can only choose one point at any single point in time, neoclassical consumer theory must be able to explain not only why the one point was chosen but also why all other affordable points were not chosen. Along the lines of the two-step procedure noted at the beginning of this section, the assumption of a strictly convex preference ordering appears to be essential since it does help solve the problem of assuring a unique best point without making prices irrelevant.

AD HOC VS ARBITRARY

A slight digression on these words '*ad hoc*' and 'arbitrary'. The *ad hoc* characteristic of any assumption is not necessarily a criticism since assumptions are usually conjectures or guesses as to the nature of the universe. If the purpose of constructing any theory (i.e. specifying a set of assumptions) is to attempt to understand some aspect of our universe, then any *ad hoc* assumption which would insulate our understanding (viz. our theory) from criticism or from critical testing is to be avoided unless it too can be open to criticism. An assumption is arbitrary if we are unwilling to give reasons for why the assumption might be true independently of the purposes of the theory itself. Arbitrariness often occurs when the possibility of an infinite regress arises, such as when we ask for reasons for our reasons for our reasons ... , then arbitrarily stop to say that we will give no more reasons in this chain. Such arbitrariness is problematic only when we are expected to go on, for example when our reasons are suspect and are to be criticized. These methodological concepts play an important role in the understanding of the dissatisfaction with *L*-orderings.

MULTIPLE CRITERIA VS *L*-ORDERINGS IN A CHOICE PROCESS

Since all creations of human beings can be considered to be solutions to specific problems, we can ask, 'What is the problem solved by such and such tool or assumption?' Of course, it is sometimes necessary to conjecture the problem since the creator of the tool (or idea) may not have been successful in realizing his or her intention. And, regardless of success, the unintended consequences may still be interesting. It turns out that the *L*-ordering is usually seen to be an attempt to solve a problem created by the mere existence of more than one relevant non-economic ordering for any choice (among bundles or points in goods-space). While multiple criteria are sometimes necessary to 'narrow the choice', as noted above, if the goods-space in question contains an infinity of points (such as when assuming infinite divisibility) we cannot always narrow the choice to one point in the two-step manner of neoclassical theory.

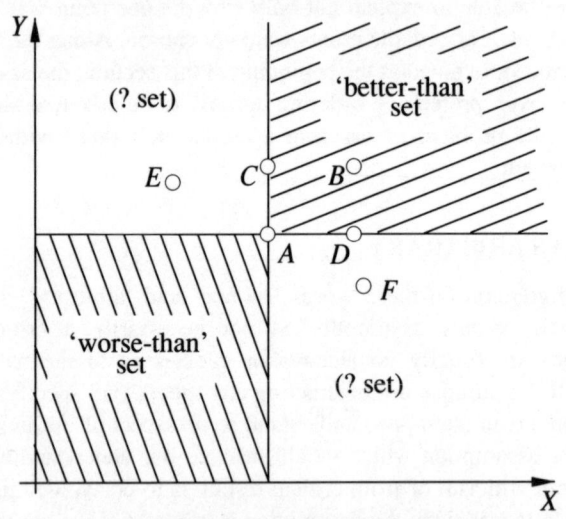

Figure 12.4 *Incomplete ordering*

To understand more clearly the problem thought to be solved by assuming that any consumer's preferences can be represented by an *L*-ordering, let us consider a situation where a person has multiple criteria that are not ordered in any way – that is, a situation only slightly different from the example of Figure 12.1. Specifically, in Figure 12.4, the consumer claims to be better off if he or she has more of either good. This would mean the consumer cannot compare point *A* with points not in the 'better than' or 'worse than' sets (the cross-hatched areas). With such an application of this non-ordered criterion, we have 'holes in the map' since there are large areas where there are many points (such as *E* and *F*) which represent more of one good and less of the other. Without introducing more criteria, points in these 'holes' cannot be compared with point *A* and thus the ordering is incomplete, another type of discontinuity. A slightly more general case is illustrated in Figure 12.5 where the consumer compares any two points by means of two separate criteria rather than by amounts of the goods themselves.

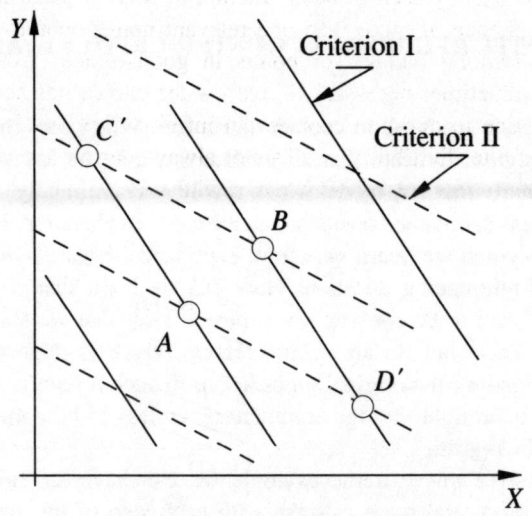

Figure 12.5 *Multiple criteria*

In Figure 12.4, without in some way ordering the two goods themselves the consumer cannot compare points C and D. Similarly, in Figure 12.5, without ranking the criteria themselves the consumer is unable to compare similar points C' and D'. Now, in either case, if the consumer ranks the criteria lexicographically he or she can compare these points. For example, in Figure 12.5, if the consumer first orders by Criterion I, then by Criterion II, the consumer would say that D' is preferred to C'. So we can see that, at least, L-orderings can help do the job of narrowing the choice to a single point (on the given budget line). However, they do so at the cost of (possible) arbitrariness. If Criterion II were given priority over Criterion I, the consumer would then prefer point C' to point D'. In other words, changing the ordering of the criteria changes the ordering of the points in question.

To explain completely the rank ordering of the points we must explain the consumer's rank ordering of the criteria. Should the ordering of orderings be lexicographic, or should we opt for some *ad hoc* utility function over the criteria such as the higher-level utility function that is integral to Kelvin Lancaster's well-known characteristics approach to consumer theory,[6] we could try to order the criteria lexicographically.

Opting for the exclusive use of L-orderings in our explanation in order to avoid the *ad hoc* assumption of a monotonic utility function (as in either Lancaster's or the ordinary neoclassical approach to the explanation of consumer choice) leads, however, to an infinite regress.

THE INFINITE REGRESS VS COUNTER-CRITICAL 'AD HOCERY'

This observation leads me to another digression. When does the possibility of infinite regress indicate that an explanation may be inadequate? The answer is clearly that any model which involves a continually self-referring infinite regress cannot be considered an adequate explanation. For example, we cannot say that we 'learn *only* from experience' because we can always ask the self-referencing question 'How did we learn that we learn from experience?' and to be consistent we must answer that we learned that by experience. This leads to an infinite regress which is impossible to stop except by violating the original proposition. In such a regress nothing new or different is brought into the argument regardless of how many steps we go back in the regress.

In contrast to this extreme example we can have an infinite regress which puts more and more at stake with each step of the argument. The latter type of infinite regress is typical of any theoretical science. One begins usually with some proposition (e.g. a policy recommendation) and attempts to rationalize this with some set of theoretical propositions. If these are in turn questioned, then broader theoretical propositions are brought up for support (e.g. neoclassical theory). If questioned further we begin to examine our basic concepts which were brought in for support (e.g. of information needed for profit maximization, the sufficiency of utility as a measure of the intrinsic quality in goods, the ability to rationalize social welfare functions, etc.).[7] Each step is offered as an explanation of the previous step in the regress – but in no way is each next step necessary in the sense that there is no other possible explanation. But to say it is not a necessary step is not to say that it is *ad hoc* or arbitrary. We can always turn to our independently established views of the matter at hand which may be broader but which may not have been seen to be important for the original issue. This progressive type of infinite regress in effect makes our original proposition more testable by allowing us to examine more and more. An *ad hoc* stopping of such an infinite regress may be against our best scientific interests.

UTILITY FUNCTIONS VS *L*-ORDERINGS

Now the importance of this digression is to argue that, when viewed as alternative to a static utility function, any *L*-ordering may only be slightly better than a self-referring infinite regress as opposed to a jeopardizing infinite regress. It is difficult to see how anything new can be brought into the infinite regress of an *L*-ordering method of explaining consumer behaviour in the two-step manner of neoclassical demand theory. That is, nothing new may be put at stake except the next higher *L*-ordering in the regress. This criticism of *L*-orderings, however, cannot be considered an argument in favour of any utility functions which are clearly *ad hoc*. Counter-critical 'ad hocery' cannot be any better than the infinite regress of 'learning only by experience'.

Casual empiricism might indicate that lexicographic behaviour is more prevalent than utility maximization primarily because, as a multi-step *process*, an *L*-ordering is easier to learn or teach than a static utility function. Utility maximization may even require more introspective, more self-reliant individuals than is allowed by modern, highly structured societies where self-reliant individualism is not always appreciated. The neoclassical theorist's rejection of *L*-orderings and the assumption of the existence of utility functions have only been supported by the assumption that the neoclassical theory of the consumer is true (i.e. that consumers act to maximize their utility in a two-step manner using a static utility function). To have a maximum in a calculus sense requires a static monotonic utility index or function or something sufficiently similar which a static *L*-ordering can never be. The assumption that such a static utility function exists is necessarily *ad hoc* unless there can be constructed an independent test of its existence – that is, independent of the theory in question. Since such a test has yet to be devised (let alone applied), lexicographic orderings need not be rejected only because they cannot *formally* represent a usable utility index.

While one can recognize that a choice can be made with multiple criteria (e.g. Figures 12.4 and 12.5), such an ordering can never be complete (there are always 'holes in the map') until one orders the criteria. A strictly convex preference ordering (such as one implied by a utility function) over criteria performs this task. But there is no reason why the assumed preference ordering is the only conceivable ordering. This consideration of the non-uniqueness of utility functions then leads to an infinite regress since a complete explanation must explain why one utility function was chosen over any other conceivable alternative. This line of criticism will lead to yet a higher-ordered preference ordering which must implicitly recognize alternative higher-ordered preference orderings between which the question is begged as to why one was chosen rather than any of the others. And so on.

A lexicographic ordering is always a conceivable alternative but only if it is seen to represent a process rather than the preference ordering used in the second step of the neoclassical explanation of demand. Since neoclassical economics is more concerned with representing choice in a manner analogous to the calculus-type constrained maximization, neoclassical economists will always choose convex preference orderings that can be represented by ordinary utility functions. What is the basis for this choice? The only reason lexicographic orderings are rejected is that they cannot be represented by formal utility functions even though they can perform the task of eliminating arbitrariness or incompleteness for the purpose of explaining a unique choice. It is clear to me that neoclassical economists put methodological considerations of mathematical formalism before even casual empirical questions whenever it comes to choosing an assumption to represent the non-economic basis of consumer choice.

NOTES

1 Note, however, that this ordinal ranking does work for the line Z–Z' of Figure 12.1 so long as we do not attempt to say anything about points off that line.
2 Technically, this procedure constitutes a rudimentary lexicographic ordering. Goods are first ordered by increasing costs, then by increasing utility. However, this is not usually the aspect of L-orderings that is put at issue in the criticism of such orderings.
3 Note that we would also have to rule out incomes so low that an individual could not afford the minimum level of utility that is necessary for survival. In this sense it could be said that neoclassical economics is middle-class economics since we are thereby ruling out both very high and very low incomes.
4 The curve through point B would allow us to pick two points such as G and H where all points on the line between them are not preferred to G and H (they are equivalent). In the case of the indifference curve through point C, at point C the curve is actually concave to the origin, that is, we can draw a line between points D and E such that points D and E are preferred to all other points on that line (e.g. point F).
5 Accepting stochasticism has similar consequences [see Boland 1986a, Chapter 8].
6 In his approach [Lancaster 1966], the consumer can order points on the basis of intrinsic characteristics such as vitamin content, salt content, or other criteria for which the content is proportional to the amount consumed. The consumer then forms a utility function over the amounts obtained of the characteristics to determine the best point and works backward to determine which bundle of goods provides the best characteristics point.
7 Such an infinite regress as this may seem risky and undesirable to some theoretical economists *because* more and more is put at stake at each step.

13 Revealed Preference vs Ordinal Demand

> Instead of dallying in the theory of consistency tests, an older writer on demand theory (one, that is, who was writing before Samuelson) would have proceeded at once, having laid his foundations, to the derivation of a much more famous principle – the principle that the demand curve for a commodity is downward sloping. We, in our turn, must now consider this basic proposition, which remains what it always was, the centre of the whole matter.
>
> John Hicks [1956, p. 59]

In 1938 Samuelson offered what he thought was a clear alternative to the unobservable static utility functions needed in the two-step procedure inherent in the neoclassical demand theory. Rather than having us assume the individual faces a preference ordering that is assumed to have the correct shape (convex, no bliss points, etc.), Samuelson would only require us to assume that the consumer makes well-defined, consistent choices. Choice will be consistent and well-defined if the individual will (a) choose the same bundle whenever he or she faces the same prices and income and (b) never choose any of the other affordable bundles except when prices and incomes change to levels that make the first (or preferred) bundle unaffordable. Armed with this notion of consistency and well-defined choices, Samuelson claimed we could dispense with assumptions about utility functions. Moreover, he claimed that everything necessary for a demand theory was observable (we can observe when a consumer makes an inconsistent choice).

At first it seemed that Samuelson had successfully developed an alternative to the neoclassical Ordinal Demand Theory of Hicks and Allen [1934] which was based on the two-step procedure with static utility functions being represented by indifference maps. Samuelson eventually reintroduced the notion of 'preferences' by claiming that consistent choices reveal the consumer's preferences since the chosen point is revealed to be preferred to all the other affordable points. Unfortunately, it never seems to have been asked why it is sensible to think of individuals being slaves to all of their past choices. Moreover, such consistency in behaviour is indistinguishable from individuals who are slaves to static utility functions.

It seems now that everyone agrees that the Ordinal Demand Theory of Hicks and Allen, which is based on assumptions concerning ordinal utility functions or preference orderings, and Revealed Preference Analysis, which is based on Samuelson's early work, are in some sense formally equivalent. The primary evidence for this equivalence is that the famous Slutsky equation can be derived either from conditions placed on ordinal utility functions or from some version of Wald's or Samuelson's Axiom of Revealed Preference, as applied to price–quantity situations.[1] Samuelson [1953, p. 2] and Hicks [1956, p. 139] even went as far as establishing what is called the 'generalized law of demand', namely that, *for normal goods*, the quantity demanded varies inversely with the price.[2] Consumer theory, whether based on the Ordinal Demand Theory of Hicks and Allen [1934] or on Samuelson's [1938, 1948] Revealed Preference Analysis, is a major part of the neoclassical theory of prices and, as such, has as its purpose the explanation of demand in general and the Law of Demand in particular. The Law of Demand is the commonly accepted notion that the demand curve for any commodity is downward sloping. This 'basic proposition', says Hicks [1956, p. 59], 'remains ... the centre of the whole matter'. Unlike 'the generalized law of demand', the Law of Demand is not restricted only to 'normal goods'.

The essentialness of the Law of Demand will not be put at stake in this chapter. I will take up that matter in Chapter 14. Here I want to critically examine the alleged equivalence of Ordinal Demand Theory and Revealed Preference Analysis with regard to the Law of Demand.

It is well known that necessary and sufficient reasons for the Law of Demand have yet to be established using Ordinal Demand Theory with a set of conditions or specification that are placed on preference orderings (except, of course, by ruling out inferior goods).[3] Contrary to the popular opinions concerning equivalence [e.g. Samuelson 1950; Houthakker 1961], in this chapter I will *attempt* to provide necessary and sufficient reasons for the Law of Demand by showing how the Axiom of Revealed Preference can be interpreted as saying *more* than Ordinal Demand Theory about the Law of Demand. The approach taken here is to examine consumer behaviour without first specifying an *ex ante* preference ordering (such a specification would not be directly testable anyway) and I will not be requiring that we must have observed all possible points in goods-space so as to construct *ex post* a preference ordering.[4] I shall develop the primary entailment of consumer behaviour that is directly relevant for the Law of

Demand: the price–consumption curve (PCC) which I briefly discussed in Chapter 4.

Unlike Gustav Cassel [1918] or Henry Moore [1929] there is no intention here to eliminate utility or preference orderings – such orderings will always be assumed to exist. On the basis of maximizing choice, and somewhat like Cassel, the basic empirical assumptions will be to conjecture specific demand curves directly. However, where Cassel would simply assume that they are properly shaped [1918, pp. 66–88], I will put that assumption at stake since it is the moot point. That is to say, I will examine the explicit or implicit conditions that must be satisfied by any given *set* of demand curves rather than just examine as usual the implicit conditions based on properties of metaphysical utility functions. Unlike Moore [1929, pp. 5–10], here it will not be presumed that the theory of consumer behaviour can be *induced* from observations – statistical or otherwise.

CONSUMER THEORY AND INDIVIDUALISM

As one half of a neoclassical theory of prices, consumer theory is a particular conjunction of ideas that is intended to explain why the quantity demanded is what it is at the going *market price*. In neoclassical economics it is usually taken for granted that no individual in society should have the power to influence (substantially) the going prices *directly*, yet together (in conjunction with supply) large groups of individuals do determine the prices of all the goods that they buy. Although the *necessity* that this determination involves only downward sloping market demand curves will not be examined until Chapter 14, in this chapter that requirement will be assumed to hold. Moreover, it is a sufficient argument that *if* all individuals have downward sloping demand curves for any particular good, *then* the market demand curve will be downward sloping for that good. The neoclassical notion of demand curves is always in terms of partial equilibrium – that is, nothing is required regarding other individuals, other markets, etc. Particularly, we do not require that other markets be in equilibrium. This is the basic feature of both Marshall's and Pareto's approaches to economics [Pareto 1916/35, footnote to Section 1978; Marshall 1920/49, Book V]. This approach reveals their view of what is 'scientific': one *must* begin with the smallest element and work up to broad generalities [Pareto 1916/35, Section 2078; Marshall 1920/49, footnote p. 315; see also Schumpeter 1909, pp. 214–17]. If in our theory we allow any individual to have an upward sloping demand curve, we must then explain why the net outcome for the whole market will still be a downward sloping demand curve as required. This would in turn require some theoretical statement about consumers as a group (perhaps, about the distribution of people with negative sloping demand curves[5]). That everyone has a downward sloping demand curve is not merely sufficient but also desirable for the maintenance of strict methodological individualism.[6] For the purpose of this chapter, the *necessity* of downward sloping demand curves will continue to be accepted without question as well as the necessity of maintaining the strict methodological individualistic view of economics. So I will thus assume that we must explain why every individual's demand curve is negatively sloped. This, I think, is the meaning of Hick's statement that the Law of Demand is 'the centre of the whole matter' and that 'centre' is focused on the individual's demand curve as the outcome of the individual's behavioural response both to his or her economic constraints (going prices and income) and to his or her disposition regarding the goods bought (i.e. tastes).

THE LOGIC OF EXPLANATION

Let us then begin with a general look at the two-step logic of explaining all individuals' behaviour regarding their choice of the quantities of goods that they buy. We say that consumers are maximizing when they buy the best quantity combination subject to *their* economic constraints and subject to *their* criterion as to what is 'best'. We say, in effect, that their choice of quantities is optimally *determined* conjointly by the state of those constraints *and* the nature (shape) of their criterion. We say that their choice is optimal, hence it can be rationalized by *anyone* whenever the consumers can clearly state the nature of their tastes. That is, given a specified preference ordering, if the choice is optimal, then we can independently *determine* what that choice would be. In that manner we say that we can explain the consumer's choice. The *determinateness* is the crucial element in this theory of explanation. To summarize schematically, we have the following elements in our explanation of the consumer's choice of quantities of n goods:

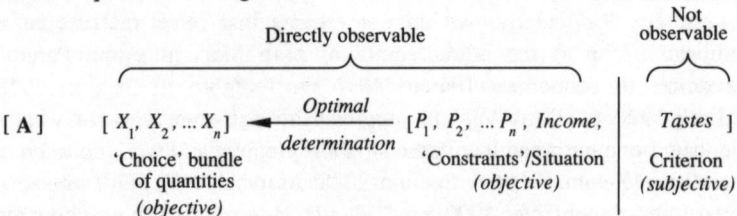

	Directly observable	Not observable
[A]	$[X_1, X_2, ... X_n]$ ⟵ Optimal determination ⟶ $[P_1, P_2, ... P_n,$ Income,	Tastes]
	'Choice' bundle of quantities (objective)	'Constraints'/Situation (objective)	Criterion (subjective)

where X_i is the quantity of good i purchased at price P_i.

That the consumer optimally picks the best point (or bundle) in no way requires that the tastes as represented by a preference ordering be of any particular shape whatsoever, except that the 'best' be well defined. What does limit the shape of the consumer's preferences is the requirement that the individual be *responsive* to changes in his or her constraints[7] – without responsiveness we could not say that prices in any way influence the consumer's choice. The only place where *all* of the consumer's constraints are influential is on the boundary of his or her 'attainable set', that is, where the consumer is spending all of his or her income (or budget) on the goods in question.

The question of *determinateness* of the choice situation facing an optimizing consumer leaves open several different ways for the theorist to approach the explanation of the consumer's behaviour. We could, on the one hand, begin with a consumer's fully specified ordering (i.e. with *ex ante* specified properties) and then examine the expected logical consequences of that consumer facing different price and income situations. On the other hand, we might avoid the requirement that the consumer in question be able to specify *ex ante* his or her preferences, and instead attempt to deduce the nature of those preferences from observed coincidence of different price–income situations and actual choices made on the basis of a static preference ordering. We could then use the deduced preference ordering as a basis for our 'prediction' of the consumer's behaviour.[8]

On the basis of *our theory* that the consumer wishes to maximize his or her utility (or, equivalently, pick the 'best' point), certain logical requirements must be satisfied either by the unobservable *ex ante* preference ordering *or* by the revealed *ex post* behaviour in observable price–income–choice situations. Because of the *determinateness* of our explanations and the *responsiveness* of the consumer's behaviour to all aspects of the price–income situation, satisfaction by one implies satisfaction by the other. That is to say, the theoretical and philosophical necessity of *determinateness* and *responsiveness* is what gives rise to the apparent equivalence between Ordinal Demand Theory and Revealed Preference Analysis. I say 'apparent' because it is only true in the case where the Marshallian requirement of being able to rationalize the Law of Demand is *not* imposed upon the optimal choice determination. As yet, the recognized conditions for an optimal choice determination that is placed on ordinal preferences are either insufficient or unnecessary for the exclusion of 'Giffen goods'. I will try to show here that the Axiom of Revealed Preference can be interpreted *consistently with the above dual approach to consumer behaviour* to show that it does seem to say something more than the assumptions of Ordinal Demand Theory can and also try to show that some well-known interpretations of demand theory are contradicted by this interpretation of the Axiom of Revealed Preference. More specifically, I will attempt to use the *determinateness* to specify *indirectly* the nature of the preferences which allow inferior goods while still excluding Giffen

182 *Principles of economics*

goods. This indirect specification will be based on the properties of price–consumption curves.

PRICE–CONSUMPTION CURVES (PCCS)

To compare the assumptions of Ordinal Demand Theory with those of Revealed Preference Analysis I need to identify something that they have in common. The one thing that they do have in common is the behavioural consequences entailed in the assumptions. The Slutsky equation, for example, is entailed in both sets of assumptions, and both seem to be insufficient to deal with the Law of Demand – they only describe the behaviour at one point, and do not help us to explain it in relation to other points. My approach here will be to examine the behaviour by first examining the families of the PCCs which can be considered either the logical consequences of using any preference ordering (map) or the implications of any set of observed choices. The properties of these PCCs are *the* central concern of the theory of consumer behaviour. To examine the properties of a PCC family or grid, I will lay out all the conceivable options which must be dealt with and then try to explain the significance of the various options with respect to either Ordinal Demand Theory or Revealed Preference Analysis. To keep this task manageable in two-dimensional diagrams, I will deal only with two-good cases. And to assist in the task, I am again going to enhance the usual representation of a PCC by adding an arrowhead to indicate in which direction (along the PCC) the price rises for the good in question.

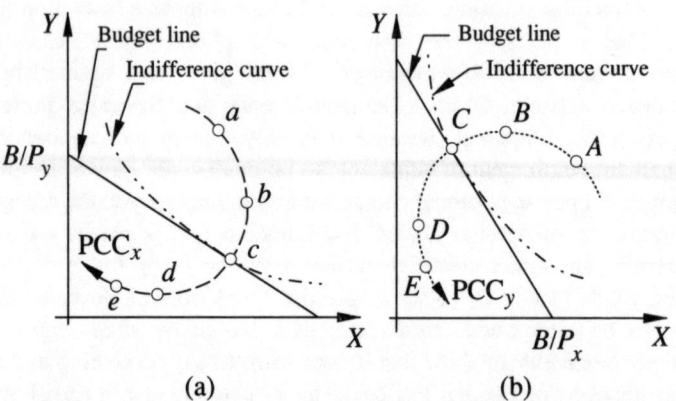

Figure 13.1 *Possible slopes of price–consumption curves*

In Figure 13.1(a), I have drawn a PCC for good X representing all five possible slopes.[9] At point *a* the implicit *demand curve* would be positively sloped since as the price of X rises the consumer will move from point *a* toward *b*, and thus we note that the consumer must buy more of good X (a Giffen good situation). At point *b* the demand would be perfectly inelastic; relatively inelastic at point *c*; at point *d* it would have 'unit' elasticity; and at point *e* it would be relatively elastic.[10] Similarly, in Figure 13.1(b), I have represented the possible cases for good Y. This means that (ignoring collinear configurations) there are five cases for each good which in turn can be combined in twenty-five different ways, see Figure 13.2. Since passing through every point on a consumer's indifference map there will be one PCC_x and one PCC_y (each with its own slope), with Figure 13.2 I have catalogued each point as being one of the twenty-five cases.[11]

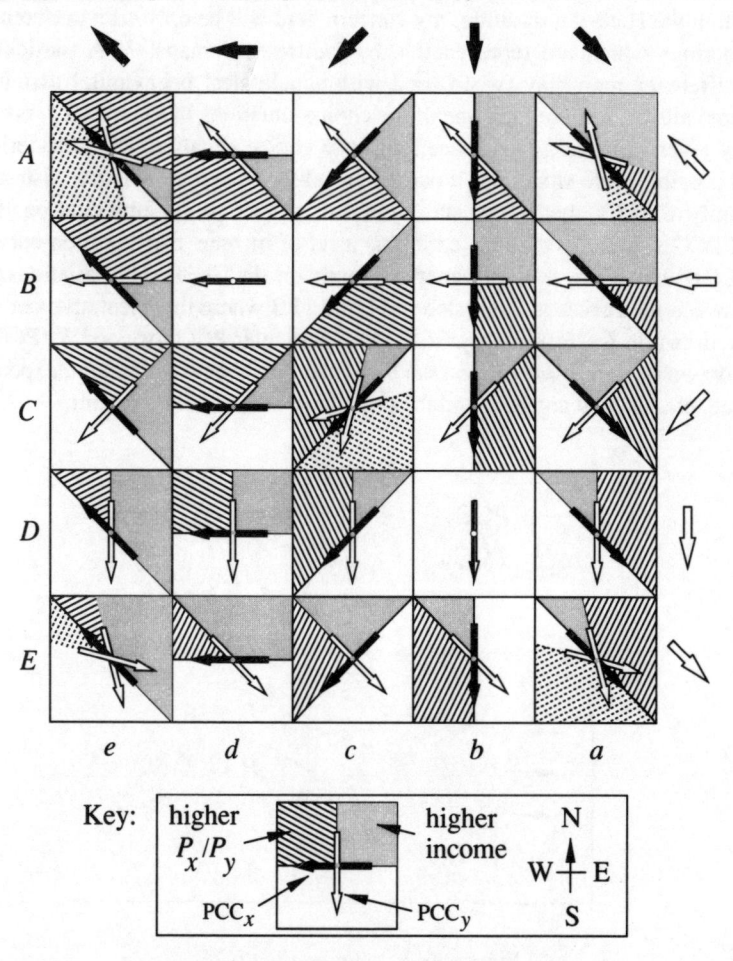

Figure 13.2 *Possible relative slopes of PCCs*

184 Principles of economics

Now, before examining the logic of the situation, we need to get a clear idea of what is meant by 'responsiveness' and 'determinateness' in our explanation of behaviour. *Responsiveness* means simply that whenever the consumer faces significantly different price–income situations,[12] the consumer will choose to buy different combinations of quantities of goods. That is, no two different price–income situations determine the same goods-quantity combination. In other words, the mapping from goods-space into situation-space is *unique*. *Determinateness* means that for any particular price–income situation there is *only one* particular goods–quantity combination that will be chosen – the *mapping* from situation-space into goods-space is *unique* (i.e. 'well defined'). To keep within the Hicksian tradition, my concern here will be only with preference orderings which are representable by indifference maps.[13] A particular indifference map may (when used with neoclassical behavioural assumptions) allow for more than one of the choice situations of Figure 13.2, but at any given point in goods-space, only one choice situation. By considering all possible price situations, a particular indifference map will give rise to a family of PCCs, that is, one sub-family for all PCC_xs and implicitly one for all PCC_ys in the two-goods case plus a set of income–consumption curves (ICCs) which are merely generated from the PCCs.[14] This relationship between the curves is illustrated in Figure 13.3 where representative curves are drawn in the form of a grid.[15] Any particular PCC for good X (PCC_x) is drawn by definition only on the basis that the income (or budget, expenditure, etc.) is held constant and the price of good Y is held constant.

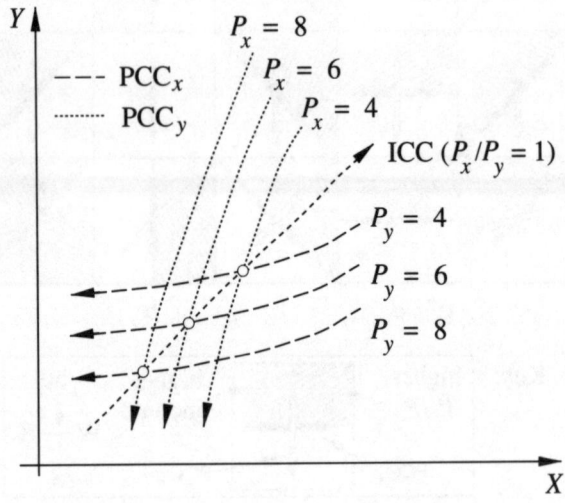

Figure 13.3   *An implicit ICC*

As the major concern of this chapter is the ability to derive the Law of Demand and hence explain price behaviour, I will always assume that income or budget, B, is fixed and thus the same for all PCCs considered. This is only a minor concern since all income changes can be represented (inversely) by proportional changes in all prices simultaneously. This leaves only P_y, the fixed price of Y, to be the identifying feature of any particular PCC for good X. If we change the fixed and given P_y we will get a different PCC_x. Similarly P_x, the price of X, is the identifying feature of any particular PCC_y. If we assume the budget or income is fixed, then to be on any particular PCC_x, the consumer is faced with an implied P_y and thus the PCC_x is labelled with the given P_y. Figure 13.3 thereby represents a grid of PCCs or more important a grid of iso-price lines where at each line there is a PCC_x and a PCC_y for the given prices, P_x and P_y. Armed with such a grid we can say what the prices must be for the consumer to choose any point in the goods-space (given a fixed income, of course). The usual income–consumption curve will be generated as the locus of intersecting PCCs with the labels in a constant ratio, P_x/P_y. In Figure 13.3 the line representing the ICC has an arrowhead indicating the direction of increasing income. The map formed for all the implicit PCCs for any particular indifference map will be called the 'PCC grid' for that indifference map. On the basis of either responsiveness or determinateness there is a one-to-one correspondence between PCC grids and indifference maps.

Assuming income constant, note that if we consider a *particular* PCC as a vector function on goods-space into price-space, $P = \phi(X)$, or an inverse function on price-space into goods-space, $X = \phi^{-1}(P)$, then its projection, $X_i = \phi_i^{-1}(P_i)$, is the individual's demand function but the projection need not be 'well defined' even though the PCC itself is. The PCCs can be interpreted in other ways: as a mapping from all-goods-space into one-price-space, $X \rightarrow P_i$, such as Wald's demand function[16] or a mapping from all-price-space into one-good-space, $P \rightarrow X_i$ such as Cassel's demand functions [Cassel 1918, p. 80]. But the entire PCC grid is not in any way an indirect utility function.[17]

The importance of PCC grids here is that the PCC grid is the one thing that Ordinal Demand Theory and Revealed Preference Analysis *necessarily* have in common. Conditions placed on preference orderings of demand theory ultimately must be reflected in the nature of the consequential PCC grid. Likewise, 'axioms' of Revealed Preference Analysis are direct statements about the nature of the implicit PCC grid.

CHOICE ANALYSIS WITH PREFERENCE THEORY ASSUMPTIONS

It would seem that the alleged equivalence between the Revealed Preference Analysis and Ordinal Demand Theory should be apparent in the categorical logic of the consumer's situation that has been outlined in Figure 13.2. In particular, the logical significance of the assumptions concerning preferences or choices is always in terms of which PCC situations (of Figure 13.2) are *ruled out* as impossible by those behavioural assumptions.

The primary tool in this section will be the array of cells illustrated in Figure 13.2. Let me be clear about what that figure shows. Each cell is drawn for one point with the two PCCs intersecting as shown. Note that at each point of an indifference map there is a PCC_x for a given price of Y and a PCC_y for a given price of X and implicitly a specific P_x/P_y. Relative to this P_x/P_y I have identified the cross-hatched areas (points) where P_x/P_y would *definitely* have to be higher for those points to be chosen. Similarly, there are shaded areas (points) where *income* would definitely have to be greater for those points to be chosen. With Figure 13.2 in mind, I will now examine the consequences of some of the usual assumptions concerning the shape of preferences. Throughout this examination I will be referring to the various cells in Figure 13.2 by identifying the row with a capital letter and a column with a lower-case letter, (e.g. the lower left cell is Ee). Each cell in Figure 13.2 represents the possible relative slopes of the two PCCs at the point of intersection and corresponding to the points labelled in Figures 13.1(a) and 13.1(b).

Greed (dominance, non-satiation)

The most common neoclassical assumption is to rule out 'bliss points'. The effect of ruling out bliss points is that people will always prefer more of any good if none of any other has to be given up. The major implication of this assumption is that indifference curves are always negatively sloped. For my purposes here, this assumption rules out those situations in Figure 13.2 where the ICC is positively sloped *but* has the arrowhead (increasing income) pointing 'south-west'.[18] Such cases as those represented by the dotted lines in Aa and Ee become problematic here if we require that the slope of the PCCs *guarantee* that this assumption is fulfilled.[19]

Hicksian assumption of diminishing MRS (convexity)

Next let us consider the effect of utilizing the Hicksian assumption that indifference curves should be convex to the origin. Convexity is assured by an assumption about the 'marginal rate of substitution' (MRS) – that is, about the slope of an indifference curve. Since the PCC grid is based on maximization, we can easily determine the value of the marginal rate of substitution. Specifically, a necessary condition for maximization is that MRS equals the given P_x/P_y. To see what the Hicksian assumption of a diminishing MRS means, consider any indifference curve drawn through the point of intersection of two PCCs. If the MRS is diminishing then (1) at all points along the curve that are 'north-west' of the intersection point, the slope of the indifference curve[20] must be higher (i.e. steeper) than the slope at the intersection point and (2) at all points along the curve that are 'south-east' of the intersection, the slope must *not* be higher. In Figure 13.2 there are a few cells which would contradict this requirement. This is most clearly seen in situation *Bb* where below and to the right all points (whether or not they are on the one indifference curve in question) must necessarily have a steeper MRS[21] which contradicts directly the assumption of diminishing MRS. Note that so long as indifference curves are negatively sloped (which is the only way we would ever use them)[22] and they are not straight lines, indifference curves must be drawn in a direction which lies in the angle formed by the arrowhead of one PCC and the tail end of the other PCC. That is, as one moves along a curved indifference locus, MRS is changing (diminishing or increasing). Now, in the context of diminishing MRS along a negatively sloped indifference curve, one can see that more situations are ruled out. In addition to *Bb*, situations *Ab*, *Aa* and *Ba* are clearly seen as logically impossible. Recognizing that 'greed' implies negatively sloped indifference curves,[23] situations *Ad*, *Ac*, *Bc*, *Cb*, *Ca* and *Da* are also impossible. Situations *Bd* and *Db*, and the conceivable cases represented by the dotted lines in cell *Cc*, are also impossible. The situations *Ae* and *Ea* are problematic under the assumption of diminishing MRS since some of the cases allowed contradict diminishing MRS. But since they are extreme cases, Hicks argued, they are unlikely.[24] If his argument were considered sufficient we could see how Hicks' assumption might eliminate Giffen goods since they are to be found anywhere in rows A and B or columns *b* and *a*.

Assumption of 'normal goods'

There is one assumption which is more than sufficient for ruling out Giffen goods. If one assumes that all goods are such that any increase in income (or lowering of all prices) would mean that more of all goods would be bought, then the ICC would always be positively sloped with its arrowhead pointing 'north-east' (i.e. the shaded area would be restricted to appear *only* 'north-east' of the intersection point). This assumption can be seen in

Figure 13.2 to rule out the situations *Ae*, *Ad*, *Be*, *Bd*, *Db*, *Da*, *Eb* and *Ea* as being impossible (since they contradict this assumption). Also, the additional situations *Ac*, *Ab*, *Aa*, *Ba*, *Ca*, *Ce*, *De*, *Ee*, *Ed* and *Ec* would be problematic as above. If the assumption is that the goods must *necessarily* be 'normal' (never inferior) then only the remaining situations would be possible. If one uses both the diminishing MRS and the 'normality' assumptions then only situations *Cd*, *Cc*, *Dd* and *Dc* are possible (i.e. no elastic demand for any good!). Obviously this conjunction of assumptions rules out too much if we only want to rule out Giffen goods.

Interdependence of elasticities

On the assumption that the consumer's income is entirely spent, the following simple situation is always maintained:

$$P_x \cdot X + P_y \cdot Y = B \qquad [13.1]$$

And, using a little calculus, for any PCC one can generate the following relationship involving the elasticity of demand, ε_i, for good i, and the slope of the PCC, $(\partial Y/\partial X)_i$, for PCC_i:

for good X,

$$[1 + (1/\varepsilon_x)] + [(\partial Y / \partial X)_x / (P_x / P_y)] = 0 \qquad [13.2a]$$

for good Y,

$$[1 + (1/\varepsilon_y)] + [(P_x / P_y) / (\partial Y / \partial X)_y] = 0 \qquad [13.2b]$$

which taken together gives the following relationship between elasticities at one chosen point in X–Y space since at any one point these two relationships must have the same (P_x/P_y):

$$[1 + (1/\varepsilon_x)] \cdot [1 + (1/\varepsilon_y)] = (\partial Y/\partial X)_x / (\partial Y/\partial X)_y \qquad [13.3]$$

That is to say, the ratio of the slopes of the two PCCs indicates directly the product involving the two demand elasticities. This result only conflicts with the conceivable situation *Ee* represented by the dotted lines and the solid case *Ae*. The ratio of the slopes of PCC_x to PCC_y must be less than one, by definition of demand elasticities, but in the *Ee* dotted case and the *Ae* solid case that ratio would be greater than one.

CHOICE THEORY FROM REVEALED PREFERENCE ANALYSIS

Referring back to the schemata [A], one can see the logic of options available to the ordinary neoclassical demand theorist. Neoclassical demand theorists up to the time of the acceptance of Samuelson's Revealed Preference Analysis would have us assume a given and known ordinal preference map [e.g. Hicks and Allen 1934, pp. 55, 198]. With a known map and any given price–income situation, we can deduce the optimal choice in goods-space. Unfortunately, this approach is based on a presumption of the availability of the consumers' subjective knowledge. Without such knowledge, it would be impossible to apply this version of demand theory directly to any person without some heroic philosophical jumps.[25] Many thought that this was merely a minor difficulty since we could ask the individual what his or her relative preferences were at any given point [e.g. Hicks and Allen 1934, Part II; Allen 1950], even though a complete map still requires more information than is conceivably possible.[26] At one time many thought that there might be a short-cut to actually constructing the map; we could observe the person's choices and *ex post* deduce from the actual observations what the person's preference ordering was [e.g. Little 1949]. Without a known ordinal preference map it would seem to be quite arbitrary whether we specify *ex ante* certain properties of the map that are assumed to exist, or deduce that map *ex post* on the basis of a simple notion of consistent choice.[27] The question then is, when does a particular difference in price–income–choice combinations imply different preferences? Samuelson's answer [1948, pp. 243-4] was in effect that any time two different price–income–choice combinations satisfy the Axiom of Revealed Preference, we can utilize the neoclassical theory of the consumer (i.e. utility maximization or optimum choice) to infer the preference map that this individual consumer was assumed to be using. As it turns out, satisfying the Axiom of Revealed Preference is like satisfying the usual conditions of Ordinal Demand Theory. These two approaches are sufficiently alike that they have important consequences in common which have led Houthakker [1961] and others to consider them equivalent.

What I am going to do here is a little different. Since it has been shown that certain versions of the axioms of Revealed Preference Analysis imply the existence of a preference ordering [Houthakker 1950, 1961; Arrow 1959a], I want to apply one of the axioms, the Axiom of Revealed Preference, to specific situations which were derived from preferences. There should be no danger of contradiction here even though I may be violating the intentions for inventing the Axiom of Revealed Preference. In particular, I am going to apply the Axiom of Revealed Preference to two points on any given PCC. There is no way two points on the same PCC can directly violate the Axiom of Revealed Preference if we always assume 'greed' (lowering one price alone always means that the consumer's real income has increased). The question here is, what are the implications of the Axiom of Revealed Preference for the shape of the PCC?

To answer this, a way must be found to express that axiom in terms of PCCs and budget lines rather than in terms of quantities of goods and/or indifference curves. It will be recalled from Chapter 4 that the Axiom of

Revealed Preference says that point A (in X–Y space) is 'revealed preferred' to point B when A is bought at prices P_x^A and P_y^A and B is bought at prices P_x^B and P_y^B such that

if $\quad P_x^A \cdot X_A + P_y^A \cdot Y_A \geq P_x^A \cdot X_B + P_y^A \cdot Y_B \quad$ [13.4a]

then $\quad P_x^B \cdot X_A + P_y^B \cdot Y_A > P_x^B \cdot X_B + P_y^B \cdot Y_B \quad$ [13.4b]

Of course, this must be true for any two points on any PCC_x where by definition $P_y^A = P_y^B$ $(= P_y)$. Hence the Axiom of Revealed Preference can be stated in this particular case as:

if $\quad P_x^A \cdot (X_A - X_B) \geq P_y \cdot (Y_B - Y_A) \quad$ [13.5a]

then $\quad P_x^B \cdot (X_A - X_B) > P_y \cdot (Y_B - Y_A) \quad$ [13.5b]

Parenthetically, at this point it becomes possible to point out a potential error in Houthakker's [1961] famous survey of consumer theory. He says that the Axiom of Revealed Preference

> is nothing but a generalization of the Law of Demand to arbitrary price changes. To see how it relates to the ordinary Law of Demand we need only put $\Sigma_i P^A \cdot Q^B$ equal to $\Sigma_i P^A \cdot Q^A$ and assume vectors P^A and P^B are identical except for one (say [good X]) price. After some subtractions we then get that
>
> if $\quad \Sigma_i P^A \cdot Q^B = \Sigma_i P^A \cdot Q^A \quad$ then $\quad \Sigma_i (P_x^A - P_x^B) \cdot (X_A - X_B) < 0$
>
> or in words: if a price changes in such a way that in the new situation the consumer can buy what he bought in the old, then the price change and the quantity change are necessarily of opposite signs. [1961, p. 707]

Unfortunately for Houthakker's attempt to apply the Axiom of Revealed Preference to demand theory, his 'if-clause' can never be satisfied on any one PCC curve (and hence on a demand curve). It must always be an inequality if only one price is varied and all the income is spent because all the points on any PCC are optimum ('equilibrium') points. In neoclassical textbook terms, no two different points on one budget line can be on the same PCC as PCCs and budget lines necessarily cross at only one point.

Perhaps I am misinterpreting Houthakker, so I will push on. If one defines $\partial X = (X_A - X_B)$ and $\partial Y = (Y_A - Y_B)$ then the Axiom of Revealed Preference in this particular case says that:

if $\quad P_x^A \cdot \partial X \geq - P_y \cdot \partial Y \quad$ [13.6a]

then $\quad P_x^B \cdot \partial X > - P_y \cdot \partial Y \quad$ [13.6b]

By specifying merely that $\partial X > 0$ and $P_y > 0$, one can say that

if $\quad (P_x^A / P_y) \geq - (\partial Y / \partial X) \quad$ [13.7a]

then $\quad (P_x^B / P_y) > - (\partial Y / \partial X) \quad$ [13.7b]

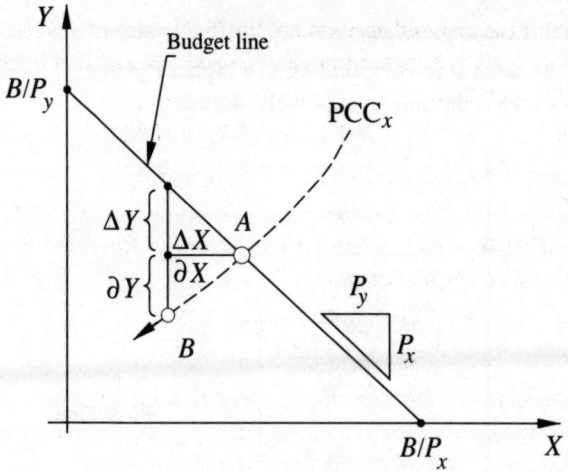

Figure 13.4 *Comparing slopes of PCC and budget line at a point*

If, as is usual, the consumer is assumed to be maximizing his or her satisfaction, then the slope of the budget line, ($\Delta Y/\Delta X$), equals the negative of the going price ratio, that is, $-(P_x/P_y) = (\Delta Y/\Delta X)$, (see Figure 13.4) then one gets the following:

if the slope of $PCC_x \geq$ the slope of the budget line of the preferred point

then the slope of $PCC_x >$ the slope of the budget line of the inferior point

that is,

if $(\partial Y/\partial X) \geq (\Delta Y/\Delta X)$ at A [13.8a]

then $(\partial Y/\partial X) > (\Delta Y/\Delta X)$ at B [13.8b]

When the slope of the PCC_x along that curve between the two points is positive (i.e. demand is relatively inelastic) this hypothetical condition is easily satisfied. When the slope of PCC_x is negative, the situation gets problematic again. In this case, the Axiom of Revealed Preference says that the slope of the budget line must be steeper than the slope of the PCC_x at point B if the slope of the PCC_x is not steeper than the budget line's slope at A. To see what this says, consider the two cases shown in Figures 13.5a and 13.5b which represent columns *a* and *e*, respectively, of Figure 13.2. Since the slopes can be compared directly by comparing ∂Y with ΔY for a $\partial X = \Delta X > 0$, the first clause of the Axiom of Revealed Preference requires that

$$\partial Y \geq \Delta Y \text{ at } A \quad [13.9]$$

and this is true in Figure 13.5b and is false in Figure 13.5a since both ∂Y and ΔY are negative. Now the Axiom of Revealed Preference can be restated as follows:

if at point *A* the *demand curve* is not positively sloped [13.10a]

then at any point *B* (corresponding to a higher P_x) that demand curve is definitely negatively sloped. [13.10b]

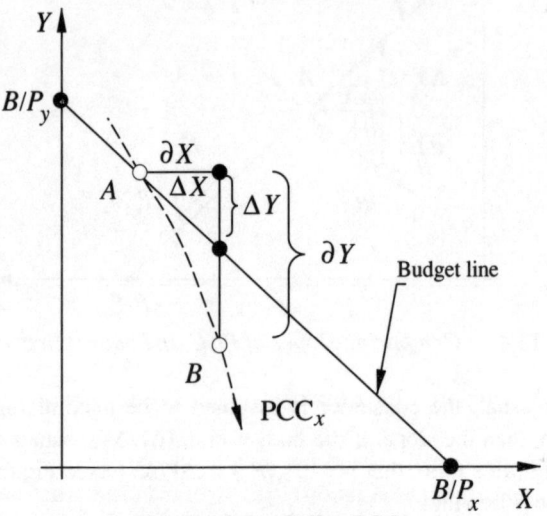

Figure 13.5a *Giffen PCC*

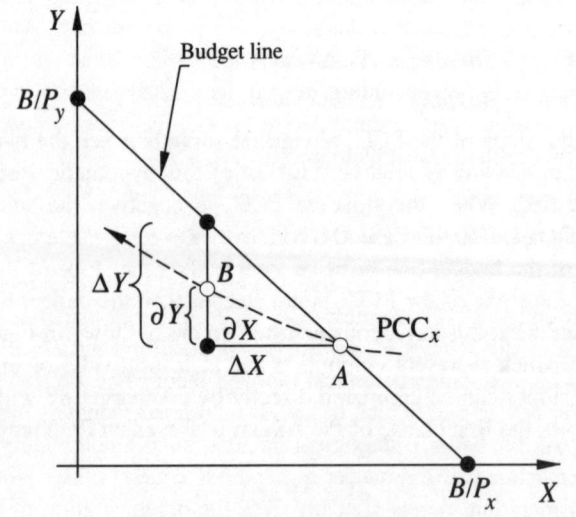

Figure 13.5b *Non-Giffen PCC*

The direct implication of this reformulation (at least in the case used here) is that demand curves as shown in Figure 13.6(a) are made impossible by the Axiom of Revealed Preference (although those as in Figure 13.6(b) are still possible).

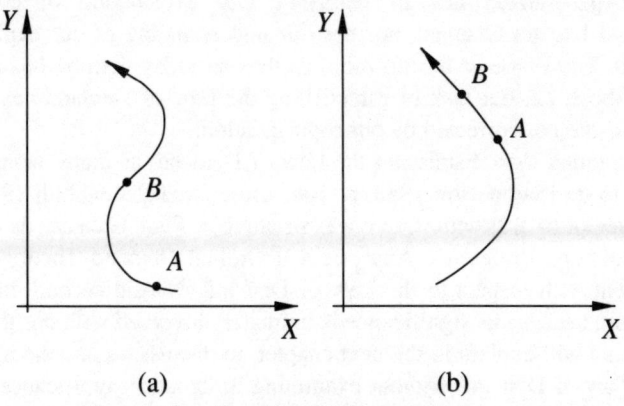

Figure 13.6 *Possible Giffen demand curves*

While this interpretation and use of the Axiom of Revealed Preference may not seem surprising on its own, it is still interesting to note that Hicks gives precisely the demand curve of Figure 13.6(a) as the *plausible* description of the case of a Giffen good [see Hicks and Allen 1934, Figure 6, p. 68]. If my interpretation of the Axiom of Revealed Preference is correct, then one can see that the axiom does say something more than the Ordinal Demand Theory (of Hicks and Allen) which alone will not exclude Giffen goods except by excluding 'inferior goods'. By adding the Axiom of Revealed Preference to Ordinal Demand Theory, however, we can get *slightly* closer to the Law of Demand.

METHODOLOGICAL EPILOGUE

Clearly, writing about a subject that has received so much attention in the past is difficult to justify. Some would accept this reconsideration if it had pedagogical utility – that is, on the presupposition that we all know all there is to know about neoclassical demand theory but we always can use some clever device with which to help teach undergraduates. I think that if there is a use for better pedagogical devices, such a potentiality reflects a poor understanding of the matter at hand. Of course, others would accept this reconsideration merely if it involves the demonstration of some new mathematical devices or techniques. Although most seem unwilling to admit it, the application of a complicated mathematical technique to a simple concept always 'costs' more than the resulting 'benefits' warrant.

The years of clothing demand theory in a mathematized fabric has left us where we began – Hicks' half of the 1934 Hicks and Allen article. All that we have to show for our heroic efforts are a few vacuous generalities such as 'the generalized law of demand'. Our explanation of consumer behaviour has not changed, nor has our understanding of our explanation changed. The Emperor has no more clothes on today than he had prior to 1934. Above all, our task of establishing the Law of Demand has neither been assisted nor corrected by our sophistication.

Now, rather than dismissing the Law of Demand, as many would seem willing to do [Samuelson 1953, p. 106; Lipsey and Rosenbluth 1971], we must attempt to deal with it, one way or another. First, because, as claimed here, Revealed Preference Analysis and Ordinal Demand Theory are not equivalent with respect to the Law of Demand.[28] And second, but more important, because its significance is intimately involved with our theory of prices, as I will explain in the next chapter, to dismiss *ad hoc* the necessity of the Law of Demand without examining its broader significance cannot help us understand economic behaviour, nor can it foster the development of 'testable' implications of neoclassical theories.

NOTES

1. For the derivation of the Slutsky equation from Revealed Preference Analysis, see McKenzie [1957] and Samuelson [1947/65, Chapter 5].
2. Samuelson calls this the 'Fundamental Theorem of Consumption Theory'.
3. See further Lipsey and Rosenbluth [1971, p. 132] and Samuelson [1947/65, p. 115, footnote 17].
4. Such a task is impossible, quite apart from the 'integrability problem', since it requires an impossibly faultless inductive logic [see further, Wong 1978].
5. For example, one person may be allowed to have a positively sloping demand curve as long as no other person does.
6. I discussed the methodology of individualism in Chapter 2, note 8 and Chapter 8, note 14. For more detail see Boland [1982a, Chapter 2].
7. Except we do exclude a change in response to any homogeneous change where all prices and income are multiplied by the same scalar.
8. Not a very 'risky' prediction, however.
9. Note that I have not included a point representing where the slope would be positive and the arrowhead would indicate a rising price. The reason is simple. Since the income and the price of Y are assumed fixed, whenever only the price of X increases, the purchasing power of the income must fall, yet the excluded point would imply the opposite, which is impossible (viz. more of both goods is bought as the price of X rises).
10. The relationship between the elasticity of the implied demand curve and the slope of the PCC is entirely mechanical. Recall that the definition of demand elasticity of good X says that if the price of good X rises by 10 percent, an elastic demand means that the consumer buys more than 10 percent *less* of good X. Since the budget (or income) and the price of good Y are fixed (by definition

of the demand curve for good X), buying more than 10 percent less of good X whose price has risen by 10 percent means that the consumer is spending less on good X. This leaves more money to be spent on good Y with its price fixed. To keep the budget fixed, the consumer must buy more of the good with the fixed price. Thus we see that at point e an increase in the price of X means that the consumer buys more Y, which fulfills the definition of a point of elastic demand.

11 Actually there are thirty cases since five of the cells represent two cases. I have represented the two alternative cases by representing one of them with dotted rather than solid lines.
12 As always, multiplying all prices and income by the same scalar does not constitute a changed situation.
13 Of course, L-orderings are excluded, too.
14 Once you know the family of PCCs for good X, you have enough information to determine the family of PCCs for good Y as well as the implicit family of ICCs. In other words, there is sufficient information in any one set of PCCs to deduce the other PCCs and thus the ICCs.
15 Specifically, in Figure 13.3 every intersection point can be represented by the solid lines of cell Cc of Figure 13.2.
16 See above, pp. 52-60.
17 They may be in some sense 'inverse demand functions' but they contain more information than a single inverted demand function.
18 The arrowhead of the ICC will always be in the shaded area.
19 Consider the location of the ICC's arrowhead in the dual-purpose cells. When considering the dotted-line PPC_y, higher income is represented by the white area demarcated by the extensions of the tail ends of the two PCC arrows. While there are parts of this area that are not 'south-west' of the intersection, if we wish to preclude the *possibility* of violation of the assumption of 'greed' it is the possibility of any higher-income points being 'south-west' of the intersection which necessitates the exclusion of cells Aa and Ee.
20 That is, the $\Delta Y/\Delta X$ needed to remain on the same indifference curve.
21 That is, $\Delta Y/\Delta X$, which is the measure of the slope of the indifference curve, must be more negative.
22 That is, we are not comparing 'goods' with 'bads'.
23 Which means that the indifference curves cannot pass through the intersection point in question and be found 'south-west'.
24 This occurs in both Hicks [1956] and [1939], which has been copied by virtually everyone who has wanted to assume the possibility of inferior goods.
25 Quite apart from the problem of induction if *we* know the consumer's preferences, they are no longer subjective.
26 This is the problem of induction – more information is required than is conceivably possible.
27 This, too, is probably arbitrary without a known map (*ex post* or *ex ante*).
28 The late Cliff Lloyd suggested to me that I have said the following. Since the Axiom of Revealed Preference implies *more* than the Slutsky relations ($S+$) and the Axiom of Revealed Preference can be deduced from Ordinal Demand Theory (ODT), then, it must be true that ODT implies $S+$, which is contrary to what seems to be the consensus concerning ODT. If Cliff was correct then we should be able, by means of the PCC analysis of this chapter, to show that ODT does imply $S+$.

14 Giffen goods vs market-determined prices

> Marshall modified his theory on two points. The first was that he slightly modified his assertion of the universality of negatively sloping demand curves and in fact introduced the Giffen paradox as an exception. The second alteration was in his treatment of consumers' surplus: 'When the total utilities of two commodities which contribute to the same purpose are calculated on this plan, we cannot say that the total utility of the two together is equal to the sum of the total utilities of each separately.'
>
> George Stigler [1950, p. 327]

The idea of the Law of Demand was commonly accepted long before Marshall mentioned the Giffen paradox. The Giffen paradox has always been interpreted as a problem for demand theorists.[1] They were required to somehow assure us that their theories of consumer behaviour imply the allegedly observed regularity of the absence of Giffen goods – that is, imply the 'universal rule' of negatively inclined demand curves. The basis of this requirement is usually viewed as a matter imposed on us by tradition or casual knowledge rather than as a matter of an interaction of demand theory with the other parts of price theory. If the Law of Demand is retained as a matter of tradition it can be callously abandoned. If it is a matter of casual knowledge we might wish to be more careful. But if it is a matter of dealing with the interaction with other parts of price theory, the Law of Demand may actually be an imperative.

With little doubt the task facing any demand theorist is to explain the quantity demanded in the market. For some the task is to go as far as explaining the lawness of the Law of Demand. If there were a problem over the insufficiency of the usual conditions placed on utility functions with respect to establishing the Law of Demand, one could simply drop all utility analysis, as was suggested long ago by Gustav Cassel. Or one could even declare the neoclassical assumptions about utility analysis to be obviously false, as some of the critics noted in Chapter 1 have done.

Tradition, casual knowledge or perhaps theoretical imperatives have ruled out these two approaches to demand theory. George Stigler, decades ago, noted that although the dictates of casual knowledge were strong enough to reject Cassel's notions on the utility of utility analysis, 'it could not reject even the imaginary Giffen paradox' [1950, p. 395]. I will argue in this chapter that the Giffen paradox is important because it is contrary to a market equilibrium theory of prices and not because it might be seen to be contrary to any theory of demand. I will discuss both aspects of the significance of Giffen goods.

The inability of demand theorists to specify conditions on utility functions or indifference maps that would preclude Giffen goods without excluding inferior goods has been a skeleton in our closet which if let out would create a scandal. In the interests of professional stability and security, the tradition has been to accept almost any *ad hoc* argument which would do the job of eliminating the logical possibility of upward sloping demand curves. All this tradition has existed without ever manifesting a clear understanding as to why they must be eliminated.

It will be argued here that the exclusion of Giffen goods is an important methodological constraint on the development of neoclassical demand theory because that theory is part of a larger theory based on the 'going prices' that are market-determined. And further, if we are free to ignore Giffen goods, then we are free to ignore the remainder of neoclassical demand theory as well. Stated another way, Giffen goods and market-determined prices do not go together. It should be recognized that, above all, neoclassical demand theory was created to explain the quantities demanded which in turn are to be used in the explanation of prices. Contrary to popular views of methodology, it is my view that neoclassical theory should be expected first to conform to the theoretical job to be done (explain prices in this case) more than to the nature of the real world that the theory intends to explain or describe. This is not to say we should ignore the 'realism of the assumptions' but that the realism is not the guiding factor in the development of neoclassical theory [Stigler 1950, pp. 394–6]. If my view is correct it means that there may be more at stake with Giffen goods than merely trying to get one logical consequence to conform to the nature of the real world.

By viewing the Law of Demand as an imperative for demand theorists we may have only two options available to us. One option is to drop all of neoclassical demand theory and start from scratch. The other option is to retain as much as possible of neoclassical theory and choose between the following: (1) an *ad hoc* exclusion of the logical possibility of Giffen goods in demand theory; or (2) an *ad hoc* dropping of any reference to market-determined prices in demand theory. The maintenance of neoclassical demand theory with either of these latter choices requires 'ad hocery'. A possible third choice might be suggested, namely, to 'rehabilitate Giffen goods' [e.g. Lipsey and Rosenbluth 1971] without giving up market-determined prices (and hence without giving up most of neoclassical theory). But this possible third option, I will argue, is self-contradictory. And furthermore, it may render neoclassical price theory untestable or, worse, irrelevant.

Any argument over the purposes of any theory in question should be resolvable merely by consulting the history of that theory. Unfortunately, demand theory has a long history involving too many contributors whose individual aims differed widely. Although economics textbooks may agree to a great extent, they still vary widely in some of the details discussed in this chapter. One could probably construct an historical, episodic account of every version of neoclassical demand theory. However, I think one could understand our present theory more clearly if one were to attempt seeing each of its details as a timely and rationalizable solution to a particular theoretical problem involving the aims of the theorist and the obstacles to fulfilling those aims. This method, called 'rational reconstruction', will be used to present neoclassical demand theory as an outcome of certain intended consequences of the problem–solution based development of that theory. Criticism and understanding in this context will always be 'internal', having to do with the chosen means of overcoming obstacles rather than be 'external' by objecting to the aims of the theorist [see Wong 1978].

So long as we find neoclassical demand theory interesting, I think the job remains to rehabilitate the Hicksian version. If this is to be done in the context of market-determined prices then some way must be found to replace John Hicks' weak argument against the existence of Giffen goods (which I discussed in Chapter 13). But since this rehabilitation may involve some 'ad hocery', I will again offer a brief digression on 'good' and 'bad' ad hocery. So as not to keep the reader in suspense, I can give the following hint: 'good' ad hocery exposes skeletons whereas 'bad' ad hocery hides them either by closing the closet door or by moving to another house (i.e. to another set of intended consequences).

A RATIONAL RECONSTRUCTION OF NEOCLASSICAL DEMAND THEORY

In this section I present my rational reconstruction of neoclassical demand theory. The overall purpose is to understand the methodological and theoretical constraints on any attempt to develop or repair neoclassical demand theory. My rational reconstruction of demand theory will lay out the logic of the situation to explain why that theory exists in its present form. In short, I will present what I think is the theoretical problem that is solved by neoclassical demand theory. I will again be concerned precisely with the allegation of Hicks that the central purpose of demand theory is to provide a rational basis for the Law of Demand [Hicks 1956, p. 59]. The issue can be put simply: in economics (or even physics) we usually call any hypothesis a 'Law' only when, if it were false, everything we consider important falls with it. For example, without the 'Law of Gravity' there would be no Newtonian physics; without the Law of Thermodynamics there would be no explanation of engines or refrigerators, and so on. In this case, without the Law of Demand, I will argue, there would be no complete theory of *market*-determined prices.

The question at issue: Why is the Law of Demand so central to demand theory? The answer, as I shall show, is simply that the Law of Demand is necessary for any neoclassical explanation which claims or assumes that all prices are exclusively determined by market equilibria. In other words, the Law is necessary for the completion of each and every neoclassical explanation. It will be a sufficient argument that any criticism of the Law of Demand (or of the non-existence of Giffen goods) must be a criticism of the entire neoclassical demand theory if it can be shown (1) that the Law of Demand is necessarily true whenever the neoclassical theory of market prices is true and (2) that together the basic assumptions of neoclassical demand theory are sufficient but individually are not necessary for the explanation of consumer demand. Moreover, it will be apparent that the basic assumptions exist in neoclassical demand theory only by virtue of the necessity of the Law of Demand. A corollary is thus that any criticism of market-determined prices is also a criticism of the necessity of the *entire* theory and its use as a basis for understanding the economy.

Walrasian stability and Marshallian stability

I begin now by showing why I think the Law of Demand is a necessity whenever we wish to explain prices as being determined in the market. The basic focus of neoclassical price theory is to explain why the price of any good is what it is *and* not what it is not. The neoclassical reason given is that the price of any good is a market *equilibrium* price, which is to say, if for any reason the price were higher than it is now it would fall back to the equilibrium level (and rise when it is lower). This raises certain questions which are essentially about specifying requirements for a successful 'equilibrium explanation'. The first requirement is simply a set of reasons why the price must fall when it is higher (and rise when it is lower) than the 'equilibrium level'.

200 *Principles of economics*

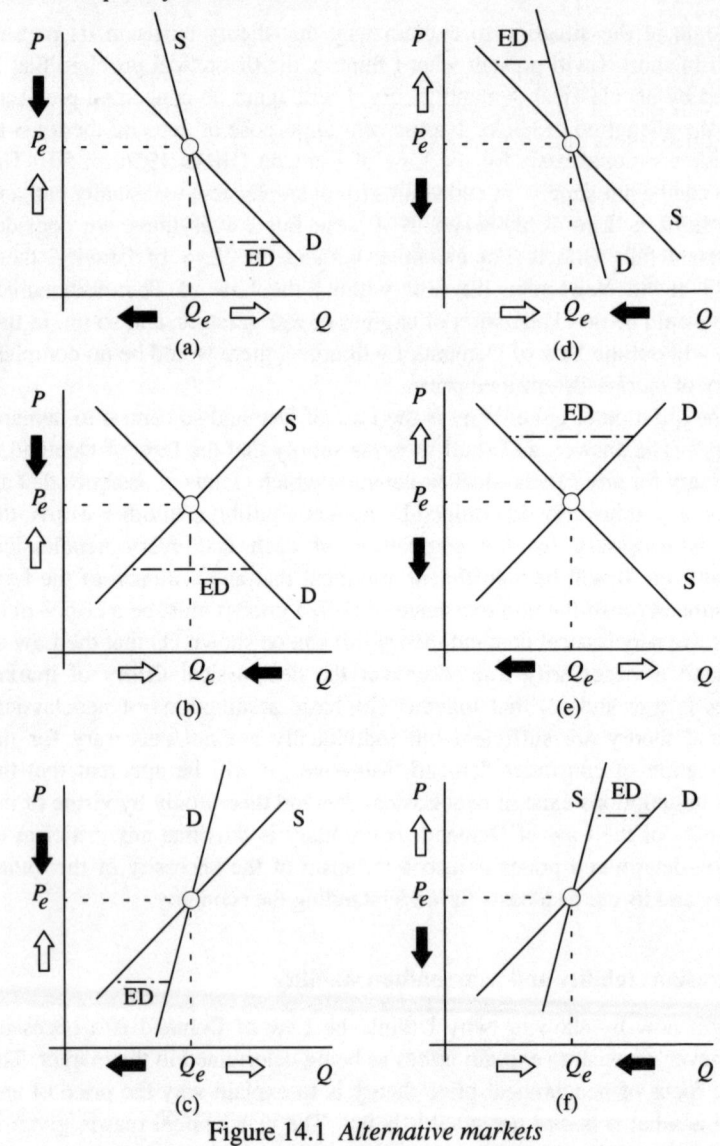

Figure 14.1 *Alternative markets*

The reasons usually given broadly define what is traditionally called 'Walrasian stability'. Specifically, it is claimed that the world is such that:

(1) Any time the quantity supplied exceeds demand, there is at least one person, a seller who will offer to sell at a lower price to achieve his or her own goals (and when demand exceeds supply, a buyer will offer a

higher price) *and*

(2) Any time the going price is greater than the equilibrium price there will exist a situation where supply exceeds demand (and when the price is less there will be excess demand).

Walrasian stability then involves these two behavioural *assumptions* about the nature of the real world, neither of which is necessary or sufficient for the question[2] but it can be argued that they are together sufficient. They hang together. One can only criticize their sufficiency,[3] which is always easy, much easier than criticizing their necessity.[4] What, then, are the implicit assumptions that underlie the presumed sufficiency of these behavioural assumptions, (1) and (2)?

The first behavioural assumption is seldom suspect, it is merely accepted either as a direct behavioural assumption or as a definition of competition which is assumed to exist. The second can be rationalized, that is, we can give a rational argument for why, when the going price is greater than the equilibrium price, there will exist an excess supply. To understand this second behavioural assumption we need to examine the logic of the situation. Consider the following question. If our assumptions are true then what logically *possible* states of the world are thereby claimed *not* to represent the real world? To answer this question I note that there are six possible situations that might be found in the world, that is, six combinations of demand and supply curves, as shown in Figure 14.1.[5]

In a Walrasian world the behavioural assumption (1) will work to promote equilibrium only if the assumption (2) is true, that is, only if the world is not like situations (d), (e) or (f) of Figure 14.1. Thus assumption (2) implicitly asserts that the world is like (a), (b) or (c). Now without support assumption (2) becomes a mere *ad hoc* empirical assumption about the real world. To avoid the ad hocery, we must be able to explain why the relative slopes of the demand and supply curves are as indicated in (a), (b) or (c) and not like (d), (e) or (f). This *might* require a joint explanation of demand and supply. Such a joint explanation is precluded by the ideology behind much of neoclassical theory, viz. *laissez-faire* individualism where all individuals, whether buyers or sellers, must be independent. Particularly, demand must be independent of supply. Without our providing a joint explanation, assumption (2) is simply an *ad hoc* attempt to save the equilibrium theory of prices. And furthermore, without a joint explanation, there is no way to distinguish worlds (a) and (d), or (c) and (f), without violating the independence of buyers' and sellers' decision-making. In these cases, demand and supply are both negatively or both positively sloped and, to distinguish (a) from (d) or (c) from (f), one has to specify which curve is steeper.[6]

Fortunately, there could be another way to avoid this ad hocery. Implicit in the neoclassical theory of the competitive firm there is an additional equilibrium theory, namely, Marshall's theory of quantity adjustment which is formally the same as that described so far for prices. In the Walrasian view of stability we have one price and two different quantities, the quantity demanded and the quantity supplied. In Marshall's theory of the firm we find one quantity (the supply) and two prices, the offering price (which is the price at which all demanders would be maximizing their utility with their contribution to the market demand) and the asking price (which is merely the marginal cost of the quantity being supplied by the firm). Thus, it can be shown that

(1′) Any time the quantity bought and sold in the market, Q, is greater than the equilibrium quantity, Q_e, the quantity will fall (when less, the quantity will rise).

This follows directly from the neoclassical theory of the firm. For example, if the offering price is greater than the asking price, the firm will increase its output to increase its profit.[7] To form a sufficient argument for a so-called Marshallian stability of the equilibrium quantities, the real world must be such that

(2′) Any time $Q>Q_e$ the asking price must be greater than the offering price (and when $Q<Q_e$, the asking price must be less).

This assertion about the nature of the real world is similar to the one made to define Walrasian stability, and needs likewise to be rationally supported or to be acceptably *ad hoc*. To assure Marshallian stability, another empirical assumption is thus required, namely, one that would now assure that the market situation in the real world not be like (a), (c) or (e) of Figure 14.1 and that the real world is like (b), (d) or (f). Now it turns out that by itself this Marshallian assertion about the nature of the real world would require an argument involving the joint behaviour of demand and supply prices similar to the previous discussion. Note also that there is something else in common between the two market equilibrium theories: they both exclude the possibility of the world being like situation (e) of Figure 14.1 and both allow situation (b). If we could independently argue why the world is like (b) and is not like (a), (c), (d), (e) or (f), we then could avoid the ad hocery of asserting Walrasian stability or its counterpart in terms of quantity, Marshallian stability. Such is the task of our independent theories of demand and of supply. Situation (b) is merely a joint statement of the Law of Demand and an analogous Law of Supply, which says that as the price rises the quantity demanded must always be falling and the quantity supplied must always be rising. If an explanation of the Law of Demand can be given independently of an explanation for the Law of Supply, then ad hocery can be avoided and prices be explained as market-determined without the risk of condoning a methodologically dangerous interaction between any buyer and any seller, as such interaction might undermine the virtues of a competitive price system.[8]

It may be distasteful for recently trained economists to admit that there is a lot of silly philosophy underlying ordinary neoclassical economics, but I think such is the case. It is seldom recognized because our textbooks try to socialize us into believing that our theories are merely descriptions of the real world and those theories were actually derived from observations of the real world, or worse, it is all a game of logic and language, of *a priori* assumptions and all that. To some extent all theories are descriptions but only to the extent that they are empirical. Of course, anyone can make an empirical statement without deriving it from the real world; for example, by conjecture or by accident. Moreover, not all empirical statements are true. The Law of Demand has always been a fiction (abstraction, non-description, generalization, etc.) to the extent that we present it as an inductively proven empirical truth instead of a possible empirical challenge to our understanding of prices.

In spite of the long history of believing in the empirical fact of the Law of Demand, I think it should be obvious that the necessity of the Law of Demand for an explanation of equilibrium prices is the outcome of avoiding either ad hocery or undesirable ideological implications of our theory, or both. But my argument intends to go further by showing that neoclassical demand theory can be rationally reconstructed *only* if we see that theory as an attempt to rationalize the Law of Demand.

There is only one fundamental behavioural assumption made about the process of consumption, namely, that consumers are maximizing utility (or, which amounts to the same thing, choosing the 'best' bundle). The rest of the assumptions are made in an attempt to facilitate the conjunction of the maximization assumption and the Law of Demand. To facilitate the maximization assumption we use assumptions which limit the shape of the assumed utility function or preference ordering (e.g. greed, diminishing MRS, transitivity, continuity, etc.). But as discussed in Chapter 13, these assumptions are usually insufficient to rule out the logical possibility of Giffen goods – that is, the demand curves could be upward sloping without violating the axioms of consumer theory. Several additional assumptions have been attempted. All seem to be unsatisfactory for one reason or another.

As was seen in Chapter 13, the most effective way to rule out Giffen goods is to rule out 'inferior goods'. Of course, this is unsatisfactory because it does too much. It is a case which Martin Hollis and Edward Nell

[1975, p. 61] describe as solving a New York City slum problem by redefining the city boundaries. Another *ad hoc* method considered has been to require the satisfaction of the Axiom of Revealed Preference which, as I have shown in Chapter 13, does not rule out entirely Giffen goods although it does limit them somewhat. Unfortunately, the limits placed on the slope of the demand curve are insufficient to assure that the market demand curve intersects the market supply curve as shown in case (b) of Figure 14.1 and thereby leaves open the question of market stability. Thus it might seem that we must choose between *ad hoc* eliminations of inferior goods or *ad hoc* assertions that markets are stable.

The imperatives of demand theory

Now I would like to present neoclassical demand theory in a slightly different way to show why it is important to avoid this choice problem. The central question of neoclassical demand theory is: Why is the quantity demanded at the going price what it is? And why would that quantity demanded fall if the price rose? To be neoclassical it is required that the theory of demand not only assume maximizing behaviour but that it be consistent with *laissez-faire* individualism, that is, with the philosophy that everyone *should* make independent rational decisions in the market – or as, Voltaire said in *Candide*, we should till our own gardens. As noted above, this leads us to argue that, to assure Marshallian and Walrasian stability, the real world would have to be like (b) of Figure 14.1 since that would allow us to explain demand and supply independently. That is, if we have separate arguments for why demand curves are always negatively sloped and for why supply curves are always upwardly sloped, then we would never have to consider a violation of the independence of the decision-makers. Without the 'always' we could never rationally reconstruct demand theory.

This then is the task facing any neoclassical demand theorist: to give reasons why the Law of Demand is true without assuming anything which would have us violate the rationality or the independence prescribed by *laissez-faire* individualism. However, there is a slight complication. The arguments about stability are relevant for *market* demand curves, and neoclassical demand theory is about the behaviour of the *individual* consumer. Thus we have an added problem facing the demand theorist. The reasons given for the slope of the market demand curve must be seen as a consequence of the individuals' demand curves. On the surface this would seem to allow much more latitude for maintaining independence of consumers' decisions, but that latitude would be at the expense of the strength of our arguments for the Law of Demand. Specifically we say that the quantity demanded is the aggregate effect of all the individual consumers' rational attempts to maximize their (independent) personal utility.

It is a sufficient argument that if *all* individual demand curves are negatively sloped their aggregation, the market demand curve, will also be negatively sloped. If one could show that rational maximization necessarily leads to negatively sloped *individual* demand curves, then the central task of demand theory would be fulfilled. Unfortunately, that has not yet been shown by anyone. But, the question might be asked, is it necessary for all individuals to have negatively sloped demand curves? The obvious response would be to say 'No' [see Lloyd 1967, p. 24; De Alessi 1968, pp. 290–1]. For example, one or two demanders could easily have upward sloping demand curves, yet in the aggregation the negative slope of all the other demanders could cancel out the positive slope. Unfortunately, that reasonable response leads to problems over the independence of the demanders themselves.

Let me try to explain. Say there are N demanders whose respective demands at the going price are d_1, d_2, d_3 ... d_m, d_{m+1} ... d_{N-1}, d_N. And say that the first m demanders, who respectively demand d_1 through d_m, each have negatively sloped demand curves and that demanders of d_{m+1} through d_{N-1} have upward sloped demand curves such that a slight change in price would leave the aggregate demand of the $N-1$ demanders unchanged (the positive and negative slopes just cancel out). If this market is to be both Marshallian and Walrasian stable and preserve the independence of suppliers and demanders, then the Nth demander's behaviour is no longer independent of the other $N-1$ demanders. This is because to avoid an embarrassing contradiction of the philosophically desirable independence between suppliers and demanders, the Nth demander's demand curve must be negatively sloped.[9] It clearly would be best if *all* individuals' demand curves could be shown to be negatively sloped as a consequence of the logic of their *individual* situations, namely, as a result of their *rational* maximization and the *nature* of their situational constraints.

AD HOCERY VS TESTABILITY

I now turn to some general questions of methodology that are raised in this consideration of Giffen goods. What is the difference between (1) straightforwardly ruling out Giffen goods as Cassel [1918] or Moore [1929] might, and (2) setting out a group of assumptions (with, or within, the theory) which if taken together logically exclude Giffen goods as Hicks [1956] tried to do? Is this merely the difference between 'good' and 'bad' ad hocery?

It must be realized that to a certain extent both options are *ad hoc*. Every assumption is *ad hoc* in one sense. If an assumption is formally a strictly universal proposition (e.g. 'all swans are white') it cannot be empirically demonstrated to be true even if it is true. Hence, assuming it to be true without such a demonstration of its truth can be viewed as being *ad hoc*. It is *ad hoc* merely because it may be necessary or sufficient for the theory in which it is assumed. Since all assumptions, all observations, are in some way dependent on the acceptance of certain universals, the acceptance of assumptions, theories and observations is in this sense *ad hoc*. Ad hocery in this fundamental sense can neither be criticized nor recommended (because the criticism or recommendation would also be *ad hoc* in the same sense). The ad hocery that might be criticized is that which arises when counter-examples are arbitrarily ruled out when the theorist narrows the 'applicability' of his or her theory – for example, by assuming that our theory applies only to 'normal goods'. Such ad hocery might be criticized because it avoids criticism or it handicaps the theorist's understanding of the objects of his or her study. In general, we can say that any ad hocery which reduces the testability of a theory is considered 'bad' by most theorists today. Conversely, any ad hocery which increases the testability is considered 'good'.

The question arises as to how one increases the testability of a theory. I have previously dealt with the subject of how model-building assumptions can affect testability [Boland 1989, Chapters 2 and 3] where I have set out an analysis of the ingredients of a model (viz. the number of parameters, standard-form coefficients, exogenous variables, endogenous variables, etc.) and demonstrated a measure of a model's testability such that it is possible to say when a model is 'more testable'. The basic idea is that the more information needed to test a newly modified model than was needed without the modification, the less testable the model becomes. Such a modification would constitute 'bad' ad hocery. Testability, however, need not be viewed as an *ad hoc* test of ad hocery. Testability is closely linked with the explanatory power of any theory, or with its empirical 'meaningfulness' as followers of Paul Samuelson's methodology [1947/65] like to say. An *ad hoc* specification of a theory which would make it possible to test the theory with less information would be considered an improvement – that is, it would be 'good' ad hocery. Testability, however, can only be viewed as a means to an end, never as an end in itself. Even when the good *ad hoc* modification produces a model which turns out to be false (when tested), we still do not know whether it is the modification or it is something in the original model which is yielding the contradictions between the modified model and the test evidence.[10]

Now *ad hoc* modifications such as limiting the applicability of a model or theory not only increase the amount of information needed to test the model (since we would now also need to know the 'applicability' of the model), they also insulate the model from empirical criticisms. If our objective in constructing a model or theory is to understand the subject in question (e.g. consumer behaviour) then, as most followers of Samuelson's methodology realize, our understanding must deny the existence of something in the real world. If our understanding is to be an improvement over past understanding the new understanding must contradict some of the old understanding. Any *ad hoc* modification which avoids such contradictions can only be a loss, a backward step.

In summary, *ad hoc* specifications that limit further the conceivable states of the real world (which possibly can be compatible with the model or theory) are 'good' since they increase testability. *Ad hoc* specifications which increase the content by increasing the number of exogenous variables that might affect the determination of the endogenous variables can also increase the testability since more possible counter-examples can be deduced from the model and thus be used as indirect tests of the model.

With regard to the *ad hoc* models of consumer theory being considered in this and the previous chapter, we can say the following: Hicks' assumption that extremely inferior goods are less likely than slightly inferior goods is probably false. But that does not jeopardize the original consumer theory if it is still possible to exclude Giffen goods by specifying directly the nature of preferences. However, all specifications of preferences need not be improvements. Some of the specifications may increase the 'likelihood' of Giffen goods, but those specifications which do increase the 'likelihood' may themselves be 'unlikely', since they may be very special (*ad hoc*) cases.[11]

GIFFEN GOODS AND THE TESTABILITY OF DEMAND THEORY

A couple decades ago the issue of the testability of demand theory itself was actually publicly debated. The debaters were Cliff Lloyd [1965, 1969] and Gordon Welty [1969]. The importance of Giffen goods for the testability of demand theory was only implicitly raised in their debate. However, Giffen goods were the explicit topic of Welty's [1971] critique of Louis De Alessi's [1968] views on the Giffen paradox. I will comment here on the Welty–Lloyd debate and Welty's critique of De Alessi's views in hopes of furthering the understanding of the significance of Giffen goods or upward sloping demand curves.

Lloyd [1965] discusses the general issue of the falsifiability of demand theory. Lloyd seems to think that 'traditional demand theory' can be tested. For him a prerequisite of testability would be falsifiability. He outlines what he considers to be testable 'implications' of demand theory. Basically, if one can determine whether a good is not an inferior good, we can test the Slutsky equation (which presumes maximization of utility). An upward sloping demand curve for a non-inferior good is clearly contrary to traditional demand theory. Whether one can actually test demand theory in this case would depend on the acceptance of the conventions used to establish the non-inferiority of the good in question and to measure the slope of the demand curve. The test will only be as good as the testing conventions used. But, as a matter of logic, Lloyd argues that demand theory is falsifiable, hence not untestable for reasons of internal logic of the individual consumer.

Many economists may think that limiting any testing of demand theory to non-inferior goods renders the theory irrefutable. As De Alessi put it in 1968,

> The theoretical admission that the income effect may dominate the substitution effect in the case of inferior goods implies that the demand curve of an individual, derived holding money income constant, may be either positively or negatively sloped; it follows that the sign of the slope of the corresponding aggregate demand curve is also indeterminate, and thus cannot be refuted by experience. [p. 287]

If Lloyd's proposed test is only a test of an individual's behaviour, De Alessi claims,

> Under no circumstances a single observation pertaining to a single individual would provide a test of any economic hypothesis. [p. 290]

And further,

> in the final analysis, ... economists accept negatively sloped demand curves ... because empirical evidence suggests that negatively sloped demand curves work. [p. 291]

It seems that De Alessi sides with George Stigler [1950] in accepting negatively sloped demand curves as a fact until hard evidence to the contrary is provided. And until this occurs, the job of any demand theorist is to explain the implicit regularity – the non-existence of Giffen goods. De Alessi suggests a possible modification of traditional demand theory.[12]

Welty argues that Lloyd and De Alessi are both wrong as the former's testing conventions and the latter's modification would each make the traditional theory unfalsifiable. The basis of Welty's critique of Lloyd is the role of *ceteris paribus* clauses and to what extent such clauses refer to unspecified variables. If one were to say the Law of Demand is true *ceteris paribus* then one could always use the *ceteris paribus* clause as an escape hatch to avoid almost any conceivable refutation.[13]

Welty's arguments concerning *ceteris paribus* clauses are based on a simple matter of logic. Adding extra clauses to any theory can insulate that theory from refutation. By the well known property of logic called *modus tollens*, we know that a false conclusion derived from a valid logical argument implies the existence of at least one false statement contained in that argument. Unfortunately, *modus tollens* cannot usually indicate which statement (of the valid argument) is false. If the argument consists of the original theory plus some additional clauses, then a false conclusion (or prediction) does not tell us whether it is the original theory or the added clause which is at fault.[14] However, if the added clause can be independently tested, then this matter of logic – the ambiguity of *modus tollens* – need not concern us.[15]

Implicit in this debate and criticism is the view that the existence of the possibility of deducing upward sloping demand curves from a given theory of the consumer is evidence of the failure of demand theory. Not everyone would accept this view. Many seem to think that neoclassical (microeconomic) consumer theory can be refuted without negating either the Law of Demand or neoclassical price theory. For example, observance of conceivable counter-evidence would lead Lloyd to reject Ordinal Demand Theory, yet, as he said, there are an infinity of possible theories of the consumer. What one replaces it with need not be anything like the original consumer theory. However, the given refuting evidence would now have to be explained by the replacement. Lloyd's notion of convincing refuting evidence is the observation of upward sloping demand curves for non-inferior goods (as well as Giffen goods). But, if my arguments in this chapter are correct, his counter-evidence would overturn neoclassical price theory as well. Of course, neoclassical price theory can be false and the traditional demand theory true without any need for *ad hoc* modifications. In this case the indeterminacy that De Alessi and others point out would not matter. It would not matter because if price theory were false and Giffen goods were considered possible, demand theory would no longer be interesting as it would not have any intellectual purpose. However, in this latter case, if price theory is false, there are no market-determined prices in the neoclassical sense.

In the absence of a successful test of demand theory as suggested by Lloyd, what are we to conclude? Should we accept *ad hoc* modifications in order to explain the presumed regularity inferred from the absence of conclusive evidence of the Giffen paradox? De Alessi seems to think we should. Others such as Stigler can argue that there is no independent evidence of such a regularity either and thus we can drop the necessity of being able to deduce only negatively sloped demand curves. Welty seems to think that such a weak approach would make demand theory untestable but his conclusion is based on what may be a mistake, the alleged indeterminacy of the slope of the demand curve. Lloyd and others have shown, however, that the slope may always be determinate. It is only that the slope is indeterminate with the *a priori* conditions placed on utility functions or indifference maps.

CONCLUDING REMARKS

This brings us full circle. I have argued that the Giffen paradox is contrary to our market equilibrium theory of prices. Apart from our neoclassical price theory, the existence of the Giffen paradox would not be a refutation of consumer theory. Lloyd's positively sloped individual demand curve for a non-inferior good would be a refutation of both traditional consumer and traditional price theories, but that is still not a case of a Giffen good in the Hicksian sense. Giffen goods themselves are still consistent with Ordinal Demand Theory. The problem is that Ordinal Demand Theory which allows Giffen goods may not be consistent with our individualist theory of market prices.

If the existence of Giffen goods has never been empirically established then a realistic theory of demand should at least explain the fact of their non-existence. Any demand theory which does not explain that 'fact' (if it is agreed that it is a fact) has not done its empirical job, let alone whether or not it has done its intellectual job with regard to explaining the demand side of price theory consistent with *laissez-faire* individualism. More subtly, in any given demand theory, if Giffen goods are allowed as a possibility for the individual but not for the aggregate demand curve, then such a theory puts the desired independence of decision-makers into jeopardy whenever market-determined prices are to be the 'given prices' upon which the individual consumers base their demand decisions. If Giffen goods are allowed in consumer theory but not in price theory, then some explanation must be provided concerning the given income distribution. That is to say, we would have to explain why income is sufficiently well distributed such that the kind of income–expenditure situation Hicks and Marshall describe for the Giffen paradox could never occur. Of course, that theory of income distribution must also avoid contradictions with our *laissez-faire* individualism. If the so-called Cambridge controversy over capital and distribution is any indication, the possibility of such a neutral theory of income distribution does not seem promising.

NOTES

1. It should again be noted that Marshall's concern for Giffen goods was due to doubts not about his theory of demand but instead about the ability to calculate consumers' surplus since such a calculation would require a downward sloping demand curve [see further Dooley 1983].
2. For example, we could have publicly or privately administered prices. And with (1) excess demand does not necessarily lead to a rising price without someone having the notion that by raising the price the situation will somehow be improved.
3. The existence of a counter-example (a case where the world is as described here, but there still is no movement toward equilibrium) will be sufficient evidence for the insufficiency of the combination of (1) and (2). Their necessity has never been asserted except by those who might wish to claim that is the way the world *should* be.
4. To successfully criticize the necessity we would have to produce a successful theory that did not explicitly or implicitly use both of these assumptions (1) and (2).
5. I will ignore the cases that cannot be represented as 'well defined functions' (viz. vertical and horizontal lines) and those cases of parallel demand and supply curves which imply a covariance that would contradict independent decision-making.
6. For example, if both curves are positively sloped (e.g. a case involving a Giffen good), Walrasian stability would not be assured if the market is characterized as case (f). Thus we must be able to explain why the supply curve will be steeper than the demand curve as in case (c).
7. In other words, if the price is above marginal cost, the firm will increase the quantity produced.
8. It is interesting to note that one can argue that both Marshall and Walras used both stability concepts. So-called Walrasian stability must hold in the short run and Marshallian stability in the long run [see Davies 1963]. In this light, note also that most neoclassical arguments involving prices in applied economics presume the existence of a long-run equilibrium. And since the long run is but a special short-run equilibrium, both stability conditions must hold in applied neoclassical economics based on market-determined prices. Some Post-Keynesian economists may wish to dismiss the long-run aspect but the fulfillment of Marshallian stability is already built into the neoclassical short-run theory of supply. Other more mathematically minded economists may argue that neither condition needs to hold if one merely adds an appropriate time-differential function for price changes to assure convergence to an equilibrium price over time. The stability of such a market determination of price depends entirely on an *arbitrarily* chosen coefficient representing the speed of response [see Lancaster 1968, p. 201]. For a discussion of the methodological problem posed by this *ad hoc* dynamics strategy, see Boland [1986a, Chapter 9].
9. Or at least not positively sloped if the supply curve is not vertical. Note that the argument would hold even if we were only concerned with one type of stability as we would still have to distinguish between (a) and (d) or between (c) and (e) of Figure 14.1.
10. For a discussion of using models to test theory, see further Boland [1989, Chapters 1 and 7].

11 In particular, Lipsey and Rosenbluth [1971] argue that Giffen goods are more likely when we base utility on 'characteristics' rather than the goods themselves. Unfortunately, they use Lancaster's *linear* model of the relationship between goods and characteristics and it is the linearity *alone* which produces their result. There are many possible non-linear models of characteristics production which would yield the Hicksian conclusions concerning 'likelihood'.

12 He suggests that we assume that 'individual utility functions [are such] that the absolute value of the deduced income effect is less than the absolute value of the deduced substitution effect in the case of inferior goods' [De Alessi 1968, p. 293]. This would seem to be as testable as Lloyd's considerations, only a little more complicated.

13 For example, the Giffen paradox can be avoided by assuming *ceteris paribus* the constancy of the marginal utility of money and then with an additive utility function using diminishing marginal utility we can explain the Law of Demand. Any substitution as the result of a change in price would change the marginal utility of money, hence rendering this theory of demand untestable. With regard to such counter-critical uses of *ceteris paribus* clauses Welty would be quite correct but Lloyd does not use *ceteris paribus* in this manner.

14 In philosophy literature, this is known as the 'Duhem–Quine' thesis, see further, Boland [1989, Chapter 7].

15 De Alessi's added clause might not be independently testable or it might only be more difficult to test than other statements contained in the traditional theory (such as the fixity of money income, fixity of prices of other goods, etc.). On this matter De Alessi's modification may not seem to be very problematic. The only criticism Welty can give reduces to the accusation that De Alessi offers a 'demonstrably arbitrary' modification of traditional demand theory. That is, De Alessi's modification is *ad hoc*.

Epilogue

Learning economic theory through criticism

Some opponents of neoclassical economics will complain that my exploration of ways to criticize neoclassical theories was not exhaustive. I welcome them to take up any other line of criticism they might have in mind. My interest has been to develop a clear understanding of neoclassical theory by determining the essential ideas that are used to form *any* neoclassical explanation. Trying to pin down the essential ideas is sometimes difficult because neoclassical economics always seems to be a moving target. I remember conversations (arguments?) with radical Marxist students in the 1960s who often would claim to have the definitive critique of neoclassical economics. Whenever they explained their criticism to me it always seemed that they were criticizing economics as it was understood about 1870. These conversations convinced me that if the critics really wanted to form effective criticisms of neoclassical economics they should learn more about how neoclassical economics is understood today. The more they understand neoclassical economics the better will be their critiques. The fear in the 1960s was always that one would be indoctrinated if one went through a formal process of learning neoclassical economics. Indoctrination might be possible but nevertheless I cannot see how one can form an effective criticism of neoclassical economics without a clear understanding of neoclassical theory.

When it comes down to its essential ideas, neoclassical economics seems now to have settled down into the clear research programme which was fairly well defined in the 1930s. Of course, the techniques of modelling neoclassical theories have changed significantly over the last fifty years and it is all too easy to confuse advancements in techniques with improvements in essential ideas. While some of the rhetoric is different, there are two identifiable streams. On the one hand there is the approach of Marshall and his followers. On the other there is the one developed by Hicks and Samuelson which follows Walras. Both are based on the neoclassical maximization assumption. Both are concerned with the necessary conditions which follow from the existence of a competitive equilibrium. While over the years the means of determining the necessary conditions have varied widely, the necessary conditions of interest are the same for both.

The source of the necessary conditions is the maximization assumption and the details are due to the particular *form* assumed for the objective functions (utility or profit). But Marshall, the mathematician, had a deeper understanding of necessary conditions than mere technical questions concerning the form of the objective functions. The questions that have preoccupied the followers of Walras are almost exclusively concerned with what assumptions one must make about the form of the objective functions to assure an equilibrium. Marshall clearly understood that one cannot explain an individual's behaviour as a matter of *choosing* the optimum unless there is sufficient freedom to choose other options. This he expressed with his Principle of Continuity which is a reflection of his approach that focuses on the necessary conditions by analyzing the calculus-based neighbourhood properties of any equilibrium. For Marshall the idea of the availability of alternative options translates into the requirement of a continuum of options. So, from Marshall's perspective, one says that one *understands* phenomenon X because one has assumed that X is the logical result of maximization given that the decision-makers had numerous alternative options from which to choose. Moreover, prices must matter in the individual's choice if the logic of the choice process is to be used to explain prices. If one's choice is limited to an extreme point on the continuum then one can explain the choice without reference to prices and thus prices do not matter. Clearly, one cannot explain or understand prices with a model in which prices might not matter!

Marshall's [1920/49, p. 449] understanding that one cannot generally assume that knowledge is perfect implicitly recognizes that knowledge is important. Yet few if any neoclassical models try to explain how the maximizing individual decision-maker knows the prices or income or even knows the utility or profit functions. Attempts to give a neoclassical explanation of knowledge by explaining the economics of information [e.g. Stigler 1961] begs the question of how information becomes knowledge – do we always have to assume knowledge is acquired inductively?

Leaving aside the difficult question of explaining knowledge, to what extent do we understand fundamental things like prices with neoclassical models? If our understanding is that all prices are general *equilibrium* prices then at least logically the explanatory basis will be adequate but only if those prices are the only prices implied by our model. This raises the old problem of whether one must require uniqueness or completeness in models. If we are only interested in local maximization then a successful neoclassical model would seem not to require uniqueness or completeness. But the question remains whether a neoclassical model based on local maximization can be a basis for *understanding* why prices are what they are and not what they are not. Unless one has shown that the prices are consistent with global maximization the possibility exists that there are multiple local optimal prices that could have been obtained. Whenever there are many possible sets of general equilibrium prices within an offered explanatory model, the question is begged as to why the world faces the one set of equilibrium prices rather than any other logically possible set of equilibrium prices. If we understand prices by being able to explain them then the basis of our explanation is a critical issue. The basis for understanding is not just the neoclassical maximization hypothesis but, I am arguing, it also includes the assertion that those are the only possible prices.

What I am saying here about the requirement of understanding is not widely accepted by economic theorists today. This is partly because most economists today think that if there is any problem with neoclassical economics it is most likely a technical modelling issue. Few economists think there is anything fundamentally wrong with their notion of explanation or understanding. Unfortunately, if the question of uniqueness and completeness is considered to be a mere technical modelling question, it can be dismissed since any model which might provide uniqueness or completeness is usually 'intractable'. So much for tractable models! The question I ask is just how do we understand prices?

Put in more methodological terms, how do we know when a neoclassical explanation of price is false? If we say we *understand* prices with a neoclassical explanation then conceivably we must be recognizing the possibility that such an explanation could be false – otherwise it would be a vacuous tautology! Any claim that says you know why the world is what it is must entail an assertion that you know why the world is not what it is not. Whenever people claim to have explained something, the challenge is for them to explain what evidence it would take for them to admit that their explanation is false (if it is false). This is my challenge to believers in neoclassical economic explanations of prices. What would neoclassical economists accept as a situation that would force them to admit that they might not actually understand why prices are what they are?

Bibliography

Agassi, J. [1963] *Towards an Historiography of Science, History and Theory, Beiheft 2* (The Hague: Mouton)
Agassi, J. [1966] Confusion between science and technology in the standard philosophies of science, *Technology and Culture*, 7, 348–66
Agassi, J. [1969] Unity and diversity in science, in R. Cohen and M. Wartofsky (eds) *Boston Studies in the Philosophy of Science*, 4 (New York: Humanities Press), 463–522
Agassi, J. [1974] Institutional individualism, *British Journal of Sociology*, 26, 144–55
Allen, R.G.D. [1950] The substitution effect in value theory, *Economic Journal*, 60, 675–85
Archibald, G.C. and Lipsey, R. [1958] Monetary and value theory: a critique of Lange and Patinkin, *Review of Economic Studies*, 27, 1–22
Arrow, K. [1951/63] *Social Choice and Individual Values* (New York: Wiley)
Arrow, K. [1959a] Rational choice functions and orderings, *Economica* (NS), 26, 121–7
Arrow, K. [1959b] Towards a theory of price adjustment, in M. Abramovitz (ed) *Allocation of Economic Resources* (Stanford: Stanford University Press), 41–51
Arrow, K. [1962] The economic implications of learning by doing, *Review of Economic Studies*, 29, 155–73
Arrow, K. [1974] *Limits of organization* (New York: Norton)
Arrow, K. and G. Debreu [1954] Existence of an equilibrium for a competitive economy, *Econometrica*, 22, 265–90
Arrow, K. and F. Hahn [1971] *General Competitive Analysis* (San Francisco: Holden-Day)
Barro, R. and H. Grossman [1971] A general disequilibrium model of income and employment, *American Economic Review*, 61, 82–93
Baumol, W. [1977] *Economic Theory and Operations Analysis*, 4th edn (Englewood Cliffs: Prentice Hall)
Bear D. and D. Orr [1967] Logic and expediency in economic theorizing, *Journal of Political Economy*, 75, 188–96
Becker, G. [1962] Irrational behavior and economic theory, *Journal of Political Economy*, 70, 1–13
Becker, G. [1976] *The Economic Approach to Human Behavior* (Chicago: University of Chicago Press)
Blanché, R. [1965] *Axiomatics* (New York: The Free Press of Glencoe)

Boland, L. [1970] Axiomatic analysis and economic understanding, *Australian Economic Papers*, 9, 62–75

Boland, L. [1971] An institutional theory of economic technology and change, *Philosophy of the Social Sciences*, 1, 253–8

Boland, L. [1974] Lexicographic orderings, multiple criteria, and 'ad hocery', *Australian Economic Papers*, 13, 152–7

Boland, L. [1975] The law of demand, weak axiom of revealed preference and price–consumption curves, *Australian Economic Papers*, 14, 104–19

Boland, L. [1977] Giffen goods, market prices and testability, *Australian Economic Papers*, 16, 72–85

Boland, L. [1979a] A critique of Friedman's critics, *Journal of Economic Literature*, 17, 503–22

Boland, L. [1979b] Knowledge and the role of institutions in economic theory, *Journal of Economic Issues*, 8, 957–72

Boland, L. [1981] On the futility of criticizing the neoclassical maximization hypothesis, *American Economic Review*, 71, 1031–6

Boland, L. [1982a] *The Foundations of Economic Method* (London: Geo. Allen & Unwin)

Boland, L. [1982b] 'Difficulties with the element of Time' and the 'Principles' of economics or some lies my teachers told me, *Eastern Economic Journal*, 3, 47–58

Boland, L. [1985] The foundations of Keynes' methodology: the *General Theory*, in T. Lawson and H. Pesaran [1985], 181–94

Boland, L. [1986a] *Methodology for a New Microeconomics* (Boston: Allen & Unwin)

Boland, L. [1986b] Methdology and the individual decision-maker, in I. Kirzner [1986], 30–8

Boland, L. [1988] Individualist economics without psychology, in P. Earl [1988], 163–8

Boland, L. [1989] *The Methodology of Economic Model Building* (London: Routledge)

Boland, L. [1990] The methodology of Marshall's 'Principle of Continuity', *Économie Appliquée*, 43, 145–59

Boland, L. and G. Newman [1979] On the role of knowledge in economic theory, *Austrialian Economic Papers*, 18, 71–80

Bonanno, G. [1990] General equilibrium theory with imperfect competition, *Journal of Economic Surveys*, 4, 297–328

Buchanan, J. and G. Tullock [1962] *The Calculus of Consent* (Ann Arbor: University of Michigan Press)

Cassel, G. [1918] *The Theory of Social Economy* (London: Unwin [English edn 1923])

Chiang, A. [1974] *Fundamental Methods of Mathematical Economics*, 2nd edn (New York: McGraw-Hill)

Chipman, J. [1960] The foundations of utility, *Econometrica*, 28, 193–224

Clower, R. [1965] The Keynesian counterrevolution: a theoretical appraisal, in F. Hahn and F. Brechling (eds) *The Theory of Interest Rates* (London: Macmillan), 103–25

Coase, R. [1960] The problem of social cost, *Journal of Law and Economics*, 3, 1–44

Davies, D. [1963] A note on Marshallian versus Walrasian stability conditions,

Canadian Journal of Economics and Political Science, 29, 535–40

Davis, L. and D. North [1971] *Institutional Change and American Economic Growth* (Cambridge: Cambridge University Press)

De Alessi, L. [1968] A methodological appraisal of Giffen's paradox, *Weltwirtschaftliches Archiv, 101*, 287–96

Debreu, G. [1959] *Theory of Value: An Axiomatic Analysis of Economic Equilibrium* (New York: Wiley)

Debreu, G. [1962] New concepts and techniques for equilibrium analysis, *International Economic Review, 3*, 257–73

Dooley, P. [1983] Consumer's surplus: Marshall and his critics, *Canadian Journal of Economics, 16*, 26–38

Earl, P. (ed) [1988] *Psychological Economics: Development, Tensions, Prospects* (Boston: Kluwer Academic Publishers)

Edgeworth, F. [1881/1961] *Mathematical Psychics* (London: Kegan Paul)

Encarnacion, J. [1964] A note on lexicographical preferences, *Econometrica, 32*, 215–17

Fisher, F. [1981] Stability, disequilibrium awareness, and the perception of new opportunities, *Econometrica, 49*, 279–317

Fisher, F. [1983] *Disequilibrium Foundations of Equilibrium Economics* (Cambridge: Cambridge University Press)

Friedman, M. [1953] *Essays in Positive Economics* (Chicago: University of Chicago Press)

Gale, D. [1955] The law of supply and demand, *Mathematica Scandinavica, 3*, 155–69

Georgescu-Roegen, N. [1954] Choice, expectations and measurability, *Quarterly Journal of Economics, 68*, 503–34

Gordon, D. and A. Hynes [1970] On the theory of price dynamics, in E. Phelps (ed) *Microeconomic Foundations of Employment and Inflation Theory* (New York: Norton), 369–93

Haavelmo, T. [1960] *A Study in the Theory of Investment* (Chicago: University of Chicago Press)

Hague, D.C. [1958] Alfred Marshall and the competitive firm, *Economic Journal, 68*, 673–90

Hahn, F. [1970] Some adjustment problems, *Econometrica, 38*, 1–17

Hahn, F. [1973] *On the Notion of Equilibrium in Economics* (Cambridge: Cambridge University Press)

Hart, O. [1985] Imperfect competition in general equilibrium: an overview of recent work, in K. Arrow and S. Honkapohja (eds) *Frontiers of Economics* (Oxford: Basil Blackwell), 100–49

Hayakawa, H and Y. Venieris [1977] Consumer interdependence via reference groups, *Journal of Political Economy, 83*, 599–615

Hayek, F. [1933/39] Price expectations, monetary disturbances and malinvestments, reprinted in *Profits, Interest and Investments* (London: Routledge)

Hayek, F. [1937/48] Economics and knowledge, *Economica, 4* (NS), 33–54 (reprinted in Hayek [1948])

Hayek, F. [1945/48] Uses of knowledge in society, *American Economic Review, 35*, 519–30 (reprinted in Hayek [1948])

Hayek, F. [1948] *Individualism and Economic Order* (Chicago: University of Chicago Press)

Hicks, J. [1939] *Value and Capital* (Oxford: Clarendon Press)

Hicks, J. [1956] *A Revision of Demand Theory* (Oxford: Clarendon Press)
Hicks, J. [1976] Some questions of time in economics, in A. Tang, F. Westfield and J. Worley (eds) *Evolution, Welfare and Time in Economics* (Toronto: D.C. Heath), 135–51
Hicks, J. [1979] *Causality in Economics* (Oxford: Blackwell)
Hicks, J. and R.G.D. Allen [1934] A reconsideration of the theory of value, *Economica, 1* (NS), 52–76 and 196–219
Hollis, M. and E. Nell [1975] *Rational Economic Man* (Cambridge: Cambridge University Press)
Houthakker, H.S. [1950] Revealed preference and the utility function, *Economica, 17* (NS), 159–74
Houthakker, H.S. [1961] The present state of consumption theory, *Econometrica, 29*, 704–40
Kalecki, M. [1938] The determinants of the distribution of the national income, *Econometrica, 6*, 97–112
Keynes, J.M. [1934] *The General Theory of Employment, Interest and Money* (New York: McGraw-Hill)
Keynes, J.M. [1937] The general theory of employment, *Quarterly Journal of Economics, 51*, 209–23
Kirzner, I. (ed) [1986] *Subjectivism, Intelligibility and Economic Understanding* (New York: New York University Press)
Koopmans, T. [1957] *Three Essays on the State of Economic Science* (New York: McGraw-Hill)
Kornai, J. [1971] *Anti-equilibrium* (Amsterdam: North-Holland)
Kuhn, H. [1956] On a theorem of Wald, in H. Kuhn and A. Tucker (eds) *Linear Inequalities and Related Systems* (Princeton: Princeton University Press), 265–74
Lachmann, L. [1970] *Legacy of Max Weber* (London: Heinemann)
Lachmann, L. [1976] From Mises to Shackle: an essay on Austrian economics and the kaleidic society, *Journal of Economic Literature, 14*, 54–65
Lachmann, L. [1982] The salvage of ideas, *Zeitschrift für die gesamte Staatswissenschaft, 138*, 629–45
Lancaster, K. [1966] A new approach to consumer theory, *Journal of Political Economy, 74*, 132–57
Lancaster, K. [1968] *Mathematical Economics* (London: Macmillan)
Lange, O. [1935/36] The place of interest in the theory of production, *Review of Economic Studies, 3*, 159–92
Latsis, S. [1972] Situational determinism in economics, *British Journal for the Philosophy of Science, 23*, 207–45
Lawson, T. and H. Pesaran [1985] *Keynes' Economics: Methodological Issues* (London: Croom Helm)
Leibenstein, H. [1979] A branch of economics is missing: micro-micro theory, *Journal of Economic Literature, 17*, 477–502
Leijonhufvud, A. [1968] *On Keynesian Economics and the Economics of Keynes* (New York: Oxford University Press)
Lerner, A. [1934] The concept of monopoly and the measurement of monopoly power, *Review of Economic Studies, 1*, 157–75
Lipsey R. and G. Rosenbluth [1971] A contribution to the new theory of demand: a rehabilitation of the Giffen good, *Canadian Journal of Economics, 4*, 131–63
Little, I.M.D. [1949] A reformulation of the theory of consumer's behaviour,

Oxford Economic Papers, *1*, 90–9

Lloyd, C. [1965] On the falsifiability of traditional demand theory, *Metroeconomica*, *17*, 17–23

Lloyd, C. [1967] *Microeconomic Analysis* (Homewood, Illinois: Irwin)

Lloyd, C. [1969] Ceteris paribus, etc., *Metroeconomica*, *22*, 86–9

Loasby, B. [1978] Whatever happened to Marshall's theory of value?, *Scottish Journal of Political Economy*, *25*, 1–12

Lucas, R. [1980] Methods and problems in business cycle theory, *Journal of Money, Credit and Banking*, *12*, 696–715

Marshall, A. [1920/49] *Principles of Economics*, 8th edn (London: Macmillan)

Mason, R. [1988] The psychological economics of conspicuous consumption, in P. Earl [1988], 147–62

McKenzie, L. [1954] On equilibrium in Graham's model of world trade and other competitive systems, *Econometrica*, *22*, 147–61

McKenzie, L. [1957] Demand theory without a utility index, *Review of Economic Studies*, *24*, 185–9

McKenzie, L. [1959] On the existence of general equilibrium for a competitive economy, *Econometrica*, *27*, 54–71

Mill, J. S. [1843] *System of Logic* (London: Longman)

Mises, L. [1949] *Human Action* (New Haven: Yale University Press)

Modigliani, F. [1944] Liquidity preference and the theory of interest and money, *Econometrica*, *12*, 45–88

Mongin, P. [1986] Are 'all-and-some' statements falsifiable after all?, *Economics and Philosophy*, *2*, 185–95

Moore, H. [1929] *Synthetic Economics* (New York: Macmillan)

Muth, J. [1961] Rational expectations and the theory of price movements, *Econometrica*, *29*, 315–35

Negishi, T. [1961] Monopolistic competition and general equilibrium, *Review of Economic Studies*, *28*, 196–201

Negishi, T. [1985] *Economic Theories in a Non-Walrasian Tradition* (Cambridge: Cambridge University Press)

Newman, G. [1972] Institutional choices and the theory of consumer behavior, unpublished MA thesis, Simon Fraser University

Newman, G. [1976] An institutional perspective on information, *International Social Science Journal*, *28*, 466–92

Newman, P. [1965] *Theory of Exchange* (Englewood Cliffs, N.J.: Prentice Hall)

North, D. [1978] Structure and performance: the task of economic history, *Journal of Economic Literature*, *16*, 963–78

Pareto, V. [1916/35] *Mind and Society*, *4* (New York: Harcourt Brace [English edn 1935])

Patinkin, D. [1956] *Money, Interest and Prices* (Evanston: Row Peterson)

Quirk, J. and R. Saposnik [1968] *Introduction to General Equilibrium Theory and Welfare Economics* (New York: McGraw-Hill)

Roberts, D.J. and H. Sonnenschein [1977] On the foundations of the theory of monopolistic competition, *Econometrica*, *45*, 101–13

Robinson, J. [1933/69] *Economics of Imperfect Competition* (London: Macmillan)

Robinson, J. [1974] History versus equilibrium, *Thames Papers in Political Economy*

Roemer, J. [1988] *Free to Lose: An Introduction to Marxist Economic Philosophy* (Cambridge, Mass.: Harvard University Press)

Rotwein, E. [1980] Friedman's critics: a critic's reply to Boland, *Journal of Economic Literature*, *18*, 1553-5

Samuelson, P. [1938] A note on the pure theory of consumer behaviour, *Economica*, *5* (NS), 61-71

Samuelson, P. [1947/65] *Foundations of Economic Analysis* (New York: Atheneum)

Samuelson, P. [1948] Consumption theory in terms of revealed preference, *Economica*, *15* (NS), 243-53

Samuelson, P. [1950] Evaluation of real national income, *Oxford Economic Papers*, *2* (NS), 1-29

Samuelson, P. [1953] Consumption theorems in terms of overcompensation rather than indifference comparisons, *Economica*, *20* (NS), 1-9

Samuelson, P. [1972] The consumer does benefit from feasible price stability, *Quarterly Journal of Economics*, *86*, 476-93

Schumpeter, J. [1909] On the concept of social value, *Quarterly Journal of Economics*, *23*, 213-32

Scitovsky, T. [1976] *Joyless Economy* (New York: Oxford University Press)

Shackle, G. [1972] *Epistemics and Economics: A Critique of Economic Doctrines* (Cambridge: Cambridge University Press)

Shove, G. [1942] The place of the 'Principles' in the development of economic theory, *Economic Journal*, *52*, 294-329

Simon, H. [1979] Rational decision making in business organizations, *American Economic Review, Papers and Proceedings*, *69*, 493-513

Simon, H. [1987] Bounded rationality, in J. Eatwell, M. Milgate and P. Newman (eds) *The New Palgrave: A Dictionary of Economics, 1* (New York: The Stockton Press), 266-8

Solow, R. [1979] Alternative approaches to macroeconomic theory: a partial view, *Canadian Journal of Economics*, *12*, 339-54

Sraffa, P. [1926] The laws of returns under competitive conditions, *Economic Journal*, *38*, 535-50

Sraffa, P. [1960] *Production of Commodities by Means of Commodities* (Cambridge: Cambridge University Press)

Stigler, G. [1950] The development of utility theory, *Journal of Political Economy*, *48*, 307-27 and 373-96

Stigler, G. [1961] The economics of information, *Journal of Political Economy*, *69*, 213-25

Stigler, G. and G. Becker [1977] De gustibus non est disputandum, *American Economic Review*, *67*, 76-90

Tarascio, V. and B. Caldwell [1979] Theory choice in economics: philosophy and practice, *Journal of Economic Issues*, *13*, 983-1006

Tisdell, C. [1975] Concepts of rationality in economics, *Philosophy of the Social Sciences*, *5*, 259-72

Veblen, T. [1899/1934] *The Theory of the Leisure Class* (New York: Modern Library)

Wald, A. [1933/34] Über die eindeutige positive Lösbarkeit der neuen Produktionsgleichungen, *Ergebnisse eines mathematischen Kolloquiums, Heft 6*, 12-20

Wald, A. [1934/35] Über die Produktionsgleichungen ökonomischen Wertlehre, *Ergebnisse eines mathematischen Kolloquiums, Heft 7*, 1-6

Wald, A. [1936/51] On some systems of equations of mathematical economics, *Econometrica*, *19*, 368-403

Weintraub, S. [1949] *Price Theory* (New York: Pitman Publishing Corporation)

Welty, G. [1969] Lloyd on the falsifiability of economic theory, *Metroeconomica*, 21, 81–5

Welty, G. [1971] Giffen's paradox and falsifiability, *Weltwirtschaftliches Archiv*, 107, 139–46

Wong, S. [1978] *The Foundations of Paul Samuelson's Revealed Preference Theory* (London: Routledge & Kegan Paul)

Name index

Agassi, J. 38, 93, 120–1, 148, 217
Allen, R.G.D. 8, 62, 177–8, 188–9, 193–4, 217–18, 220
Archibald, G.C. 135, 217
Arrow, K. 62, 95, 124, 189, 217, 219

Barro, R 85, 217
Baumol, W 34, 68, 217
Bear, D. 104, 217
Becker, G. 3, 45–6, 152, 217, 222
Blanché, R. 62, 217
Boland, L. 5, 37–8, 47, 63, 87, 104, 120, 125–7, 146, 152, 161, 176, 194, 206, 211–12, 218, 222
Bonanno, G. 86, 218
Buchanan, J. 112–13, 218

Caldwell, B. 38, 222
Cassel, G. 179, 185, 196–7, 205, 218
Chamberlin, E. 21
Chiang, A. 8, 218
Chipman, J. 37, 40, 218
Clower, R. 85, 91, 132, 138, 218
Coase, R. 49, 115, 135, 218
Cournot, A. 24, 37

Davies, D. 211, 218
Davis, L. 113, 219
De Alessi, L. 205, 207–9, 212, 219
Debreu, G. 62, 217, 219
Dooley, P. 211, 219

Earl, P. 152, 218–9, 221
Edgeworth, F. 138–9, 146–7, 219
Encarnacion, J. 166, 219

Fisher, F 85, 144, 219
Fisher, I 144
Friedman, M. 3, 5–6, 18, 31, 37, 159, 218–9, 222

Gale, D. 62, 219
Georgescu-Roegen, N. 166, 169, 219
Gordon, D. 95, 112, 207, 219
Grossman, H. 85, 217

Haavelmo, T. 219
Hague, D.C. 30, 217, 219
Hahn, F. 48, 62, 64, 85, 217–19
Hart, O. 86, 219
Hayakawa, H. 152, 219
Hayek, F. 13, 92, 96, 98, 118, 124, 146, 153–7, 160, 219
Hicks, J. 8, 21, 62, 112, 124, 131, 139–41, 146, 177–8, 187–9, 193–5, 198–9, 205, 207, 210, 213, 219–20
Hollis, M. 203, 220
Houthakker, H. 63, 178, 189–90, 220
Hynes, A. 95, 219

Jevons, W.S. 43, 115

Kalecki, M. 83–4, 220
Keynes, J.M. 7, 13, 21, 43–4, 62, 125, 131–7, 139–41, 143–5, 218, 220
Kirzner, I. 161, 218, 220
Koopmans, T. 50, 114, 220
Kornai, J. 91, 220
Kuhn, H. 62, 220
Kuhn, T. 20

226　Principles of economics

Lachmann, L. 91–2, 94–5, 97–104, 126, 154–8, 160–1, 220
Lancaster, K. 173–4, 176, 211–12, 220
Lange, O. 81–2, 87, 217, 220
Latsis, S. 136, 220
Lawson, T. 146, 218, 220
Leibenstein, H. 11, 14, 16, 220
Leijonhufvud, A. 91, 220
Lerner, A. 83, 220
Lipsey, R. 135, 194, 198, 212, 217, 220
Little, I.M.D. 85, 189, 220
Lloyd, C. 20, 195, 205, 207–10, 212, 221, 223
Loasby, B. 30, 221
Lucas, R. 135, 221

Marshall, A. 6, 7, 21–37, 39–46, 52, 65, 85, 112, 115–17, 123, 125, 132–3, 137–8, 140, 153, 165, 179, 196, 202, 210–11, 213–14, 218–9, 221
Mason, R. 149, 221
Mill, J.S. 44, 134, 221
Mises, L. 92, 96, 98–100, 220–1
Modigliani, F. 62, 221
Mongin, P. 20, 221
Moore, H. 179, 205, 221
Muth, J. 221

Negishi, T. 37, 86, 221
Nell, E. 203, 220
Newman, G. 104, 123, 152, 218, 221–2
Newman, P. 166, 221–2
North, D. 112–13, 117–20, 219–1

Orr, D. 104, 217

Pareto, V. 82, 138, 147, 179, 221
Patinkin, D. 62, 132, 217, 221
Pesaran, H. 146, 218, 220

Quirk, J. 62, 166, 221

Roberts, D.J. 86, 221
Robinson, J. 21, 35, 62, 80, 83, 113, 221
Roemer, J. 83, 221
Rosenbluth, G. 194, 198, 212, 220
Rotwein, E. 5, 222

Samuelson, P. 8, 21, 23, 47, 62–3, 87, 93, 131, 146, 177–8, 188–9, 194, 206–7, 213, 222–3
Saposnik, R. 62, 166, 221
Schumpeter, J. 127, 179, 222
Scitovsky, T. 150, 222
Shackle, G. 11–14, 19, 91–2, 94–104, 112, 220, 222
Shove, G. 43, 222
Simon, H. 5, 11, 14, 16, 19–20, 221–2
Solow, R. 8, 222
Sonnenschein, H. 221
Sraffa, P. 21, 35, 126, 222
Stigler, G. 45–6, 152, 196–7, 208–9, 214, 222

Tisdell, C. 97, 222
Triffin, R. 21
Tullock, G. 112–13, 218

Veblen, T. 152, 222
Venieris, Y. 152, 219
Voltaire 93, 204

Wald, A. 48, 51–6, 58–63, 178, 185, 220, 222
Walras, L. 25–6, 42, 52–4, 61, 115, 211, 213–14
Weintraub, S. 83–4, 223
Welty, G. 207–9, 212, 223
Wong, S. 194, 198, 223

Subject index

ad hocery 167, 174–5, 198, 201–3, 205–6
  counter-critical 174–5
average-net-product
  of capital (ANP_K) 74–5, 77, 86–7
  of labour (ANP_L) 77
axiom of revealed preference 55, 62–3, 93, 178, 181, 189–91, 193, 195, 204; see also revealed preference analysis
axiomatic analysis (axiomatics) 4, 48, 50–1, 53, 60, 62, 64
  completeness 50–3, 60–1, 64, 85, 152, 214–15
  consistency 11, 29, 49–51, 56, 60, 64, 85, 91, 93, 177–8
  existence of equilibria 47, 49
  and geometry 62
  theory of completeness 52, 61
  uniqueness 55, 60–1, 93–4, 149, 171, 175, 214–15

behaviour
  dynamic 26, 125
  maximizing 1, 5, 14, 18, 39, 149, 204
  see also maximization
biological analogies 40–1, 43–4

capital
  as embodied technology 108, 109
  homogeneous 109
  optimum quantity of 65, 67
  optimum type of 65
  quality of 108
  stock 107–8, 115
  theory of 106, 108–10

Coase theorem 49
competition
  free enterprise 67
  imperfect 3, 7, 62, 66, 68, 71, 73, 75, 78, 81, 83, 86
  perfect 3, 7, 70, 81
constraints
  fixed 33
  institutional 108, 116–18
  natural 134–6, 147
  non-natural 135
  short-run 33, 135
  static 113, 118–19
consumer theory, see demand theory
consumers, types of
  apriorist 99, 159
  conventionalist 159
  instrumentalist 160
  positivist 99
  scepticist 99, 160
  sophisticated inductivist 159
continuity 27, 31, 39–41, 44–7, 55, 203
  and connectedness 37, 40
  mathematical conception of 24
  of options 27, 46
continuum
  historical vs logical time- 134
  historical-time 132
  Keynes' 133–4, 137
  logical 132–3
  logical-time 135
  Marshall's 36, 40-2, 46, 133, 137–8, 214
  methodological-cum-historical 132
criteria
  multiple 166, 169, 171–3, 175

rank ordering of 173
criticism 1–8, 11–16, 18–21, 50–1, 94–7, 113–14, 213
and completeness 60–1
direct 12–13, 46
effective 1, 5–6, 144–5, 213
external 3, 11
indirect 4
internal 3
internal vs external 3
criticizing critiques 5–6

decision(s), irreversible 35–6, 46, 114
decision-makers, methodology of 158
decision-making, successful 100, 117–19, 124
demand curves
  downward (negatively) sloping 8, 29, 34, 37, 61, 70, 72–3, 179–80, 196, 205, 208–9, 211
  Giffen 193
  market 54–5, 179, 204
  upward (positively) sloping 156, 166, 179, 194, 197, 205, 207–9
demand, inverse 56, 59, 195
demand theory
  characteristics 173, 176, 212
  choice-theory 157
  consumer surplus 165
  determinateness 180–2, 184–5
  diminishing MRS 186–8, 203
  explicitness 91, 101
  Giffen good(s) 165, 182–3, 187–8, 193, 196–9, 203–4, 206–12
  Giffen paradox 196–7, 207, 209–10, 212
  income–consumption curves (ICCs) 57–8, 184–7, 195
  and individualism 150–2, 179–80
  inferior good(s) 178, 181, 193, 195, 197, 203–4, 207–10, 212
  interdependence of elasticities 188
  iso-price lines 185
  law of demand 2, 178–82, 185, 190, 193–4, 196–7, 199, 202–4, 208–9, 212
  marginal rate of substitution (MRS) 186–8, 203
  marginal utility 12, 17, 41, 150, 212
  monotonic utility 166, 174–5

non-Giffen PCC 192
non-inferior 208–10
non-inferiority 208
normal goods 178, 187, 206
ordinal demand theory (ODT) 8, 158, 177–8, 181–2, 185–6, 189, 193–5, 209–10
price–consumption curves (PCCs) 56–9, 63, 179, 182–92, 195
responsiveness 100, 181–2, 184–5
Slutsky equation (Theorem) 15, 20, 178, 182, 194, 208
static utility 175, 177–8
substitution effect 20, 208, 212
utility function 3, 14–15, 19, 94, 136, 147, 149–52, 158–60, 165–9, 173–6, 185, 203, 212
disequilibrium (disequilibria) 124, 135, 140
general theory of 84–5
as involuntary unemployment 2, 49
long-run 77
measures of 81–4; degree of monopoly 83–4; index of less-than-optimum output 83; index of monopoly power 83; interest rate 81; *see also* exploitation
state of 64–5, 75–87, 132
and transaction costs 3
vs universal maximization 18, 45
dynamics
  economic 96
  institutional 114, 119
  knowledge 7, 92–3, 95, 103, 105
  learning 97
  long-run 26
  price adjustment 61

Edgeworth–Bowley box 138–9
elasticity 70, 73, 83, 86, 100, 183, 188, 194
  elasticity of demand 70, 83, 188
  and the relationship between the marginal and the average 73, 82
epistemics 154
epistemology (epistemologies) 13, 92–3, 100–4
  inductivist 102–3
  interdependence of methodology and 100

Subject index

Lachmann–Shackle 92, 101
equilibrium (equilibria)
  vs balance 61
  criticism of 48, 84
  general 52–3, 65, 86, 91, 146, 214–15; competitive 44, 52; market 52
  intermediate-run 66–9, 73, 75, 86, 108
  long-run 27–32, 34, 37, 66–9, 71, 73–8, 95, 101–3, 114, 116, 125–6, 136, 211
  market-determined 66
  market-run 29
  multiple 50, 61, 63
  neighbourhood properties of 214
  nesting of 29–30
  partial 27, 52, 179
  short-run 29, 66–7, 69, 77, 86, 95, 103, 211
  stable 23, 59, 61, 64
  state of 4, 49, 52, 67, 95
  and transaction costs 45, 49, 78–9
  unstable 51, 61, 100, 102, 156, 159
expectations 93–104, 134, 139, 143
  rational 146
  and sociology 119–20
explaining vs explaining away 2–3
explanation
  cause and effect 23–4, 42
  ceteris paribus 52, 208–9, 212
  circular 98; vs incomplete 98; vs infinite regress 42; vs tautological 17; without exogenous variables 26, 118, 126
  comparative statics 140
  complete 11, 27–8, 30, 49, 95, 117, 175
  equilibrium 50, 199
  incomplete 27, 63
  long-run 26, 117
  problem of 22, 25–7, 35
  psychologistic 44
  Walrasian vs Marshallian 42
explanatory principles 22, 25, 34
exploitation 80–1, 133
  measure of 83

firm 24, 30–7, 65–87, 131, 136–4, 202, 211
  excess capacity 74–5, 78, 140–2, 144–5
  excess profits 29, 33, 35, 45, 74
  imperfectly competitive 78
  as institution 105–11
  life-cycle of 30–2, 35, 41–2
  marginal cost 32, 35, 67, 70, 76–7, 79, 85–6, 202, 211
  marginal revenue 34–5, 70, 79
  maximizing profit 15, 69, 74, 143
  as monopolist 66
  perfectly competitive 65–6
  as price setter 66
  price-taking 28, 44–5, 76
  representative 31–2, 34
  size, irreversible 30
  stationary state 30–1, 37
  turning point 31–4

general theory 7, 84, 144–5
givens
  endogenous 114
  exogenous 25–6, 76, 101, 116, 124, 134, 147
  natural 37, 127, 132, 134–5
  non-individualist 146
  non-natural 134

Hatter, the 21
hedonism 43–4
high theory 8
holism
  institutional 121, 126, 148
  psychologistic 148

ideology 117–18, 124, 201
incentives to change 29, 115
indifference curves 62, 170–1, 176, 186–7, 189, 195
indifference map(s) 55, 57, 169, 177, 183–6, 197, 210
  and attainable set 181
  and bliss points 170, 177, 186
  and budget line(s) 59, 138, 146, 169–70, 173, 189–91
  community 55
  and non-satiation 186
individualism
  institutional 120, 127, 146, 148

230 Principles of economics

laissez-faire 201, 204, 210
methodological 37, 127, 134–6, 147–8, 150–2, 180
neoclassical 136
and psychological states 126–7, 134, 147
psychologistic 121, 126–7, 134–5, 145, 148
vs psychologism 147–8
inductive logic 13, 94, 118, 194
inductive process 157
inductive proof(s) 13–14, 19, 38, 104, 157–9, 161
information 13, 174, 189, 195
economics of 214
and the role of institutions 119, 123, 142
and 'the news' 98
and testability 206–7
institutional arrangement 113, 116
institutional change 106–8, 112, 117, 119, 123–4
theory of 110
institutional economics 112
institutional environment 46, 113
institutional reforms 106, 108
institutionalism 124, 127, 148
and evolutionary economics 113, 125
institutions
and circular causation 122–3
changeability of 123
concrete 120, 122–3, 126
consensus 120, 123–4
dynamic theory of 120
endogenous 116
and knowledge 113
neoclassical view of 110, 112–14, 116
as organizational structure 118
social 85, 106, 110, 112, 114, 119–20, 126
as social technology 110
and sociological acts 119
successful 124
theory of 106, 110, 119, 126
instruments of change 121
inter-generational changes 116–17
inter-generational comparisons 105
inter-generational 'secular' periods 132

intermediate run 65–8, 71, 74–5, 86
involuntary unemployment 2, 49

kaleido-statics 101
knowledge 60–1, 91–109, 153–8, 161
adequate 100, 102
casual 196–7
endogenous 92
epistemological problem of 98
epistemological role of 100, 102
exogenous 96, 101
exogenously-fixed 98
fixed 96
growth of 106, 108, 116
Hayek–Lachmann distinction 155, 157
imperfect 101
induction-based 118, 161
knowledge acquisition 154, 157
methodological role of 102, 153
perfect 27, 91, 95–7, 101, 153, 214
positivist view of 99
potentially-variable 97
practical 154–7
problem of 91–4, 98, 105, 157
propositional 154, 157
Scepticist theory of 99
scientific 154–7
social 119–20, 125–6
and social institutions 112–26
sociology of 117
subjective 189
technical 105, 135
theories of 13, 19, 61, 93, 98–100, 102–3, 157–8
true 13–14, 18, 94, 118, 161
variability of 96–7

learning
and criticism 1, 6, 213
by doing 108, 156, 158
inductive 154, 157, 161, 175
and life-cycle of firm 30, 36
methods of 159
progressive 160
social 106, 110, 120
takes time 27, 97
liquidity 131, 136–7, 139–42, 144–6
and flexibility 141–2
Keynes' use of 140

in general 141
preference 131
long period(s) 23, 26, 28–31, 33,
  104–5, 116, 132
  and changeability of inputs 33
long run 26, 33–5, 65–6, 78, 80, 85,
  95–6, 105–6, 116–17, 126, 136, 146,
  211

macroeconomics 8, 85, 145
March Hare 21
market(s)
  excess demand 45, 156, 201, 211
  excess supply 85, 141, 156, 201
  spoiling 35
  stable 155–6, 199–205; and convex
    preferences 160–1
  stability conditions 28, 30, 36, 47,
    61, 199–205, 211
  unstable 157
market periods 132
Marshall's Book V
  insufficiency of Book V 28
  methodology of Book V 30
Marshall's economics 22, 24, 26, 125
Marshall's 'element of Time' 21–4,
  26–8, 30, 32, 35, 42, 46, 115
Marshall's 'Principles' 7, 21, 32, 36,
  40, 115
Marshall's strategy 27, 138
mathematical economics 2, 52, 55
  formalism 176
maximization 3–8, 11–23, 25–6,
  39–41, 44–7, 80, 83–4, 92–4, 144–5,
  149–50, 213
  constrained 23, 136–8, 169, 176
  vs conventional judgement 144
  empirical critique of 14
  global 17, 19–20, 215
  vs follow-the-leader behaviour 144
  as global optimum 82
  vs irrationality 3, 93, 152
  Lagrange multiplier(s) 19, 87
  local 12, 17, 20, 214–15
  as optimum choice 133, 140, 166,
    189
  possibilities critique of 13
  of profit 7, 11, 29, 33–5, 44–5,
    65–87, 108, 142–3, 155, 174
  as rationality 93, 114

vs rules-of-thumb 144
vs satisficing 11, 20
secondary assumptions 19
universal 11, 16, 44, 45, 150, 157
of utility 15, 20, 35, 44, 136, 149,
  156–61, 165, 175, 189, 191,
  202–5, 208
maximization hypothesis 11–18, 20–2,
  39, 45–6, 49, 110, 215
methodological doctrines
  Apriorism 98, 104, 159
  Conventionalism 36, 38
  Inductivism 19, 37, 98, 103–4, 153,
    157, 159, 161
  Instrumentalism 3, 6, 18, 31, 37,
    159, 161
  Positivism 104
  Scepticism 100, 104, 159
methodology
  ad hoc modifications 206–7, 209; vs
    arbitrary assumptions 171
  arbitrariness 42, 171, 173, 176
  as if approach 31
  collectivist 123, 127
  constrained-optimization 136
  conventionalist 31, 159
  empirical refutation 14–15
  as hidden agenda 37, 47
  general vs special case 132–3
  generality 3, 17, 19, 25, 131–2, 134
  infinite regress 42, 104, 118, 161,
    167, 171, 174–6
  Keynes–Hicks 139
  Marshallian 22, 24, 32, 85, 115–16,
    132
  and meaningfulness 206
  vs metaphysics 17–19
  neoclassical 4, 18, 125, 134–6, 145
  normative view 115
  paradigm 113, 166; as metaphysics
    20
  predictions 60, 96, 101, 137
  and the problem of induction 94,
    104, 195
  rational reconstruction 198
  rationalism 43, 93, 148–9
  realism of assumptions 19, 95, 171
  refutable 14, 16, 20
  refuting facts 99–100
  statical method 27, 29, 31–2, 35, 39,

52
stochastic theories 125
stochasticism 127, 176
tautology (tautologies) 6, 12, 16–17, 215; vs metaphysics 16–17
theory-choice 157
unscientific 16; and meaningless statements 16
unverifiable 16–17
verifiable 14, 16, 20
verifying facts 99
Walrasian 42, 47, 5–12, 62
see also explanation
micro-micro theory 11
microeconomic analysis 28
minimization 20, 33, 44, 114
satisficing as cost minimization 20
least-cost production 80
model-building 19, 62, 206
models
Austrian 37
axiomatic 40
comprehensive maximization 44
equilibrium 4, 7, 22, 49–50, 52, 64, 66, 85
neo-Walrasian 22, 37
timeless 7, 118

Pareto optimum 82, 138
phenomena
disequilibrium 2, 49, 64, 76–7, 81
equilibrium 49
preference ordering 20, 152, 166, 168–71, 176–8, 180–2, 189, 203
convex 59, 146, 161, 186
and the discontinuity problem 167
and greed 67, 186–7, 189, 195, 203
incomplete 172
integrability problem 194
lexicographic (*L*-orderings) 8, 165–7, 169, 175–6
static 181
strictly convex 170–1, 175
transitive 203
price(s)
disequilibrium 85, 154–6
equilibrium 29, 36, 52, 66, 126, 157, 199, 201, 211
market 24, 28–9, 179
market-determined 114, 197–9, 209–11
and noise 24, 28
rigidity of 115, 123
system 17, 114, 126, 203
theory of 8, 60, 99, 178–9, 194, 196–9, 201, 209–10
Principle of Continuity 7, 22–4, 27–30, 32–4, 36–7, 39–47, 115, 137, 214
Principle of Substitution 22–3, 25–7, 29, 33–4, 36, 39, 42, 46, 65, 110, 115–16, 137–8
applicability of 23, 40
Principles of Economics 1, 6–7, 21, 28, 105, 115
privatization 75
production functions 67–8, 72, 85, 146
Euler's theorem 33, 45, 68
everywhere-linear-homogeneous 68–9, 72
as iso-quants 138–9, 142
linear-homogeneous 29, 33, 67–72, 74–6, 78, 82, 84–5
locally linear-homogeneous 29, 33, 68–9, 75–6, 78, 82
marginal physical product of capital (MPP_K) 67–70, 72–4, 77, 82, 86–7
marginal physical product of labour (MPP_L) 67–70, 72–4, 77, 82, 85–6
marginal productivity 33, 41, 139, 142
marginal productivity, diminishing 41
marginal rate of technical substitution (*MRTS*) 67–8
marginal returns 41, 146
production possibilities curves (PPCs) 50–1, 136–9, 141–3
full-employment PPC 143
under-employment PPC 143
psychological economics 152
psychology 147–52
Marshall's rejection of 42–3
mass 148
vs mechanics 4, 42–4, 93, 94
and Mill 134
social psychology 7, 147
vs sociobiology 151
and rationality 93

rationality 91–4, 97, 100–1, 148–9, 151, 205
resource allocations 49, 81
returns to scale
　constant 29, 31, 34, 45, 68–9, 73–4, 81
　decreasing 31, 41, 72
　increasing 32, 35, 41, 72–4, 78–9, 81–2, 146
revealed preference analysis 8, 178, 181–2, 185–6, 188–9, 194
　see also axiom of revealed preference

schools of thought
　Austrian 7, 37, 91–2, 97–8, 100, 102–3, 139, 154–5
　Chicago 5
　Classical 27, 43, 44
　Keynesian Counter-revolutionaries 132
　neo-Keynesian 91
　Post-Keynesian(s) 7, 35, 144, 211
short period(s) 23–4, 26–8, 33, 35, 116, 132
short run 24–5, 27, 29, 33, 35, 37, 65–7, 86, 95–6, 102–3, 115–16, 126, 134–5, 140, 143, 211
social change 122–3
　theory of 106, 110
stability
　and the auctioneer 156–7
　of market 85, 199–205
　Marshallian 28, 30, 199, 202, 211
　Walrasian 199–201, 204–5, 211

technological change 110
technology 7, 24, 26, 29, 64–7, 76, 95, 101, 105–11, 114, 140
　and change 105–6
　non-autonomy of 107
testability
　ad hocery vs 205–7
　all-and-some statments 16, 61–2
　and the ambiguity of modus tollens 209

　and completeness 60–2
　as criticizability 60
　of demand theory 205–8, 212
　and the Duhem–Quine thesis 212
　of maximization 4, 6, 15–16,
　and strictly universal statements 14–15, 19, 206
time 105–7, 109, 111
　historical 35, 36
　logical 35–6, 134
　see also Marshall's 'element of Time'

understanding 1–8, 21–2, 161, 193–4, 203
　and criticism 6, 50, 171, 197–9, 206–7, 213–15
unity and diversity 150
　dilemma between 148
　and downward sloping marginal utility 150
　and psychology 150–2
universality 93–4, 148–50, 196

variables
　as exogenous conditions 24–6, 42
　as social conditions 25–6, 112, 116–17, 122–3
　changeability of 27–8, 115
　dependent 24
　endogenous 24–6, 30, 33, 37, 49, 53, 95, 114–18, 123, 126, 132, 134–5, 146, 149–50, 206–7
　exogenous 20, 24–7, 30, 37, 42, 49, 53, 76, 114–18, 126–7, 134, 138, 146, 149, 159, 206–7;
　changeability of 26, 42
　non-natural 146
　independent 24
　macro- 136, 145–6
　non-individualist 134–5
very short period 24, 28
Voltaire's Candide 93, 204